100 THINGS
49ers FANS
SHOULD KNOW & DO
BEFORE THEY DIE

Daniel Brown

TRIUMPH
BOOKS

Library of Congress Cataloging-in-Publication Data

Brown, Daniel.
100 things 49ers fans should know & do before they die / Daniel Brown.
    pages cm
    ISBN 978-1-60078-791-1
    1. San Francisco 49ers (Football team)—History. 2. San Francisco 49ers (Football team)—Miscellanea. I. Title. II. Title: One hundred things fortyniners fans should know and do before they die.
    GV956.S3B76 2013
    796.332'640979461—dc23
                                                        2013009092

This book is available in quantity at special discounts for your group or organization. For further information, contact:
    Triumph Books LLC
    814 North Franklin Street
    Chicago, Illinois 60610
    (312) 337-0747
    www.triumphbooks.com

Printed in U.S.A.
ISBN: 978-1-60078-791-1
Design by Patricia Frey
Photos courtesy of Getty Images unless otherwise indicated

To my brother, David

Contents

Foreword

I learned right away what it means to be part of the San Francisco 49ers tradition. The lesson came on the day in 1983 I reported to the locker room as a rookie. That's when Willie Harper, a veteran linebacker heading into his 10th season, sized me up. "You know why we drafted you?" Harper asked. I told him I didn't know.

"To help us win more Super Bowls," he said.

And right then and there I grew up. That gave me goose bumps. I realized I was here for a purpose. It wasn't enough that the 49ers picked me. I had to show them *why* they picked me. That's why I took pride in my work ethic and trained hard. I wanted to be accepted. I wanted them to feel like I was part of the team and part of the family. So it was a big moment for me later that '83 season when offensive lineman Keith Fahnhorst, another great veteran leader, pulled me aside and told me that even menacing linebacker Jack "Hacksaw" Reynolds was ready to welcome me aboard. "You know, you're pretty lucky," Fahnhorst told me. "Hacksaw Reynolds hates rookies. He *hates* rookies. He just despises them. He won't give them the time of day…But he likes you. He likes your work ethic."

I fit in because I understood that being part of the 49ers tradition meant aiming for an impossible standard. Anything less than a Super Bowl season was a crushing disappointment. Bill Walsh, my first coach, was a perfectionist. His offense was very complex. You had to be smart to understand the West Coast Offense, so we studied a lot. We wanted to perfect our game. From Joe Montana to Jerry Rice to John Taylor, we all took pride in perfecting our position.

And at the time, nobody could figure out how to stop us. In my first year, we made it all the way to the NFC Championship

Game. In my second year, we went 18–1 (including playoffs) and beat the Miami Dolphins in Super Bowl XIX—the second of five championships for the 49ers.

But we recognized that the greatness of the 49ers was established long before we got there. The franchise was special from its start in 1946. R.C. Owens, the great receiver from the 1950s, was my hero. He worked for the organization during my playing days and was a great ambassador for the 49ers. I would always sit and pick his brain. Joe "the Jet" Perry was such a nice man, such a gentleman. He always made time for you. Bob St. Clair was my biggest hero. I love Bob. He used to tell me about how he ate raw meat and scared the rookies in training camp. I told him, "Man, you've got to be an animal to do that!"

I appreciated those guys because I'm a history buff. I appreciate anybody who played the game before me and I respect them. They opened the doors up for us. They sacrificed for us. That's why I take the time now to visit the new generation—guys like Frank Gore, Patrick Willis, and Vernon Davis. Whenever I see them, I always have a positive message for them.

That's what makes this book by Daniel Brown so fun. In his typically informative and entertaining style, Dan is able to pass along the same stories I used to hear—about the legends of Kezar Stadium to the glory years of Joe Montana all the way through to the franchise rebirth under Jim Harbaugh.

Through this history you can understand how proud I am to have been part of the 49ers organization and to have left an impact. I won three Super Bowls, made four Pro Bowls, and in 1985 became the first running back in history to have 1,000 yards rushing and 1,000 yards receiving in a single season. But the contribution I'm most proud of is nothing you can measure with statistics. The biggest thing I brought to the table was the work ethic I was able to instill. I changed the attitude of the team, the way we practiced. Bill Walsh would even say that.

I would sprint to the end zone every time I touched the ball. *Every* time. And then I would run back to the huddle. When I first started doing that, guys would make fun of me. Here was this young guy out here sprinting 80 yards down the field on every play. But it turned out to be a way of life for us. Pretty soon when the new draft choices came in, veterans would notice if the running backs weren't sprinting the plays out. Somebody would yell, "Run it out! Run it out!" I took Jerry Rice under my wing when he got there in 1985, and he helped pass along that approach to future generations.

We pushed all the young bucks in our camp, but we didn't believe in rookie hazing. That was something Bill Walsh didn't like. He said, "Why are you going to haze these guys when you might need them?" The way Bill saw it, if you hazed rookies you might get them so scared they couldn't focus on the game. You might destroy their confidence. So Bill didn't allow that.

After all they were there to help us win more Super Bowls.

—Roger Craig

1 The Catch

On a typically sweltering training camp day in 1981, coach Bill Walsh asked quarterback Joe Montana and receiver Dwight Clark to stick around a little longer. Never mind that the sun beating down in Rocklin, California, had already taken its toll on the two exhausted players. Never mind that the play Walsh wanted them to rehearse—Sprint Right Option—was already a successful part of the 49ers playbook.

The problem was that Montana always threw to his primary receiver, Freddie Solomon. Walsh wanted his quarterback to demonstrate that he could connect with his second option, Clark.

You know, just in case.

So Montana practiced rolling to his right and lofting the ball to the receiver sprinting across the back of the end zone. Again and again. "Until I threw the ball three times an arm's length above Dwight's head, Bill wouldn't let us off the practice field," Montana said. "When we finally walked off, Dwight and I were both saying, 'That gray-haired guy is going senile. I don't know what he's thinking about, but we would never throw a ball there.'"

Montana smiled and then said: "Little did we know that it would become such a part of 49ers history."

The 49ers would practice Sprint Right Option again and again. The proof that they eventually got it down pat exists in the form of five Super Bowl trophies—and millions of replays and Dallas Cowboys nightmares.

But mostly it exists in two words: *The Catch.*

The phrase is all it takes to conjure the image of Clark soaring over defensive back Everson Walls to pluck Montana's high-arcing

Dwight Clark skies over Cowboys defensive back Everson Walls to make The Catch, the play, which launched the 49ers to their first Super Bowl and on the way to a dynasty.

pass from the evening sky. The 6-yard pass with 58 seconds left gave the 49ers a 28–27 victory against the Cowboys in the NFC Championship Game on January 10, 1982.

The Catch launched the 49ers dynasty and forever altered the NFL landscape. The team would go on to play bigger games—starting with a triumph two weeks later in Super Bowl XVI—but no moment better defines the franchise or provides a better starting place for this top 100 countdown.

The Catch embodies Walsh's genius, Montana's magic, and a generation of 49ers like Clark who managed to rise—even soar—to the occasion.

Montana, though, didn't get to witness the crowning moment. As he let the pass go, the skinny quarterback was engulfed by an avalanche of Cowboys defenders, including Ed "Too Tall" Jones. But when they heard the Candlestick Park crowd going crazy, both of them knew exactly what it meant. "You just beat America's Team," Jones told Montana.

"And you can sit at home with the rest of America and watch the Super Bowl," Montana replied.

This represented the changing of the guard. Out with the old, in with the gold. The 1981 Niners, two seasons removed from a 2–14 finish, had the seeds of a powerhouse—including a rookie defensive back named Ronnie Lott—and were ready to knock off the Tom Landry-era Cowboys.

But for long stretches during that NFC title game, it looked as though 49ers fans were going to suffer yet another heartbreak. In a game that featured seven lead changes, Cowboys quarterback Danny White connected with Doug Cosbie for a 21-yard touchdown pass with about four minutes gone in the fourth quarter.

The Cowboys led 27–21. Of course they did. Dallas had thwarted the 49ers' championship dreams in three consecutive playoffs (1970 to 1972) and looked ready to do it again. In this one the 49ers kept trying to blow it, committing six turnovers after having turned the ball over only 25 times during the regular season.

But then Montana trotted out to the huddle. "He had this look on his face," former lineman Randy Cross told NFL Films. "And he says, 'We're going to go down, we're going to score a touchdown, and we're going to win the game. We're going to stick it in their ear.'"

Taking over at their 11-yard line with 4:54 left, the 49ers unleashed a showcase for the West Coast Offense that would torment opposing defenses for years to come. Montana kept hitting short passes and Lenvil Elliott—a 30-year-old halfback cut by the Cincinnati Bengals in training camp—kept picking up key yardage. Just after the two-minute warning, Solomon ran a reverse that gained 14 yards to the Dallas 35. Solomon picked up 12 more yards on an underneath pattern, getting the ball to the 13.

Solomon, in fact, could have been the hero. With 1:15 remaining, the 49ers ran a play called 29 Scissors that dispatched Solomon to the left corner of the end zone. The receiver ran it beautifully, broke into the clear, and the greatest clutch quarterback in the history of the universe misfired. "The Catch never would have happened if I'd hit Freddie Solomon, who was wide open," Montana said. "I threw it three feet over his head."

Instead, the 49ers followed the incompletion with a draw play to Elliott that got the 49ers to the 6-yard-line. The stage was set.

Along the sidelines, Walsh gave Montana explicit instructions: "We're going to call a sprint option. He's going to break up and break into the corner. You got it? Dwight will clear. If you don't get what you want, simply throw the ball away."

And if that sounds prophetic, consider the video clip of Walsh standing in front of a chalkboard in the meeting room, drawing up the play on the chalkboard, and telling his players: "Dwight is in here sliding back out. This is great when they're tired, and they're confused and they want to get back to Dallas. This is when you knock their ass out."

Solomon lined up in the slot inside Clark. On the Sprint Right Option, Clark first runs out and shields the defender like setting a pick in basketball, so that Solomon can spring free. It almost always works like a charm—just as it had for an 8-yard touchdown earlier in the game. But this time Solomon slipped under tight coverage so Montana scrambled right. As "Too Tall" Jones, Larry Bethea, and D.D. Lewis closed in, chasing the quarterback to the sideline, Montana let it fly.

The funny thing is on all those steamy days in Rocklin, Montana kept messing up. He'd throw it too low, irritating Walsh who told him a defender would be waiting. Or he'd airmail the pass over Clark's head. This time the ball floated to where only Clark's fingertips could find it. "The only time he got it right was with everything on the line, time winding down, and the defense in his face," Clark said. "That was the magic of Joe Montana."

2 Bill Walsh

Thanks to his dizzying intellect, Bill Walsh was often cast as the NFL's white-haired professor. Don't be fooled. The Genius was tough as nails. As a promising boxer at San Jose State in the 1950s, Walsh had such a potent left hook that he briefly flirted with the idea of turning pro. "I remember telling Bill—and I swear this actually happened—to give up on that sissy football stuff," said friend Al Accurso, who helped train Walsh during his fighting days. "I said, 'Bill, you're an obscure football player at San Jose State. You're not going to go anywhere. If you went into boxing, you could really be somebody.'"

Instead, Walsh stuck to the gridiron. And he turned the 49ers from punching bags into the heavyweight champions of the world. Hired away from Stanford by desperate owner Eddie DeBartolo in 1979, Walsh went 92–59–1 (.609) during his 10 seasons as the 49ers head coach. He won three Super Bowl titles, left behind a blueprint for two more, and revolutionized the game with his choreographed artistry of Joe Montana, Jerry Rice, Roger Craig, and Steve Young. When Walsh died of leukemia at age 75 on July 30, 2007, Young called him, "the most important person in football over the last 25 years, and I don't think there's any debate about that.

"He brought into Silicon Valley—about the time Silicon Valley was being born—the same kind of innovation. When you mention Steve Jobs or Andy Grove, you just say Bill Walsh. He was doing the same thing, just in a different venue—football. I've always said Bill would have been a great CEO of anything. Luckily for us it was the 49ers."

Perhaps the most influential strategist in NFL history, Walsh was inducted into the Pro Football Hall of Fame in 1993. He popularized and perfected the West Coast Offense that paved the way for the team's five Super Bowl victories. His teams won six NFC West titles and raised the standard for an organization that had zero titles before his arrival. The new bar? Anything less than a Super Bowl was considered a crushing disappointment. "One of the things I learned from Bill Walsh," Montana said, "is that you want to be perfect."

To be fair, Walsh *did* look like a professor. As the legendary *Los Angeles Times* columnist Jim Murray wrote: "You half expect his headset is playing Mozart." Walsh made it cool to blend IQ with Xs and Os.

Montana recalled that even one of Walsh's simplest plays was a mental challenge. He pointed to one called 22-Z-In, which often came in a split-back set. The back on one side would run a 12-yard hook while the other back ran a wide flare. The tight end also ran a hook. But depending on the coverage he saw, the running back's hook could turn into a crossing route...or an out-route...or a speed-cross and a stop, which means that if the back saw a defender in front of him during a crossing route, he had the freedom to stop. At the same time, receiver John Taylor would be running one of two routes depending on the look he got from the safety in the middle of the field.

Whatever happened, it was all precisely as it had been drawn up on Walsh's chalkboard. "It was easy to believe Bill Walsh because he would tell you things that would happen," Dwight Clark told NFL Films. "He'd say, 'We're going to run this play against this defense. When you catch it, there won't be anybody within 10 yards of you.'

"Then you'd make the catch during the game and you'd turn around, and there'd be nobody there. [Walsh] would do that over and over with his designing of plays. It just got to the point where everything he said you believe."

Even as a fledgling coach, William Ernest Walsh was always one step ahead. In graduate school for physical education at San Jose State, his master's thesis was called "Flank Formation Football—Stress: Defense," a project he later dismissed as "the silliest little thing." But former Spartans coach Bob Bronzan was amazed. In a recommendation for Walsh's file, Bronzan would later write: "I predict Bill Walsh will become the outstanding football coach in the United States."

After a flurry of brief coaching stops that ranged from head coach at Washington Union High School in Fremont, California, to college assistant gigs to the San Jose Apaches of the Continental Football League, Walsh got his big break in 1968. He was hired by legendary Cincinnati Bengals coach Paul Brown to oversee quarterbacks and receivers. Under Brown, Walsh learned the value of the short, high-percentage passes, which would define his West Coast Offense.

But his tenure in Cincinnati ended on a sour note: Walsh turned down several job offers because he was certain he was in line to succeed Brown. When the Bengals instead handed the job to Bill "Tiger" Johnson in 1976, Walsh was shattered. He resigned his post and moved to San Diego, where he served one year as an assistant for Chargers coach Tommy Prothro before getting the top job at Stanford.

The 49ers lured Walsh away from Stanford after the 1978 season just as the NFL franchise was hitting rock bottom. San Francisco staggered to a 2–14 finish that season. General manager Joe Thomas had gone through four coaches in two years and traded 14 draft picks during that span. DeBartolo, the owner, fired Thomas and entrusted the roles of coach and general manager to Walsh. At 47 he was finally in charge of an NFL team. Things didn't look much different in the standings at first, as Walsh endured another 2–14 mess in '79 and sputtered to a 6–10 finish in 1980.

But the climate was changing. "There was a feeling in the air," Montana said, "that something was different."

The 49ers broke through in 1981 with Montana and Clark hooking up for The Catch. After the 49ers beat the Dallas Cowboys in the NFC title game, Walsh's first Super Bowl victory came against his old employer, the Bengals. The emotional outpouring from the Bay Area after that '81 championship season, including the 49ers' victory parade down Market Street, stayed with Walsh the rest of his life. "I thought perhaps a few thousand people might show up, and it was more like 200,000," Walsh said. "My God, it was incredible. And what I remember is one of our players, Charle Young, standing up before all those people saying, 'We are champions!'"

Walsh was the NFL's Coach of the Year in 1981 and 1984. The Hall of Famer retired after the 1988 season. After the 49ers organization hit a skid, Walsh came back as vice president and general manager from 1999 to 2001 and served three more years as a consultant, reinvigorating the franchise. But his final act as 49ers coach ended after getting carried off on his players' shoulders after winning Super Bowl XXIII.

3 Joe Cool

In addition to getting snowed in for seven days during his senior season, Joe Montana played his final game at Notre Dame during a historically wicked ice storm in Dallas. In that 1979 Cotton Bowl, the quarterback had to down two cans of chicken soup in the half-time locker room just to stave off hypothermia. That explains why some of 1979's early draft rumblings made Montana shiver. He heard that the Green Bay Packers were intrigued. New York was a possibility, too. "I was just begging that it was a little bit nicer than that," Montana said with a laugh. "I'd had enough of snow. I was fortunate to be drafted here. And even more fortunate that it was by a guy named Bill Walsh."

The sunny climate of San Francisco was the perfect spot for Joe Cool. Paired with the brilliant Walsh, who maximized Montana's gift for footwork and timing, the duo revolutionized the NFL landscape. And they forever warmed Bay Area hearts.

Montana played with an unforeseen elegance, tormenting defensive savages with nothing but his skinny legs, so-so arm, and immeasurable resolve. Montana games were part battle, part ballet. "You knew you had the opportunity to win simply because he was on the field," former running back Roger Craig said. "He kind of reminds me of players like Larry Bird, Magic Johnson, Wayne Gretzky, Michael Jordan. He's in that category of great players, being able to elevate teammates to another level."

Montana won four Super Bowls during a 49ers career that lasted from 1979 to 1992. He also won three Super Bowl MVP awards, two regular season MVP awards, eight Pro Bowl selections, and six All-Pro honors. In barstool debates over who is the best quarterback of all time, these are the stats to have handy: Montana was 4–0 in Super Bowls with 11 touchdowns, zero interceptions, and a passer rating of 127.8. He is the only player to win three Super Bowl MVP awards, and in the one game he didn't, all he did was throw the game-winning pass to John Taylor with 34 seconds left.

Then again, measuring Montana through statistics is like measuring Van Gogh by his easel. Raw numbers explain why he slid to the third round in 1979, the 82nd player taken overall. The top quarterback in the draft that year was Jack Thompson, the "Throwin' Samoan," who was a sturdy 6'3", 217 pounds and went third overall to the Cincinnati Bengals. Montana, in contrast, was scrawny. The first time Dwight Clark ever saw him, at a Howard Johnson's restaurant counter, Clark figured the lanky kid with the blond Fu Manchu must be a kicker from Sweden. "I was 6'2" and—soaking wet—maybe 185," Montana said. "If you look at the numbers, I was probably drafted in the right spot."

Luckily for him and for the course of football history, the 49ers looked at a few other things. During a pre-draft workout in Los Angeles, Walsh and quarterbacks coach Sam Wyche put Montana threw a series of drills. They made the quarterback throw short, medium, and long.

After 15 minutes, they pulled the plug. They'd found their guy. "As soon as I saw Joe's beautiful, gliding footwork—quick natural steps, just poetry in motion, I knew we could develop the disciplines in him that would have been difficult with someone slower or less athletic," the late Walsh said.

Joseph Clifford Montana Jr. was born June 11, 1956 in New Eagle, Pennsylvania. He was a sophomore languishing on Notre

Dame's quarterback depth chart when Dan Devine, who had replaced Ara Parseghian as the Fighting Irish coach a year earlier, played a hunch. When his starter went down with an injury, he tapped Montana as his new man. "To this day I can't explain exactly why," the coach told *Time magazine* in 1985. "He just impressed me as the kind of guy who you think is going to get the job done. Often his first play off the bench was a bad pass, but as the game wore on, he would do what it took to win."

Montana sat out his junior year with a broken collarbone, but by the time he graduated, he had foreshadowed the on-field magic to come, culminating in that famous 1979 Cotton Bowl. Suffering from the consequences of the worst ice storm in Dallas history, Montana wasn't allowed to return to the field after halftime until he got his body temperature up to a safe level. He finally did in the third quarter and then came off the bench to erase a 34–12 deficit as Notre Dame defeated Houston 35–34. It remains known as the Chicken Soup game. "They actually gave me my choice—chicken or beef," Montana said. "It could have just as easily been the Beef Soup game."

Comebacks like that would be the hallmark of Montana's NFL career as well. In 1980 he engineered the largest comeback in league history, beating the Saints 38–35 after San Francisco trailed 35–7 at halftime. The next season he engineered the last-minute touchdown drive that culminated in The Catch in the 1981 NFC Championship against Dallas. In Super Bowl XXIII he spotted John Candy in the stands before finding Taylor with the game-winner.

Montana did it all with a calmness that belied his inner ferocity. It looked like poetry only because Walsh and Montana suffered for their art. Montana recalls now that he would head into games with 120 to 130 pass plays to memorize plus another 35 runs. All of the plays could be run out of two or three formations. All of them had to be run with absolute precision. "There are a lot of things that I learned from Bill throughout my career, but the message that's stayed with me throughout my life is the desire to be perfect," Montana said. "He pushed me and pushed us, especially the quarterback position which he was so proud of, to want to be perfect. And if you missed perfect, you end up with great."

Montana had a similar temperament. Even after beating the Bengals in Super Bowl XVI, his father found Joe sitting in the training room, despondent. The game's MVP only completed 14-of-22 passes for 157 yards with one touchdown passing and another running. He had no interceptions. By the time his dad stumbled across him, "I was happy, but I wasn't jumping for joy," Montana said. "We'd already done all that."

When his dad asked him what was wrong, Joe admitted that he didn't feel like he played that well. "Would you just shut up?" Joe Sr. snapped. "You just won the Super Bowl! Have some fun for a change!"

Montana laughed at the memory. "But that's the point," he said. "We wanted to be perfect. We didn't even want a ball to hit the ground. We wanted to complete 100 percent of our passes. We were striving for that perfection."

4 Jerry Rice

Jerry Rice first flickered onto the 49ers' radar screen on October 20, 1984. Technically, it wasn't a radar screen. It was the television set in Bill Walsh's Houston hotel room.

The 49ers were in town for a game against the Oilers. Walsh was flipping channels and stumbled across a game featuring Mississippi Valley State. Mesmerized by a wiry and elusive wide receiver, the coach watched for a while. He then summoned executive John McVay and public relations director Jerry Walker to his room. "Bill had such an unbelievable eye for talent—it's actually spooky," McVay recalled. "He kept saying over and over again that Rice looked super. Bill would say, 'Look at the way he moves! Look at his concentration! Look at the way he uses his hands!' I saw it, too, but only because I was sitting at the hands of the master."

Soon, the rest of the world would see it, too. And chances are we'll never see someone like him again.

The 49ers traded up in the 1985 draft to acquire the kid on Walsh's TV. They bundled their three top choices and swapped them to the New England Patriots for the No. 16 spot, nabbing Rice in the first round. He would go on to break every major receiving record in the NFL, putting the new marks out of reach.

For example, his 22,895 receiving yards are about 7,000 yards more than the next person on the list. That's almost four miles.

Rice amassed 208 touchdowns. The only player within 50 of that total is former Cowboys running back Emmitt Smith (175). And he caught more touchdown passes than Hall of Famers Lynn Swann, Raymond Berry, and Charlie Joiner combined.

Catches? Rice racked up 1,549. At the start of the 2013 season, only one active receiver (tight end Tony Gonzalez) had 1,000.

Rice was a Niner from 1985 to 2000 before playing for the Oakland Raiders (2001 to 2004) and the Seattle Seahawks (2004). When reflecting on his career, however, he urges you to put away the calculator. "My legacy is that I just played the game and I loved it and I left everything on the football field," he said. "It's not about the records or being considered the best receiver or the best player to ever play the game. It's just about doing something I love."

With Rice, statistics tell only half the story. And the other half is even more fun. He was born in dinky Starkville, Mississippi, before moving to even dinkier Crawford (pop. 445). He ran four miles down a dirt road each day to get to B. L. Moor High School.

There were only 20 kids in his sophomore class, so when Rice decided to skip out and loiter in the corridor one day, it didn't take long for the principal to crack the case. As the story goes, the principal tried to confront Rice, but the kid fled the scene like a startled hummingbird. It's the first documented case of Rice being as fast as the situation required.

When the vice principal caught up to him the next day, he whipped Rice six times and ordered him to report...to the football coach. Rice fit in quickly on the team, thanks to his principal-eluding speed, sturdy body, and strong hands, the result of his summer job working for his father, Joe.

Rice's dad was a no-nonsense bricklayer who demanded that all six of his sons serve an apprenticeship. (Rice was the youngest boy; he had two younger sisters.) During shifts that could last from 5 AM to sundown in the sizzling Southern heat, Rice would stand on the scaffold or the second story of an apartment building while his dad tossed bricks from below. If Rice dropped one, the cost of the brick was deducted from his paycheck.

Rice played well at Moor High School, but the venue was hardly a showcase for his talents. The stadium seated about 100 people and had light poles on just one side of the field. The only college to recruit him in person was Mississippi Valley State, a Division I-AA school in Itta Bena with an enrollment of 2,500 at the time.

The school was too small to generate much national attention. Still, it proved big enough. "I think Mississippi Valley State gave me an opportunity to showcase my capabilities," Rice said in 2013. "I had letters from all the major big schools, but Mississippi Valley was the only school that sent someone out to talk to me face to face. In Mississippi that goes a long, long way."

The biggest knock against Rice as an NFL prospect was his lack of foot speed. He was timed at 4.6 seconds in the 40-yard dash, which made him a tortoise in a field of 4.4-second hares.

Rice's Records

The unquestioned greatest receiver of all time, Jerry Rice holds just about every major receiving record. Here is a list of some of his more impressive ones.

Most Touchdowns, Career—**208**
Most Pass Receptions, Career—**1,549**
Most Seasons, 50 or More Pass Receptions—**17**
Most Consecutive Games with Pass Reception—**274**
Most Pass Receiving Yards Gained, Career—**22,895**
Most Seasons, 1,000 or More Yards Receiving—**14**
Most Games, 100 or More Yards Receiving, Career—**76**
Most Receiving Touchdowns, Career—**197**
Most Consecutive Games with Receiving Touchdown—**13**
    (1986 to 1987)
Most Yards From Scrimmage, Career—**23,540**
Most Combined Net Yards, Career—**23,546**

But Walsh and McVay had noticed something else: Nobody ever caught him. Rice was always one step ahead regardless of the distance or how many defensive backs were in pursuit. "To get an accurate 40 time on Jerry," McVay said, "you'd have to have somebody chasing him."

Upon being drafted by the 49ers, the bricklayer's son from the dirt roads of the Deep South had a hard time adjusting to San Francisco. Rice has said that when he stepped off the plane, he wanted to turn the plane right back around. He'd dazzle on the practice field but falter under the glare of NFL gamedays. Rice would muff a pass. Joe Montana would glare. Fans would boo.

Rice flubbed so many balls in one early-season game that Ronnie Lott silently vowed to watch how the kid handled himself in the locker room. Lott found Rice sitting alone, crying. "When I saw that, I knew we had something special," the Hall of Fame defensive back recalled. "It's the guys, who don't care, that you worry about."

Rice cared so much he remained after practices for extra sessions with veteran receiver Freddie Solomon. Other veteran teammates such as Lott, Guy McIntyre, Dwight Clark, and Mike Wilson took him under their wings and helped him calm down.

In the *Monday Night Football* spotlight during the 14th game of Rice's rookie season, Rice broke loose for 10 catches and 241 yards.

He had worked his way out of the mini-slump with "work" being the operative word. For more than a decade, Rice helped set the tone for excellence at 49ers practices by treating mundane afternoons as if they were the fourth quarter of the Super Bowl. "Not only was he head and shoulders above everybody else, but he was also the hardest worker on the field," Lott recalled. "What that established for everyone—Joe, myself, Steve Young, everybody—is the idea that you couldn't relax. You couldn't rest. You practiced for the purpose of being the best."

Rice made it to the Pro Bowl 13 times and was an All-Pro 12 times. But the only number that really matters to him is three. That's the number of Super Bowl rings he owns from his 49ers days. "This is why we play the game—to win Super Bowls and be part of something special," Rice said. "You hear so many players say, 'I'm not going to let a Super Bowl define my legacy.'

"Then why are you playing the game?"

Ronnie Lott and His Pinky Finger

Upon announcing his retirement on March 12, 1996, Ronnie Lott lamented that he was leaving the game without having delivered the perfect hit. A generation of bruised and battered ball

An intimidating hitter and one of the NFL's best defensive backs ever, Ronnie Lott delivers a jarring hit during a 1988 game.

carriers—Mark Bavaro, Ickey Woods, Gerald Riggs, and Jimmie Giles among them—might beg to differ.

What did Lott consider to be the perfect hit? Vaporizing somebody?

As a defensive back who terrorized 49ers opponents from 1981 to 1990, Lott left his mark by leaving a mark. The guy hit *hard*. And though Lott, by his own estimation, may have never delivered the utopian blow, he acknowledged that he at least reached the level of "mouthwatering." That was the term he used for the shots in which his physical training, mental preparation, and natural instincts all converged upon the opponent at once. "You've done your homework and you've hit it right on the money," Lott told the *San Jose Mercury News* in 1989. "Everything tingles. You let everything out, kind of cleanse yourself. Me making a great hit is no different than Magic [Johnson] making a great pass. You don't luck into it. It's knowing the game, knowing what's going to happen, knowing what angle to take."

Lott played for four Super Bowl winners and made 10 Pro Bowls during his 15 seasons in the NFL. An eight-time first-team All-Pro, he made the NFL All-Decade Team for the 1980s and, as if that weren't enough, he went ahead and made the all-1990s team, too. He was inducted into the Pro Football Hall of Fame in 2000 at a ceremony where, fittingly, he saluted his fellow intimidators. "Thank you to the players of this great game, the warriors, the guys who love to hit," Lott told the crowd. "I'm talking about giants like Dick Butkus. I'm talking about Jack Tatum, guys like Kenny Easley and Jack Lambert. I know you're here with us. You were definitely a warrior."

Lott, however, was hardly a one-hit wonder. He displayed his diverse skills whether at cornerback (both left and right), free safety, or strong safety, earning All-Pro honors at all three positions.

And no matter the spot, he ranks among the best defensive backs in NFL history. Joe Montana recalled that on the night before games, coaches would air highlight reels of previous games— all the big plays. The majority of what they saw was Ronnie Lott. Linebacker Keena Turner said: "He was such a ferocious hitter, but he played the entire game. Nobody knew the opposition better than Ronnie. He not only was a big hitter, but he knew his stuff. Those things get lost when you're as great as he was at a certain thing."

Born on May 8, 1959, Ronald Mandel Lott spent his pre-teen years in Washington, D.C., roaming the streets looking for pickup

The Amputation

There's no arguing that Ronnie Lott is one of the NFL's all-time tough guys. And certainly no one would be foolhardy enough to argue with the man himself. But an oft-told tale about Lott's grit merits clarification.

The 49ers' Hall of Fame defensive back did lose part of his left pinky as the result of a gruesome injury. But he did not have his finger cut off in the middle of the locker room. The amputation took place in the offseason.

Here's what happened: In a game against Dallas on December 22, 1985, Lott's finger was crushed by the helmet of Cowboys fullback Tim Newsome. One of Lott's close friends told SI.com years later that the tip of his finger "exploded." During the game's broadcast, announcer John Madden watched Lott come off the field and said, "I'm sure he has one of those fractures where the bone was through the skin because there is blood involved in that thing."

Lott was indeed tough: He played the rest of the Cowboys game with his exploded pinky taped up. And then rather than miss a playoff game against the Giants, he had it taped up again the following week and took the field in the 49ers' 17–3 loss. With that his legend as a warrior was sealed. "Dark Ages, World War I, Civil War, pick the period," former teammate Randy Cross told NFL Films. "He could have fought at Troy."

It was April before doctors looked at the badly damaged finger and gave Lott two choices: They could operate, graft a bone from his wrist and have him wear a cast for eight weeks. Or they could amputate just above the first joint.

Lott chose the latter, ensuring that he'd be ready at the start of the '86 season.

But upon his first look at the whitish, rounded stump post-surgery, the legend himself teetered from a blow. "The ugliest thing I've ever seen," Lott recalled for the *San Francisco Chronicle* in August of 1986. "I was trying to laugh it off, but I felt sick. I tried to stand up, but I broke into a cold sweat. It was just a total shock. I thought, *Oh man, I should have had the pin put in.*

games—baseball, football, basketball, whatever. During one such neighborhood game, Lott scored a touchdown and celebrated so enthusiastically that his annoyed opponent smashed him in the face. "I went running in the house crying and yelling, 'Dad! Dad! He hit me in the eye!'" Lott recounted to *Mercury News* writer John Hubner. "My dad put the paper down, said, 'You don't look so bad to me. Go on back out there.'

"I did and it was a great lesson for me. It showed that getting hit isn't that bad. It showed me that you can't mouth off about how good you are. It made me tougher."

Lott went on to star at USC where he was an All-American as both a junior and a senior. The 49ers took him in the first round (eighth overall) in the 1981 draft. The team was undergoing a cultural shift, and the fiery and intense Lott helped lead the charge to a victory in Super Bowl XVI.

In that 1981 season, Lott became the second rookie in NFL history to return three interceptions for touchdowns. He finished second to Lawrence Taylor for Rookie of the Year honors. Opponents soon knew to keep an eye out for the hulking No. 42 who roamed the Niners' defensive backfield. His greatest hits album would include him crumpling Bavaro, the New York Giants tight end, on a cool Monday night at Candlestick Park and sticking Woods, the Cincinnati Bengals' mouthy running back, to turn the tide in Super Bowl XXIII. "It doesn't matter who Ronnie was hitting," Montana said, "he was going to throw his whole body at the guy."

At 6'0", 203 pounds, Lott played without fear. Dallas Cowboys coach Tom Landry once described him as being like a middle linebacker playing safety. Although Lott played all over the secondary during his career, he was at his best as a rangy free safety. From that position in 1986, he led the NFL with 10 interceptions, forced three fumbles, had two sacks, and was credited with 77 tackles.

In one of the worst decisions in franchise history, after the 1990 season the 49ers decided not to protect Lott from Plan B free agency—leaving him little choice but to move on. He then played for the Los Angeles Raiders (1991 to 1992) and New York Jets (1993 to 1994) before injuries nudged him into retirement.

When he was finished with football, the player known for his hard hits showed off his soft heart. Lott became the founder and chairman of All-Stars Helping Kids, a nonprofit organization that encourages other high-profile athletes to maximize their charity efforts. By the early 2000s he was distributing more than $1 million annually in grants to other nonprofits. "People think once you stop playing sports, you retire from everything. But it's just the beginning of life," Lott said. "You have to take action. You have to stand for something."

6 Steve Young

On the day he arrived for his first training camp with the 49ers in 1987, quarterback Steve Young needed new shoes. The equipment man, Bronco Hinek, was more than happy to help out, handing the newcomer a pair of Mizuno cleats. Hinek was a tremendous practical joker. But Young didn't know that yet. So the quarterback trotted out to the practice field blissfully unaware that his footwear actually belonged to somebody else. "Nice shoes," Joe Montana said.

Young finally noticed the No. 16 embossed on those Mizunos. Yup, he was standing in Joe Montana's footsteps. "So that was my introduction to the Bay Area," Young said.

Is there a more fitting allegory for a quarterback defined largely by the player who came before him? All Young had to do was match the standard set by Joe Cool—the man who would win four Super Bowl rings, three Super Bowl MVP trophies, and the eternal devotion of the San Francisco faithful.

But by the time Young hung up his *own* cleats, he'd left an impact: a Super Bowl MVP award, seven Pro Bowl selections, two regular season MVP awards, and enshrinement into the Pro Football Hall of Fame. Young had gone from *can't* to Canton. "Joe Montana was the greatest QB that I had ever seen. I was in awe," Young said during his induction speech in 2005. "I was tempted many times by the opportunity to play for other teams, but I was drawn to the inevitable challenge to live up to the standard that I was witnessing."

Few players took a longer or rockier path to NFL stardom. Even in college, Young had to overcome skeptics. He ranked eighth on the quarterback depth chart at the start of his BYU career. "I didn't even throw the football properly," said. "People were like, 'Good luck with this kid. He doesn't even know how to throw.'"

But in a progression that would foreshadow his NFL career, Young persevered at BYU—then thrived. Succeeding record-setting passer Jim McMahon, Young threw for at least 300 yards in all but two of his games during his senior year and completed 71.3 percent of his passes, an NCAA record at the time.

The NFL, though, would have to wait. In 1984 Young signed a 10-year, $42-million deal with the Los Angeles Express of the United States Football League. The franchise would go belly up by '85, but it was not a total loss in terms of Young's football development. His offensive coordinator in Los Angeles was Sid Gillman, the innovator best known for his revolutionary passing game with the San Diego Chargers. Gillman repeatedly told Young: "This is not a game. It is a canvas, and you are Michelangelo."

As the USFL careened toward its doom, Young wriggled out of his Express contract and signed with the Tampa Bay Buccaneers, who had taken him with the first pick of the supplemental draft a

Lawrence Phillips' Non-Block

Troubled running back Lawrence Phillips spent much of his life running afoul of the law. His biggest crime with the 49ers was something he didn't do: Phillips failed to block Arizona cornerback Aeneas Williams, whose blindside hit ended Steve Young's career.

Phillips simply whiffed when Williams raced in on a blitz on September 27, 1999. Young wound up with his fourth concussion in three years and was forced to call it a wrap—just one year after establishing career highs with 4,170 passing yards and 36 passing touchdowns.

After his blown assignment, the 49ers buried Phillips on the bench. Eventually he rebelled by refusing to practice. And by mid-November, the 49ers had seen enough: They suspended him en route to waiving him. "Lawrence said, 'You don't put me in during games anyway. So why should I practice?'" coach Steve Mariucci said. "That's conduct detrimental to the team if I ever saw it."

Phillips clearly could have used a tad more attention to detail. Just ask anybody who saw the devastating hit on Young. "We're a hard-working team," Mariucci said. "We believe [Phillips] failed to comply with those standards and began to find reasons why he wouldn't practice and shouldn't give a complete effort. It came to the point where we weren't able to work together."

year earlier. During his two miserable seasons in Tampa Bay the Bucs went 4–28, helping Young later appreciate that there are worse fates than riding the bench on an excellent team behind the greatest quarterback of all time. "Yes, there was pressure in San Francisco—the expectations, the standards," Young said. "And I would think, *Thank heavens. This is great.*"

The 49ers traded for Young by sending Tampa Bay second and fourth-round draft picks plus about a million in cash. Young arrived eager to take over. He was under the impression that Montana's bad back left the legend on the verge of retirement.

Um, no.

As early as his first practice—the day he was wearing Montana's shoes—Young realized that the rumors of Joe's demise had been greatly exaggerated. There was no sign of injury. Montana looked as healthy and as sharp as ever. Young was going to have to wait. What followed was one of the most high-voltage quarterback controversies of all time. From 1987 to 1992, the 49ers had two future Hall of Famers on the same roster, and neither one was thrilled with the arrangement. At least, though, it gave Young a firsthand look at what he was up against. "I remember watching Joe from the sideline and thinking, *How did he do that?* I don't even know how to start *thinking* about doing that," Young said. "And then by watching it, you start doing it."

Montana could dominate the meeting rooms, too. Young recalled that players would get handed the game plan every Wednesday with about 15 minutes to spare before a meeting. Young, a smart guy who earned a law degree during the NFL off-seasons, tried to cram as much info as he could during that short span. But once the meeting started, Montana always knew the right answer—in expansive detail. "I got more and more frustrated," Young said. "Finally, I turned to Mike Holmgren, one of the coaches, and said, 'How does Joe do that? He knows everything.' And Holmgren said, 'Because he gets it faxed to him on Tuesday nights.' There's no angle that Joe didn't know."

Ultimately, of course, Young got his chance. In 1992 with Montana still struggling to recover from elbow surgery, the 31-year-old left-hander started all 16 games for the first time in his career. He responded by leading the NFL in touchdown passes (25), completion percentage (66.7), yards per attempt (8.6), and passer rating (107.0). Different from Montana in style, Young was a scrambler who finished his career with 4,239 career rushing yards and 43 rushing touchdowns.

"Steve had to really work. I felt bad for him when he first took over because he was searching, trying to find himself," former running back Roger Craig said. "Steve was a running back caught in a quarterback's body. But he knew that if he was going to be great, he had to stop running. He had to learn how to be a pocket thrower and he proved that he could be a pocket thrower. And he shocked the NFL when he had the highest rating in the NFL for like four years in a row. And then he had the opportunity to taste the victory of winning the Super Bowl. And all the fans that booed him turned into cheers at the end of his career. They were cheering him big time, so I take my hat off to Steve Young. He worked his butt off to be where he is today."

And with all that work, Young left his own indelible footprints.

7 Mr. D

To understand how Eddie DeBartolo Jr. transformed the 49ers from struggling franchise into the envy of the sports world, you have to look beyond his hiring of Bill Walsh, his drafting of Joe Montana, his five Super Bowl championships, and his 13 division titles. For a full view, step inside a disquieting doctor's office in Tampa, Florida, long after he had given up his ownership of the 49ers.

It was here that Mr. DeBartolo—as players still call him—would sit and wait for ex-receiver Freddie Solomon to finish his chemotherapy treatments during his final years of life. "We're not talking about just picking up the tab. We're talking about picking up the patient," recalled former 49ers executive Carmen Policy. "He'd drive Freddie to chemotherapy, wait with him the entire time, and then drive him home. He sincerely cared. It wasn't just, 'We drafted you. You played for us. And now we're getting somebody new—see you later.' Really, it's an approach that doesn't exist today."

DeBartolo purchased the 49ers in 1977 with the goal of creating a top-notch organization on and off the field. To do so he invested enthusiastically to upgrade the front-office administration and on-field talent. Above that he created what former 49ers like to call an "atmosphere conducive to winning." That meant first-class travel, brand-new facilities, and a receptive ear to whatever the players needed.

If one of his players was injured in a road game and had to stay behind for treatment, DeBartolo would send his private jet once the player had healed enough to come home. On standard team flights, every player had at least two seats to themselves. Whenever the 49ers won the NFC West, every player would get two dozen long-stemmed roses to give to his wife or girlfriend or mother.

Word spread quickly among players about this NFL paradise. It was not uncommon for opponents to approach 49ers and ask what it was like to play for Eddie D. "If you look at today's game and how owners think in all sports, it was led by Eddie DeBartolo," Hall of Famer Ronnie Lott said. "Now you have owners that have more of an appreciation for the athletes that played for them. Other prominent teams saw that they had to raise their bar. They had to create a better environment. Now facilities are better. If you look around the league, Eddie was one of the first to build a nice facility."

Born November 6, 1946 in Youngstown, Ohio, Edward John DeBartolo Jr. was the son of a real-estate giant. The undisputed leader in the shopping-mall industry, Edward Sr. was worth an estimated $1.4 billion in personal wealth by 1990.

Edward Jr. graduated from Notre Dame in 1968 and worked for a while in the family business. But he wanted to carve his own niche. So in January 1977—when football executive Joe Thomas left a message asking Eddie Sr. if he might be interested in buying the 49ers—Eddie Jr. called him back instead. At 30 he became the proud owner of an NFL franchise.

DeBartolo's early days with the 49ers hardly had the look of a dynasty in the making. He hired Thomas as his general manager, and Thomas promptly set about tearing down the franchise with a series of personnel blunders and coaching missteps.

Fans took out their frustration on this boy prince of an owner. Late in the '77 season as the 49ers were spiraling toward a 5–9 finish, a fan fired a half-full beer can off DeBartolo's head. "At least you could've drank it first!" he shouted back in the direction of his assailant.

But his fortunes turned at the end of the 1978 season when DeBartolo fired Thomas and made way for the new general manager and head coach: Bill Walsh. The team also targeted a third-round quarterback named Joe Montana, and together they made history. "Bill and Eddie were complete opposites when it comes to temperament," Montana told me. "Bill was more quiet. But they had the same demands of perfection and wanting to win—and that's how they were united by a common bond. They were so different, but they wanted the same thing."

By 1981 the 49ers were 13–3 and on their way to their first Super Bowl title. The team averaged an astounding 13 wins per season, including playoffs during a span from 1981 to 1998 (not including strike-shortened '82.) The franchise posted the best winning percentage in the NFL in both the decades of the 1980s and 1990s.

And along the way, DeBartolo engendered an unending loyalty for his willingness to go beyond the call of duty. "When my father got sick with brain cancer—probably in my fifth or sixth year—Mr. D was instrumental in getting my father in to see some of the best doctors in the world," longtime tackle Harris Barton said. "That was an unbelievable gesture for him to do something like that. I ended up having my father come out to see Dr. Charlie Wilson, who was the noted brain tumor specialist at UCSF. Without a call from Mr. D, my dad would have never gotten in.

"There was a human connection. Mr. DeBartolo expected greatness. He expected hard work. He expected class guys. He was leading the way in being a class individual and a caring person."

8 Roger Craig

As the 1983 NFL draft approached, Roger Craig spotted an item in *Sports Illustrated* suggesting the 49ers had him in their sights. Craig's first reaction was fear.

His only previous trip to the Bay Area had consisted of a recruiting visit to the University of California at Berkeley, where the kid from a tiny town in Iowa recalled being "scared to death" by the radical scene on Telegraph Avenue. To make matters worse, a Bears assistant coach had zipped him around the California freeways—"a madman driving in a sports car," Craig remembers—before dropping him off at the doorstep of Levi Strauss, a noted Cal alum. When Craig stepped out of the car to cross the street, a taxi cab nearly mowed him down. It's no wonder he decided to go to Nebraska instead.

But when he saw that Bill Walsh wanted him? I thought, *Oh, my gosh! I have to go back to the Bay Area!* he said, laughing at the memory. "I was freaking out again." Craig's second reaction was practical. And it would alter the course of the franchise—and even the NFL itself.

Craig had remembered while watching the 1981 Super Bowl champions that Walsh's offense depended on runners catching the ball out of the backfield. This was not a grinding offense: Ricky Patton led the '81 49ers with a mere 543 rushing yards. So to make sure he'd be useful to his prospective employer, Craig started catching balls—a lot of them. He coaxed his quarterback at Nebraska, Turner Gill, to throw him passes. He got his brothers to do the same.

When the 49ers did draft him in the second round (49th overall), they envisioned a fullback who could block and share carries with running back Wendell Tyler. After all, Craig had only 16 career catches over three seasons at Nebraska. It wasn't until his first day at 49ers rookie camp that Craig showed off his new trick. Quarterbacks coach Paul Hackett threw him about 100 passes on all kinds of routes. Craig caught 98. "Their eyes lit up," Craig said.

Soon Craig was lighting up the scoreboard, too. He caught 48 passes his first season and placed second to Eric Dickerson in NFC Rookie of the Year voting. In 1984 he caught 71. In 1985 the fullback (*a fullback?*) led the NFL with 92 catches. The great Washington Redskins wideout Art Monk finished second with 91. "Monk was so funny," Craig said. "I went to the Pro Bowl that year and he said, 'Stay out of my category, man.'"

With Craig, Walsh had a 6'0", 222-pound toy for his West Coast Offense. The fullback could run (with that distinctive high-kneed style), block, and catch. Equally important, he had the IQ required to understand how any of those things could open up possibilities for Joe Montana, Jerry Rice, and John Taylor. "Within our system, it was hard for defenses to cover all of us," Craig said. "It was like playing chess, and Montana was the guy who made all the checkmates."

Craig experienced the NFC Championship Game as a rookie in 1983 and went to Super Bowl XIX the following year. Before that showdown against the Miami Dolphins at Stanford Stadium in Palo Alto, California, linebacker Jack "Hacksaw" Reynolds pulled him aside and offered a few words of advice. "He told me, 'Make sure you lay it on the line. Play every play like it's going to be your last. You don't know if you're *ever* going to be back to the Super Bowl here. So you have to take advantage of every opportunity that's given to you.' And I did. I played every play so hard. That was the most focused, most motivated I've ever been on every play. If you watch the game, you'll see how intense I was."

The 49ers defeated Miami 38–16, and Craig became the first player ever to score three touchdowns in a Super Bowl. Fittingly, he mixed things up. One touchdown came on the ground and two through the air.

But Craig's best individual season would be the one that followed, when in 1985 he became the first player in NFL history to reach both 1,000 yards rushing and 1,000 yards receiving in the same season. He also led the 49ers with 15 touchdowns. Other backs in history had made catches, but no one had ever done so as prolifically as Craig, the first running back to amass at least 500 career receptions. He has watched with an air of pride as a wave of multi-threat runners such as Marshall Faulk, Edgerrin James, Brian Westbrook, Maurice Jones-Drew, LaDainian Tomlinson, and Ray Rice have followed in his footsteps. "We were ahead of our time," Craig, the four-time Pro Bowler, said. "We had a 21st century offense back in the 1980s."

In 1988 Craig was named the AP's NFL Offensive Player of the Year. He ran for 1,502 yards and caught 76 passes for 534 more yards. Like so many other players from the 49ers' dynasty years, however, the only things he counts are the rings on his fingers. Craig was part of three Super Bowl victories—XIX, XXIII, and XXIV—during a 49ers career spanning 1983 to 1990. "I wasn't like one of those running backs that would run for 100 yards and build up the stats," he said. "Yeah, that's fine and dandy. But if you're not winning, that doesn't mean anything. Stats are great, but if you're not winning, what are stats going to do for you?

"I wouldn't trade my rings for anything. Trust me. Because that's what people remember the most."

9 Super Bowl XVI

Upon arriving in Detroit for the first Super Bowl week of his career, Joe Montana learned quickly that the atmosphere was a madhouse. By the time the bus pulled up outside the team hotel, fans were everywhere. The quarterback wanted nothing more than to push through the crowd and get to the lobby. But first Montana had to shake a pesky defender. "We get off the bus and we had to carry our bag. And all of a sudden, somebody's trying to grab my bag," he said. "I'm looking at this bellman and I'm saying, 'I got it. I got it.'"

Montana kept walking, but the bellman kept trying to yank his bag away. Irritated, the quarterback was ready to snap. "I turn," Montana said, "and it's Bill Walsh dressed as a bellman."

Their head coach's practical joke set the tone for a 26–21 victory against the Cincinnati Bengals in Super Bowl XVI at the Silverdome in Pontiac, Michigan. Needless to say, the 49ers had never played such a high stakes game, having improved from 2–14 to 6–10 to 13–3 over the span of just three seasons. They had started the 1981 season with 20 new players on the roster and they were playing a much more experienced Bengals team. But Walsh's shenanigans ensured that they would remain as confident and loose as their head coach. "He was one of the great motivators of all time," Montana said, still marveling. "He always knew when to make light of things when we were getting ready to play the game to calm everybody down."

Montana would go on to win the first of his three Super Bowl MVP awards. Some, though, thought the vote should have gone to Ray Wersching, who drilled a Super Bowl record-tying four field goals and kept the Bengals guessing with his befuddling kickoffs.

The 49ers defense fended off quarterback Ken Anderson, receiver Cris Collinsworth, and most memorably a 249-pound bruising back named Pete Johnson during a remarkable goal-line stand. In short this Super Bowl title was a team victory—an unstoppable machine made up of parts that only Walsh knew how to piece together. There were rising stars like Montana, Ronnie Lott, Randy Cross, and Dwight Hicks; grizzled veterans like Jack "Hacksaw" Reynolds and Fred Dean; and a roster of support players whose names still echo like poetry on the streets of San Francisco: Craig Puki, Bill Ring, Lenvil Elliott, John Choma, Fred Quillan, Jim Stuckey, Dan Bunz, and Dan Audick. "This was one rare moment when a team without great stars and experience raises up," Walsh said. "No one could take us. It was the highlight of my life. Anything can happen now."

The celebration had eluded the 49ers for 36 maddening years. But they welcomed it with the ease of a gracious bellman, bursting out to a 20–0 lead—the largest halftime lead in Super Bowl history. The 49ers took a 7–0 lead on a 1-yard run by Montana (a fitting player to score the first touchdown in 49ers' Super Bowl history). Then Earl Cooper caught an 11-yard pass to cap the longest drive (92 yards) in Super Bowl history—a showcase for the Walsh-Montana blend of short passes and patience.

Walsh may have been eager to leave an impression on a Bengals team that had passed him over for the head coaching job in 1976 in favor of Bill "Tiger" Johnson after Walsh had served as a Bengals assistant coach from 1968 to 1975. But if Walsh was showing off, some of his best moves went unseen.

Road conditions on the way to the game were treacherous that day. The lanes were covered with snow as the windchill factor dropped to minus-22. Compounding the 49ers' travel woes, their team bus got stuck behind a motorcade for then–vice president George Bush, who was heading to the game. Players began to squirm. Were they going to be late for the biggest game of their lives? About the only members of the 49ers' traveling party at the stadium were equipment managers Bronco Hinek and Chico Norton. Everybody else was stuck on the bus. "No traffic is moving. Nothing. We had no idea what was going on," Montana said. "Everybody is looking at their watches and thinking, *In 10 minutes we're supposed to be on the field.* That's when Bill stood up. He said, 'Guys, don't worry. I just got a call. Chico just scored, Bronco kicked the extra point, and we're up 7–0.'"

The tension was broken—again. And after the 49ers really did go up 7–0 and then 20–0, they were able to withstand the Bengals' late charge in the second half. Anderson, once a Walsh protege, took the Bengals on an 83-yard touchdown march on the opening series of the third quarter, scoring on a 5-yard scramble up the middle. That made it 20–7 with plenty of time to go.

But the Bengals' comeback express ran into a brick wall later in the third quarter. That's when Cincinnati had a first-and-goal at the 3 and walked away with nothing but bruises. Johnson managed to take the first-down play to the 1. But on second down, Reynolds blasted the fullback to stop him for no gain. On third down Anderson completed a pass to Charles Alexander in the right flat, but linebacker Dan Bunz stopped the halfback inches short of the end zone. On fourth Johnson tried to go over right tackle but was swarmed by the 49ers' line for no gain. "I figured I could go under them," Johnson said. "It just didn't work."

And while Johnson wound up at the bottom of the pile, the 49ers were finally at the top of the football world. The 49ers became the first Super Bowl winner to be outgained in yardage by the loser (356 to 275), which seemed about right for a team that had come from nowhere. "I don't know how we are ever going to top this," tackle Keith Fahnhorst said. "I'm still numb. To grasp something like this, well, it's unbelievable."

10 Frank Gore

Frank Gore demonstrated at an early age that he was coachable. Long before he took his first snap in the NFL, the kid listened to his mom whenever she asked him to clean the house or do yard work. "That's one thing I'll say about Frank," Liz Gore said. "He'll never give me any back talk."

That bond between mother and son is the reason the 49ers wound up with Gore in the first place. He entered the 2005 draft when his personal stock was at its nadir. Gore had shown promise at the University of Miami, but had suffered two torn anterior cruciate ligaments while with the Hurricanes. Scouts whispered he'd lost a step. *Sports Illustrated* labeled him the most overrated running back in the draft. Miami coach Larry Coker tried to persuade Gore to stick around for his senior season to show NFL general managers how he could really play.

For Gore, though, there was no use in waiting. His mom was 43 and had been on dialysis since Frank was in high school. No longer just intent on cleaning her house, Frank wanted to buy her a new one. So he entered the draft just to land whatever paycheck he could get. Even as a third-round pick, the 65th player overall, he earned enough to buy Liz Gore a spacious new home. As it turned out, Gore found the perfect home, too.

The back, who slipped in the draft because of concerns about his health, turned out to be one of the most relentlessly reliable offensive threats in franchise history. Tough enough to hammer his way between the tackles and fast enough to outrun defenders, Gore racked up monstrous rushing totals in good times and in bad.

And when he finally reached his long-awaited first Super Bowl, he did his part by setting a franchise Super Bowl record with 110 rushing yards. Naturally, Gore celebrated his 6-yard touchdown run against the Baltimore Ravens that day by pointing toward the sky. "I point at her," Gore said. "That's for her."

The 49ers' all-time leader in rushing yards, attempts, and 100-yard games, Gore was the first player in team history to record four consecutive 1,000-yard rushing seasons (2006 to 2009). He was also an excellent pass catcher, snagging more receptions than any 49ers running back except Roger Craig.

And Gore continued to carry himself with the air of a dutiful son. He did whatever the organization asked. Quarterbacks loved him because he was as dedicated to his blocking as he was to his carries. Reporters loved him because he was polite and approachable. And coaches? Well, don't get the coaches started. "Every day my admiration for Frank Gore as a football player grows," coach Jim Harbaugh said. "Every time you think it's as high as it can be, then he finds another rung on the ladder to go in my esteem. And then even more so as a person. He's just one of the finest guys you ever want to be around. He'd do anything for the team and is just a football player in all senses of the word, phrase."

Gore had some huge games early in his career, including a 207-yard outburst against the Seattle Seahawks in 2009 when he ripped off touchdown runs of 79 and 80 yards. (Barry Sanders is the only other running back to have two touchdown runs of 75 yards in the same game.) But for pure emotion, it would be tough to top a game in September 2007. Gore took the field just days after Liz Gore died at age 46. Her son paid tribute the best way he could, scoring two touchdowns and both times pointing up to the sky.

"When I got up this morning, it was tough getting up," Gore said, fighting his emotions in the locker room that day. "Every time that it is game time, all I know is that stadium. Me and my mom would talk on the way to the stadium. This morning, I just kept looking at my phone. She didn't call. It's tough, you know. I shed a few tears, and it was tough to get up, but I decided to play and I had to do my best for my team. And I know that my mom and the Man above are watching over me, so I would be all right."

11 Joe the Jet

During a 1948 game, rookie running back Joe Perry twice burst past Frankie Albert before the quarterback had time to deliver a handoff up the middle. "Joe, you're like a jet coming through there," Albert declared. And just like that, a nickname was born.

Joe "the Jet" Perry blasted off from the start, averaging 7.3 yards per carry and scoring 10 touchdowns in that first season. And he remained in flight with the 49ers for 14 seasons, leaving behind a franchise mark for career rushing yards that lasted until Frank Gore's arrival decades later.

A 6'0", 200-pound fullback, Perry was the first player in NFL history to record back-to-back 1,000-yard rushing seasons. He led the 49ers in rushing eight times, including seven straight seasons (1949 to 1955). "Joe Perry was a super, super superstar," quarterback Y.A. Tittle said.

Perry had a history of getting to places faster than anyone else could: He was the first black player in 49ers history when he signed

O.J. and Al

O.J. Simpson's best years in San Francisco came during his childhood not during his one season in a 49ers uniform. The running back was legendary at Galileo High School and City College of San Francisco before earning national stardom at USC (where he won the 1968 Heisman Trophy) and with the Buffalo Bills (where he won four rushing titles).

But by the time the 49ers acquired him in 1978, the Juice was just about out of juice. Simpson totaled 1,053 yards over two injury-plagued seasons before retiring at age 32.

The 49ers got him from the Bills in what Rick Reilly of *Sports Illustrated* called the Lawrence Welk trade—San Francisco gave up "a one and a two and a three," though it was actually one first, two seconds, a third, and a fourth.

Simpson didn't play that well, but as Reilly noted, Simpson still got to experience some of owner Edward DeBartolo's trademark kindness. When Simpson was going through a divorce in 1980 and was about to lose his house, DeBartolo lent him the money to keep the place. "Eddie is a hard guy not to like," Simpson said.

One of Simpson's 49ers teammates during that '79 season was defensive lineman Al Cowlings. Simpson and Cowlings had also played together at Galileo High, San Francisco City College, USC, and Buffalo.

Most notoriously they would later team up again for a slow-speed chase in a white Ford Bronco on June 17, 1994, several days after the murder of Simpson's ex-wife, Nicole Brown Simpson, and Ronald Goldman. Cowlings was the driver and Simpson the passenger.

In 1997 a civil court awarded a judgment against Simpson for the wrongful deaths of Brown Simpson and Goldman.

---

before the '48 season, the team's third in the All-America Football Conference. That milestone was not taken lightly. 49ers owner Tony Morabito offered Perry $4,500 to sign, while the Los Angeles Rams offered $9,500. But the running back later told the *San Francisco Chronicle* that there was far more than money involved. "I told [Morabito], 'They're offering me $5,000 more than you are,'" Perry said. "He said, 'Yeah, well, I know.' But he went on and said, 'We've been looking for a black player in San Francisco. I've checked you out on all facets of life and everything, and you're the guy we want. I can't afford to pay you the amount of money the Rams have offered you, but if you go with me, you'll never regret it.'

"I mulled it over for a while because $5,000 was a lot of money in 1947. But Tony sold me. He became like a father to me. I never regretted my decision."

There were only a few other black players in pro football in the 1940s. The NFL's Rams had Kenny Washington and Woody Strode while the AAFC champion Cleveland Browns featured stars Marion Motley and Bill Willis. But Perry was among that first wave of pioneers.

And he said he always felt welcome in San Francisco. In *Gridiron Gauntlet*, an oral history of black players by Andy Piascik, Perry recalled the strong support of his fellow 49ers. "If somebody on the other team ever got any idea he wanted to start something, he had to mess with our whole team," he said.

Fletcher "Joe" Perry was born on January 22, 1927 in Stevens, Arkansas, and raised in Compton, California. He wanted to attend UCLA, but the school rebuffed him—a bitter blow for a young man who idolized Jackie Robinson. So Perry headed off to community college. He scored 22 touchdowns in his lone season at Compton Junior College and was playing for the Alameda, California, Naval Air Station football team known as the Hell Cats when he earned the notice of John Woudenberg, an offensive tackle for the 49ers. Woudenberg dutifully reported his discovery to Morabito and head coach Buck Shaw.

Perry dazzled during his first two seasons while the 49ers were in the AAFC and kept right on rolling when the NFL absorbed the franchise in 1950. He gained 1,018 yards in 1953 and 1,049 more in '54. Whatever the league, Perry was a star: He was All-AAFC in '49 and All-NFL in '53 and '54.

Before the 1961 season, the 49ers traded him to the Colts. He played two seasons there before returning to the 49ers for one last go-round.

Given his pioneering ways, it was only fitting that Perry become the first player from the Million Dollar Backfield to receive induction into the Pro Football Hall of Fame in Canton, Ohio, in 1969. He was followed by Hugh McElhenny in 1970, Y.A. Tittle in '71, and John Henry Johnson in '87.

Of course, none of those players actually came close to making a million bucks. Late in life, Perry, who died in 2011 at age 84, was asked how much money he might command in the modern NFL. "How many Brink's trucks do you have?" he replied.

12 John Brodie

Long before John Brodie won the 1970 MVP award, guided the 49ers to back-to-back NFC Championship Games, or had his jersey retired, fans at Kezar Stadium booed the living daylights out of him. They could be creative. Sometimes it wasn't just a boo. "We Want Mira!" "We Want Spurrier!" or a hurled beer can could also get the fans' point across after a painful loss. But mostly they just booed. "I'd have heard 'em if I was down at Third and Market," Brodie said. "I can't turn off my ears."

In retrospect those boos are a little tricky to explain. As a 49ers quarterback from 1957 to 1973, he holds the team record as its longest-tenured player. He played 17 years for the franchise—one more than either Jerry Rice or Jimmy Johnson. Brodie's 201 games as San Francisco's quarterback rank comfortably ahead of Joe Montana (167) and Steve Young (150). "The highest tribute that can be paid a quarterback is to say that he strikes a little fear into whatever defensive team he faces," Dallas Cowboys coach Tom Landry said. "Brodie does that. I marvel at the way he has now mastered the art of quarterback."

Born August 14, 1935, John Riley Brodie grew up in Oakland as one of those kids who was good at everything. That part never changed: He would one day become a champion golfer on the Senior PGA Tour, play in the World Dominoes Championships, and was by all accounts no one to mess with in Ping-Pong, backgammon, or bowling.

There was, however, no mistaking his true calling. The 49ers selected the young quarterback out of Stanford with the third overall choice of the 1957 draft. He played sparingly at first, but got a taste of fans' fickleness that season when some, disgruntled with veteran quarterback Y.A. Tittle, chanted, "We want Brodie!" Putting in four seasons behind Tittle, Brodie took over as the 49ers' leading man after Tittle's trade to the New York Giants in 1961.

Then Brodie became the poster boy for frustration. The 49ers missed the playoffs every season from 1958 to 1969, creating restlessness among a fan base that *Sports Illustrated* once described as the "Kezar Cruelty Brigade." During that decade Brodie ran hot and cold. In 1965 he led the NFL in completion percentage (61.9), passing yards (3,112), and touchdowns (30). A year later he threw 22 interceptions against just 16 touchdowns.

So fans booed, but Brodie did his best to take it in stride. "All week long they catch hell from their bosses and maybe sometimes from their wives," he said. "They get all jammed up. Who could blame them? One day a week, they get out to the game and all of a sudden, they're my bosses. They can shout whatever they want. Okay, let 'em."

At other times Kezar crowds would fling refreshments at Brodie's head as he ran down the ramp to the locker room after a loss. "Sometimes they didn't bother to take the beer out of the

Quarterback John Brodie, who played 17 seasons for the 49ers, warms up before a game during his last season in 1973.

cans," Brodie told *Sports Illustrated.* "Finally we had to put up a cyclone fence to protect ourselves from their hardware."

Meanwhile, the rest of the football world had a better appreciation of Brodie's mighty right arm. After the 1965 season, the Houston Oilers of the rival American Football League tried to lure him away with a reported offer of $750,000 over 10 years. Instead, the 49ers arranged to keep him for a multiyear contract estimated at $1 million.

The sounds ringing in his helmet changed dramatically in 1970 when Brodie became the first 49ers player to win an MVP award. He guided the team to a 10–3–1 finish and—at last—that long-awaited playoff berth.

Brodie sealed his award with his magnificent play during the stretch drive, leading come-from-behind victories in each of the season's final three games. During that stretch he threw for 666 yards with seven touchdown passes (five of them to Gene Washington) and one interception. By the time he retired—from football that is—he ranked third in NFL history in career passing yards, trailing only Johnny Unitas and Fran Tarkenton. His 31,548 passing yards trail only Joe Montana (35,124) on the 49ers' all-time list.

Brodie had a second career to come: After he turned 50, he totaled more than $735,000 in career earnings on the Senior PGA Tour, racking up one win and 12 top 10 finishes between 1985 and 1998. Two of his daughters earned fame as well. Erin starred in the reality show *For Love or Money,* and Diane married former Atlanta Falcons quarterback—and one-time 49ers nemesis—Chris Chandler.

Considering all their father, John Brodie, accomplished with the 49ers, there are those who wonder why Brodie never made the Pro Football Hall of Fame. "I'd have to ask the same thing," said running back Ken Willard, his longtime teammate. "He was the MVP in one year. But I think it points out how important it is to win a Super Bowl. You look at the people going into the Hall now, and it's mostly people who won the Super Bowl. John had a great arm. He had a great ability to run the ballclub. I think he's very deserving of the Hall of Fame."

13 Tony Morabito

After Tony Morabito suffered a severe heart attack in 1952, his physician instructed him to sell the 49ers. Dr. William O'Grady warned the team founder and president that the stress of owning an NFL franchise would prove too much for his ticker.

Morabito agreed, flirted with a few offers—then wriggled out of several potential sales. He finally confessed to O'Grady. "I'll be worse off if I get out of football," Morabito said. "What the heck will I do with myself?"

Morabito operated on borrowed time for as long as he could. He could not imagine living without the 49ers, and the 49ers could not imagine living without him. Anthony J. Morabito had breathed life into the franchise, fighting for—and then engineering—the arrival of the first NFL team west of Chicago.

And when he suffered a fatal heart attack during the second quarter of a 49ers-Chicago Bears game on October 27, 1957, the 49ers felt as though they had lost their father. He was 47. "The 49ers could never find a better owner even if they got President Eisenhower," said coach Frankie Albert, who sobbed in the dressing room after the 49ers' emotionally charged 21–17 comeback victory against the Bears.

Morabito died, as he may have wished, at the 50-yard line at Kezar Stadium. He was with his brother and junior partner, Vic Morabito, when he slumped back into his seat. Medical personnel, including O'Grady, rushed to his aid. Instead, Father William McGuire gave Morabito final absolution. "Thank you, Father," Morabito whispered.

Those conversations are documented in Dan McGuire's *San Francisco 49ers*, which counts down the final hours of an owner whose passion, resolve, and intelligence established the foundation of one of pro football's most powerful franchises.

Morabito's stubbornness with his doctors should have come as no surprise. His feisty streak was the reason the team existed in the first place. He tried to score an NFL franchise for the West Coast as early as 1942. The native San Franciscan made his case before league officials, who promptly ushered him out of the room. In 1944 Morabito filed an application for an expansion team, traveled with his business associates to Chicago, presented his plan to commissioner Elmer Layden, and was rebuffed again.

But Morabito knew San Francisco was ready to support football. Fans had long packed the local stadiums to watch Cal (including the University of California at Berkeley's "Wonder Teams" of the 1920s) and were filling up seats to watch the "Wow Boys" of Stanford. During that era St. Mary's College in Moraga, the University of San Francisco, and Santa Clara were the top three schools in the West Coast Athletic Conference.

Morabito had business acumen, too. In 1940, at age 30, the son of Italian immigrants began amassing a fortune in the lumber carrier business. Lumber Terminals of San Francisco really took off during the Bay Area's post-war economic surge as houses were springing up for the growing population that was quickly migrating to California. At that time the NFL had no teams west of Chicago. In fact there was no major league professional team in the area, as Major League Baseball's Giants wouldn't move from New York until 1958.

Having been stonewalled by the NFL, Morabito got his team off the ground thanks to Arch Ward, the *Chicago Tribune* sports editor. Ward organized a rival league, the All-America Football

Lou Spadia

The most versatile player in franchise history never wore a uniform. Instead, Lou Spadia did just about everything else. Upon being hired by the fledgling 49ers in 1946, Spadia's roles included ticket manager, equipment manager, bed check man, media guide writer, and game program editor.

And that was just in his first year. Within two years Spadia was promoted to business manager. Within five he was the 49ers general manager. Spadia became chief executive officer and general manager in 1964 upon the death of owner Vic Morabito. He reported to Jane Morabito and Josephine Morabito, who retained ownership of the organization.

In 1967 he was named team president and in 1973 added the title of general manager, positions he held until 1976. The *San Francisco Chronicle* recalled his best management move as tapping Dick Nolan as coach in 1968. Nolan would guide the 49ers to three consecutive NFC West division titles from 1970 to 1972. "I hired him because his strength was defense," Spadia said. "I realized offense was a great show, but you didn't win with it."

Spadia remained with the 49ers until Eddie DeBartolo bought the team from the Morabito family, including Spadia's 5 percent share, in 1977. DeBartolo hired Joe Thomas to run the club.

It's a good thing Spadia cofounded the Bay Area Sports Hall of Fame in 1979. It gave him a place to be properly enshrined 20 years later. "He was one of a kind: philanthropic, creative, a born leader," former 49ers marketing man Ken Flower told the *San Francisco Chronicle* when Spadia died on February 18, 2013.

Among Spadia's many gifts was persuading his BASHOF fund-raising crew to work for free. Golfer Ken Venturi once quipped that Spadia's nickname ought to be "Crime—because crime doesn't pay, and neither does Spadia."

Conference. On June 6, 1944 in St. Louis—D-Day—Morabito agreed to form a San Francisco franchise for the AAFC, which would begin operations once World War II had ended. In that first year, 1946, Morabito co-owned the team with his lumber business partners, Allen E. Sorrell and E. J. Turre. The name "49ers" came from Sorrell, who proposed the moniker as a nod to the Northern California Gold Rush of 1849.

Hardly a hands-off owner, Morabito plucked Lawrence "Buck" Shaw from Santa Clara to serve as the 49ers' first head coach and helped stock an inaugural roster loaded with Stanford stars such as Frankie Albert, Norm Standlee, and Bruno Banducci.

The 49ers played their first (preseason) home game at Kezar Stadium on September 1, 1946. On that day the man, who was once laughed at for proposing a pro team in San Francisco, watched his franchise defeat the Chicago Rockets 34–14 before a crowd of 45,000 described as "longshoreman, draymen, mechanics, and waterfront workers."

When the AAFC folded in 1949, San Francisco was absorbed by the NFL along with the Cleveland Browns and Baltimore Colts franchises. At last, Morabito's dream had reached fruition. In fact a merger is what he'd hoped for all along, and he capitalized on it by signing future greats like Joe Perry, Hugh McElhenny, and John Henry Johnson. Morabito convinced the former to become the 49ers' first black player. "For nine years I signed blank contracts with him," Perry told the San Francisco Call-Bulletin. "I knew he'd fill in more than a fair salary figure. Many people don't know the nice things he's done. He didn't want them told, but I know lots of wonderful things about him."

When he suffered his fatal heart attack at Kezar, Morabito was taken in a stretcher to an ambulance outside the stadium. He was pronounced DOA at Mary's Help Hospital. News of his death reached the game in the third quarter with the Bears leading 17–7. His players rallied to win 21–17. Quarterback Y.A. Tittle called it "two of the most emotional quarters of football I have ever played."

A representative from the Bears approached Albert after the game. "If he was going to die," the Bears staffer said, "it would have made him happy that you beat us by four points."

"If he was going to live," a tearful Albert replied, "it would have made me happy to lose by a hundred points."

Victor Morabito kept the team in the family until 1964 when he, too, died of a heart attack. The brothers' wives, Jane and Josephine, retained control of the 49ers with Lou Spadia as team president until 1977 when Edward DeBartolo Jr. of Youngstown, Ohio, emerged to buy the franchise.

14 Super Bowl XXIII— The John Candy Game

When Cincinnati Bengals kicker Jim Breech drilled a 40-yard field goal with 3:20 left in Super Bowl XXIII, the stage was set. The 49ers trailed 16–13, meaning Joe Montana had just one chance left. Bill Walsh was in the final minutes of his coaching career. A third Super Bowl title hung in the balance. Backup quarterback Steve Young turned to Montana on the sideline. "Well," Young said. "It sets up perfectly for us."

Indeed, giving Montana the ball with the Super Bowl on the line is like putting Superman in a phone booth. He calmly—and predictably—orchestrated the most famous two-minute drill of his storied career, capped by a 10-yard touchdown pass to John Taylor with 34 seconds to spare.

The 49ers' 20–16 victory in Super Bowl XXIII represents everything that was right about the dynasty-era 49ers: a preternaturally cool quarterback, an unstoppable receiver (Jerry Rice had 11 catches for a Super Bowl–record 215 yards), and a genius who knew how to say farewell in style. (It was Walsh's last game.)

Played on January 22, 1989 at Joe Robbie Stadium in Miami, it's hard to believe that one of the most thrilling Super Bowls in

Jerry Rice races past the Bengals defense during Super Bowl XXIII. Named the game's MVP, he caught 11 passes for 215 yards.

history was just 3–3 at halftime and that the Bengals led 13–6 through three quarters. As Paul Zimmerman of *Sports Illustrated* described it: "For almost 45 minutes, it wasn't a great game at all. It was a screwup game played against the depressing backdrop of a city torn by riots and flames."

But the players saved the best for last, starting with some comic relief. As the Super Bowl pressure reached its crescendo, Montana trotted out to the huddle and spotted actor John Candy in the stands. To break the tension, the quarterback figured that his offensive tackle, Harris Barton, might appreciate the celebrity sighting.

Let's hand the play-by-play over to Montana himself: "During Super Bowl week, Bill [Walsh] always tried to keep a tight rein on us, but we got cut loose at least for dinner. Harris Barton would come in the next day and he was always talking about who he saw that night at dinner—what movie star, what model. It didn't matter. He was telling everybody who he saw. And so we got in the game, and the TV timeouts took forever. Back then they were maybe eight minutes or something. Harris would stand exactly like this," said Montana, mimicking a statue, "for eight minutes. You couldn't get him to move or anything. He was always just nervous about his performance.

"So I walked over and said, 'Harris, hey, it's John Candy.' I figured he would appreciate it. He looked over at the stands and then looked back at me and said, 'Are you crazy?' He just gave me one of those looks that said, 'Are you nuts? We're in the Super Bowl. We're trying to win a game.' But I always tried to be myself. And that's what I would have done if we weren't in the Super Bowl. If it was practice, I would have done the same thing. I think that guys learn to read each other. If you're nervous, they get nervous. So I always tried to do what I would do if it was just a normal day."

This normal day ended with an 11-play, 92-yard drive and one of the most heart-stopping finishes in Super Bowl history. The drive began with small chunks of yardage. A pass to Roger Craig for eight yards. A pass to tight end John Frank for seven. On the sideline Walsh knew the Bengals' prevent defense was leaving the door open for the short passes. "I can't say I was confident we would score," Walsh said. "But I felt good. Joe was handling the no-huddle offense beautifully. He was ice. And we were keeping our poise."

The 49ers were at their 23-yard line. Montana hit Rice for seven yards. Craig ran right for a yard. Craig ran right again for four more. Another first down. The clock now showed 1:54 left and 65 yards to go. Montana called timeout and jogged over to consult

Candyland

Joe Montana has recounted the magical final minutes of Super Bowl XXIII many times over the years, but when he told the story one night in 2010 for an intimate gathering of friends and neighbors, the audience included former 49ers general manager Carmen Policy.

That added a new twist.

As everyone already knew, Montana famously spotted comedic actor John Candy in the stands just before directing a last-minute touchdown drive. Montana capped the most memorable comeback of his career by hitting John Taylor with a touchdown pass for a 20–16 victory against the Cincinnati Bengals.

The new wrinkle to the tale? It turns out there was a reason Candy looked so familiar. "I knew him already," the quarterback admitted. Then he turned toward his former boss. "Carmen, I don't know if you know this. But at some point along the line, Candy was trying to get me to go to [the Canadian Football League]. So I had met with John a number of times. I knew John Candy very well."

Policy just laughed. He knew there was no way he would let Candy take his baby.

with Walsh. They talked about how the Bengals secondary mostly was playing man-to-man defense against wide receiver Jerry Rice. That was an open invitation.

Sure enough, on the next play, Montana hit Rice for 17 yards. Another first down. There were 48 yards to go. Montana completed another short pass to Craig. The drive stalled briefly with an incomplete pass intended for Rice and a penalty on Randy Cross, but Montana shook off the second-and-20 by simply floating a 27-yard square-in to Rice.

Now the ball was on the 18, safely in range for a tying field goal. But the 49ers didn't march all the way down to stop there. Montana found Craig crossing from right to left and hit him for eight more yards. And then: It was second-and-2 from the 10 with Rice lined up to the right and Taylor split wide left. The play call was "20 halfback curl, X up." The Niners had not used it all game.

Taylor, who had not caught a ball during the drive, made a quick out move from his wide receiver position then cut up the seam. Montana hit him five yards deep in the end zone.

Touchdown!

"Joe Montana is not human," said Cris Collinsworth, the Bengals wide receiver. "I don't want to call him a God, but he is definitely somewhere in between."

15 Dwight Clark

Dwight Clark had 560 other catches.

That might be hard to remember, considering the magnitude of a certain 6-yarder against the Dallas Cowboys on January 10, 1982. But Clark was no one-grab wonder. The two-time All-Pro was so prolific over his nine seasons in San Francisco (1979 to 1987) that he briefly held the 49ers record for career catches, surpassing the great Billy Wilson. "If anybody was going to break my record, I'm glad it was him," Wilson said at the time, "because he is one of the best receivers I have ever seen."

As was the case with so many other 49ers of that generation, Bill Walsh spotted Clark's promise before anybody else had a clue. And it happened by accident. Clark was an obscure receiver at Clemson University when his phone rang. He considered not answering, having just slung his clubs over his shoulder for a round of golf. But Clark turned around, picked up the phone, and heard Bill Walsh on other end of the line. The new 49ers coach was in town for a pre-draft workout with Clark's roommate, quarterback Steve Fuller. "I need a receiver to run some routes," Walsh said to Clark. "Can you come and run some routes?"

Clark agreed and then caught everything in sight during a practice field workout that so intrigued Walsh that the coach asked the receiver if he could watch some game film of him. That was tricky. Clark had caught just 11 passes during the 1978 season. "Are there any games where you caught two passes?" Walsh wondered. So they sat down and watched Clemson's game against North Carolina. One of Clark's two catches was a terrific leaping grab in traffic. (Foreshadowing alert!)

In the 1979 draft, the Kansas City Chiefs took Fuller in the first round; the 49ers took Joe Montana in the third round and Clark in the 10th. "Dwight looked good to me. I know he didn't look necessarily good to other scouts," Walsh said. "And as the draft progressed, our scouts said, 'Coach, you can get him in the free agent market a month from now.' I said, 'No, that man is going to be here. You watch.' So we drafted him."

In fairness to all those talent evaluators who passed on him, Clark kept his promise pretty well hidden as a teenager. At Garinger High in Charlotte, North Carolina, he'd wanted to play basketball. But he was neither quick enough to play guard nor big enough to play forward. As a quarterback on the football team, Clark was often too nervous on the field to make much of an impact.

Clemson tried him at strong safety; Clark was so discouraged that he nearly quit school after his freshman year. By the end of his college career, he'd caught all of 33 passes. "If my future in football had been decided by what I did in college, I'd be working at Wendy's right now," he told sportswriter Mike Lupica in 1985.

But Clark found football soul mates in Montana and Walsh. He caught 18 passes as a rookie, 82 the next season, and 85 the next. Along the way the rest of the football world saw what Walsh had first noticed way back on that Clemson practice field. The 6'4", 212-pounder had incredible hands, impeccable body control, and an understanding of the game that allowed him to have a synchronicity with Montana.

Clark ran midweek practice routes the same way he ran them on Sunday. During a 49ers minicamp late in his career, Clark raced 20 yards up field on a post pattern, spun between two defenders, and caught the ball at his belt before he planted his feet. Allan Webb, the 49ers director of pro personnel at the time, watched it all. "If a rookie had made that catch, you'd say, 'Whoops. Look what I found,'" Webb said. "But this was Dwight Clark. And we've all seen him do it before."

Clark finished his 49ers career with 506 catches during the regular season and 55 more in the playoffs, including one pretty famous one.

For all his production, however, Clark was never the prototypical NFL burner—and he took some ribbing for his perceived slowness. Years after they had all retired, Jerry Rice thanked Clark for taking him under his wing as a youngster and teaching him nuances like the speed route. "Wait," Montana interrupted, his eyes wide with wonder. "Dwight ran a speed route?"

16 Fred Dean

Just before Fred Dean made his debut in a San Francisco uniform on October 11, 1981, Bill Walsh approached his new defensive end with a modest plan. Walsh told Dean to prepare for a mere 10 or 11 snaps against the Dallas Cowboys. It made sense. Dean was new to the team and had barely practiced with them. "(Walsh) said he didn't know what my condition was," Dean recalled.

Instead, the 49ers turned Dean loose all afternoon, unleashing the human fireball at Cowboys quarterbacks Danny White and Glenn Carano from the first snap to the last. After the game Dean, still gasping as he caught his breath, asked Walsh what happened to the modest plan. "Your condition was good," Walsh replied.

Dean laughed at the memory. He told that story just a few weeks before being inducted into the Pro Football Hall of Fame. The funny thing is, Walsh did learn how to make life easier for Dean—even as that made things more difficult for opposing quarterbacks.

Together they concocted a plan in which Dean played mostly on passing downs, which was a way of maximizing his talent while easing the wear and tear on his body. He owes his enshrinement in Canton in part to his pioneering role as one of the NFL's first situational pass rushers. "I take a great deal of pride in that," Dean said.

Dean, who grew up in Ruston, Louisiana, was already an accomplished player by the time he arrived in San Francisco. He spent six-plus seasons with the San Diego Chargers, playing alongside fellow terror Gary "Big Hands" Johnson and Louie Kelcher, who would eventually follow Dean to San Francisco and help the 49ers win Super Bowl XIX.

Dean's quickness, speed, and strength made him one of the league's most feared pass rushers. "Defensive ends like Fred Dean—well, there just aren't any like that around," offensive tackle Keith Fahnhorst once said. "I remember playing against him in an exhibition game in '75 when he was a rookie. I looked in the program and saw 6'2", 230 pounds, and I licked my chops. On the first play, he flew by me so fast I never even saw him. I asked someone, 'Who the hell is that guy?'"

That guy forced a trade in 1981 because he wanted more money. (He'd mentioned his NFL salary to his brother-in-law, who said, "Hey, I make that much driving a truck.") In 1980 the Chargers paid $67,500 to Dean, who made his second consecutive Pro Bowl. But San Diego felt it was loaded with defensive linemen, so rather than pay him the $75,000 he was owed for '81, they traded him to San Francisco. The 49ers sent a No. 2 draft pick in 1983 and agreed to swap No. 1 draft picks that same year if the Chargers wanted. As *Sports Illustrated*'s Paul Zimmerman put it at the time: "San Francisco signed Dean for roughly double what he was making and told him to start collecting sacks."

The acquisition of the 6'2", 230-pounder turned out to be one of the greatest midseason trades of all-time. Starting with White, Dean kept tormenting quarterbacks all the way to the Super Bowl. They weren't counted as a stat until 1982, but unofficially Dean had 12 sacks in his first 11 games with the 49ers.

Also unofficial: His hard-to-quantify impact on a team about to win its first title. "Bill Walsh was putting together a puzzle. The team was just so young, and he infused Fred Dean into the team," teammate Dwaine Board told ESPN in 2008. "And [Dean] brought something to the team that was kind of missing, and that was an attitude of when you step on the field, you win. That was Fred's thing. And he won. He won at rushing the passer and was Defensive Player of the Year. What more can you say? The guy was incredible. He was a true warrior. I remember in our last Super Bowl, he had 'Warrior' written on his shoe."

Dean had a career-best 17.5 sacks in 1983, including a record six against the New Orleans Saints. He was a standout on the 49ers Super Bowl team in 1984. More than the numbers, Dean took pride in the way future pass rushers like Reggie White and Derrick Thomas followed in his footsteps—all the way to the quarterback.

17 Bryant Young

Bryant Young broke into the NFL the best way imaginable in 1994, starting on the defensive line for a juggernaut that would go on to win its fifth Super Bowl. Just 22, he figured that hoisting that hefty Lombardi Trophy over his head was going to become a habit. "You think there's many more to come," Young said. "But it didn't happen that way."

Instead, Young never reached a higher peak than he did during that rookie season. By the time he retired 14 seasons later, the 49ers had fallen on hard times. They didn't even reach the playoffs during his final five seasons. Still, Young will be remembered as a champion. Because no matter the record, no matter the score, the mammoth defensive tackle carried himself with a grace that made him royalty in the 49ers' locker room.

For those final years, when he was the last remaining link to the Super Bowl lineage, Young showed young players what it meant to be a 49er. "He's a fierce competitor, the ultimate pro," said quarterback Jeff Garcia, a longtime teammate. "Everybody should have the opportunity to have a teammate like that."

A four-time All-Pro selection, Young spent his entire career in San Francisco after the team plucked him out of Notre Dame with the seventh overall draft choice in 1994. He promptly bombarded opposing quarterbacks at a rate rarely seen for a defensive tackle. Young registered 89.5 career sacks—and zero career sack dances. "Some guys are attention seekers," 49ers linebacker Jeff Ulbrich once said. "Not him."

"Young was always a throwback, a regal warrior, a courtly gentleman in a modern-day gladiator's body," *San Jose Mercury News* columnist Ann Killion wrote. "He was the man who took the

Bryant Young's Best

Shortly after his retirement, I asked Bryant Young to look back at a some of his favorite things.

Opposing quarterback he most respected? "Brett Favre. Because of his toughness. Because he also had an ability to improvise and make something happen. He could always create time to come up with a play."

Hardest running back to bring down? "Edgerrin James. He was a guy that was very elusive. He ran so low to the ground. Even when you got him, he could wiggle his way for another two or three yards."

Toughest offensive lineman? "Larry Allen. He was playing right guard early in his career when I was the left tackle. We just had some memorable, tough matchups on gamedays."

Funniest teammate? "[Defensive tackle] Ron Fields. All that joking around went away on gamedays. But in the locker room during the week, he was definitely one of the funny guys."

Proudest moment? "Winning the Super Bowl. I realize a lot of guys don't get that chance to go to one, let alone win one. I was pretty proud and excited to do that."

Advice he wishes he had known as a rookie? "If I could go back, I would tell myself not to take as much time off after my first season. I learned the hard way that you have to get back to work."

double-team to allow someone else to get the sack, the steady presence who worked hard every day, every down, without complaint or issue."

No chapter better illustrated Young's courage than his comeback from a devastating compound fracture of his right leg late in the 1998 season. He went down in the Week 13 game against the New York Giants—a gruesome scene for a Monday night audience. The fracture was so severe that it required doctors to insert a titanium rod into his broken tibia during surgery.

Young, however, all but brushed it off. He vowed to be ready for the start of training camp in 1999. And of course, there he was, reporting for the first practice in pads right on time on August 10.

He went on to rack up 11 sacks and the NFL's Comeback Player of the Year award that season.

Young played 208 games in his career—all starts. He was held in such high esteem by teammates that his name became synonymous with the Len Eshmont Award. Considered the team's most prestigious annual honor, the award goes to the 49ers player who "best exemplifies the inspirational and courageous play" of its namesake.

That sounds like Young, which is why he won the award an unprecedented eight times, including the final four seasons of his career. Receiver Isaac Bruce, the first player to win the Eshmont after Young's retirement, wasn't surprised to hear Young's final tally. "If they were giving it for toughness and accountability," Bruce said, "he'd be up there even more."

18 Hugh McElhenny

Quarterback Frankie Albert bestowed the crown upon the King on October 19, 1952. That was the day a rookie running back, heretofore known as Hugh McElhenny, fielded a punt near the goal line, whirled around a few Chicago Bears defenders, and blazed 94 yards for a touchdown to highlight a 40–16 victory. "After the game in the locker room, Frankie Albert gave me the game ball and said, 'You're now the King,'" McElhenny said. "Then he turned to Joe Perry and said, 'Joe, you're just the Jet.'"

That's how the nickname was born, according to writer Joseph Hession in *Forty Niners: Looking Back*. Indeed, by the time McElhenny was done with his playing career in 1964, there was no arguing that he was football royalty. The speedy, powerfully built halfback ran all the way to enshrinement in Canton, Ohio.

McElhenny spent the first nine years of his 13-year NFL career in San Francisco—three of them as part of the famed Million Dollar Backfield. In the words of the Pro Football Hall of Fame, McElhenny was "an artist whose electrifying moves left opponents and observers spellbound."

It didn't take long for McElhenny to assume the throne. In that rookie season of 1952, he had the NFL's longest punt return (94 yards), longest run from scrimmage (89), and the top rushing average (7.0). "There's no question he could do everything," teammate Billy Wilson said. "He could change direction on a dime. He had great cutting ability where other backs were just slashers."

Born on New Year's Eve 1928 in Los Angeles, he emerged as an All-American halfback at the University of Washington. The 49ers took him when he was still merely a prince in the first round of the 1952 draft (ninth overall). The athletically gifted McElhenny arrived in San Francisco with all the makings of a backfield star.

- Speed? His 100-yard dash had been timed at 9.6 seconds—faster than the Pacific Coast Conference sprint champion at the time.
- Power? His 32-inch waist was part of a sculpted physique rarely seen in football's pre-weightlifting era.
- Balance? According to the *Seattle Post-Intelligencer*, McElhenny trained on high and low hurdles, regularly beating Olympic decathlete Bob Mathias.

McElhenny's bang-up rookie season with the 49ers is mostly remembered for stats like all-purpose yards (1,731, first in the NFL) and touchdowns (10, fourth). But he also rescued the San Francisco organization. "When Hugh joined the 49ers in 1952, it was questionable whether our franchise could survive," former general manager Lou Spadia said. "McElhenny removed all doubts. That's why we call him our franchise saver."

Though he did not play in enough games to officially qualify, McElhenny led the league in rushing average for a second time in 1954. That was also the season he began running with some fast company. Fullback John Henry Johnson joined a franchise that already included McElhenny, running back Joe Perry, and quarterback Y.A. Tittle. Together they formed the Million Dollar Backfield. "Tittle used to joke about trying to keep us all happy by giving us the ball," McElhenny said in *Forty Niners: Looking Back.* "He certainly had his hands full, because we all had egos."

In 1961 the 49ers sent McElhenny to the expansion Minnesota Vikings where he made his sixth and final Pro Bowl. He later spent one season with the New York Giants ('63) and his last with the Detroit Lions ('64). At the time of his retirement, McElhenny was one of only three players with 11,000 all-purpose yards, joining Perry and Ollie Matson. His career totals included six Pro Bowls, two first-team All-Pro first selections ('52 and '53), and a bust in the Hall of Fame (inducted 1970).

But he said that his greatest honor was a plaque bestowed to him by Chicago Bears fans. The inscription on the metal plate was fit for a King: "To the most respected opponent the Bears ever faced. If everyone played the game like Hugh McElhenny, wouldn't it be beautiful."

19 Patrick Willis

Patrick Willis built his reputation by virtue of his tackling, which makes sense. Willis grew up in Bruceton, Tennessee, with his siblings wrapped safely in his arms. So how hard can it be to grab just one guy at a time?

Hacksaw: The Ferocious—Yet Eccentric—Linebacker

There are players who say they eat, drink, and sleep football. And then there are guys who really do. Jack "Hacksaw" Reynolds actually lived out of his locker for about a month when he first joined the team in 1981. He slept in a nearby economy motel but kept all of his clothes and personal belongings—including eating utensils and a film projector—inside his stall at the 49ers' old Redwood City headquarters. "We all knew he could afford an apartment, but that was just Hacksaw," defensive back Ronnie Lott explained to *San Jose Mercury News* columnist Mark Purdy.

Reynolds played for the Los Angeles Rams from 1970 to 1980 before spending his final four seasons with the 49ers. He made two Pro Bowls (1975 and 1980) and left a legacy as one of the NFL's outlandish characters.

Former 49ers running back Bill Ring recalled how on road trips, Reynolds would come down from his hotel room to breakfast at 9 AM on gameday dressed in his full uniform. "I couldn't believe it," Ring said told the *Mercury News*. "He would have his eye black on, his jersey, the whole thing."

Shaking off the horrific circumstances of his childhood, Willis somehow emerged as an NFL rarity—the humble, industrious superstar. Maybe that had to do with the fact that he had to grow up fast, wresting control of his household at an early age as his father battled drinking and drugs. Maybe that had to do with the fact that Willis learned early how to focus on teammates, ensuring his sister and two brothers had enough to eat before whisking them off to school each morning. Maybe it had to do with the fact that his success in the face of adversity was so amazing that one former coach scoffed at the Hollywood blockbuster *The Blind Side*, saying, "They made the movie about the wrong guy."

Regardless of the winding road it took to get there, Willis got there, and the 49ers are glad he made it. The do-everything, tackle-anything linebacker established himself almost immediately as one of the greatest defensive players in franchise history, a fearsome and

The heart of the 49ers defense, linebacker Patrick Willis has made the Pro Bowl during each of his first six seasons.

reliable presence not seen since the days of Ronnie Lott. "I remember I asked Patrick, 'What do you want out of this game?' former running back Roger Craig said. "And he said, 'I'm playing the game to make the Hall of Fame.'

"This was just his third year. Most of these kids say, 'I want to make All-Pro…I want to make the Pro Bowl.' He said, 'I play the game to be a Hall of Famer.' Wow, that blew me away. When he told me that, I thought, *Oh, he gets it.* This was only his third year when he said this."

Willis, though, made the Pro Bowl in each of his first six seasons. He became the first 49ers defensive rookie to make the Pro Bowl and joined Bruce Taylor (1970), Dana Stubblefield (1993), and Bryant Young (1994) as 49ers who have won the Defensive Rookie of the Year award.

And to think the 49ers almost passed on him. Just before the 49ers took Willis in the first round (11th overall) in 2007, personnel chief Scot McCloughan showed then-linebackers coach Mike Singletary some game tape of Willis at Ole Miss. Singletary was unimpressed. But when McCloughan revealed that Willis was playing through a broken hand, "I realized we had something special," Singletary said. The 49ers figured that if Willis could demolish some ball carriers with a bum hand, he would be a terror at full strength. It turned out to be one of the most prescient calls in team history.

From the second he stepped on the field, Willis made an impact that helped transform the franchise. Combining sideline-to-sideline speed and Lott-esque physicality, Willis led the NFL in tackles twice in his first five seasons. In one of the signature plays of his rookie season—a play that put him on the map—Willis roared from behind to haul down Arizona Cardinals wide receiver Sean Morey after a 62-yard catch, a game-saving tackle in overtime. In another game that season, he helped hold Minnesota Vikings running back Adrian Peterson to just three yards on 14 carries—a feat akin to holding Niagara Falls to just a few drops.

With Willis at the center of their universe, the 49ers defense became a perennial powerhouse, one that got better and better with the addition of rugged defensive lineman Justin Smith and speedy linebacker Navarro Bowman.

The center of that universe uses his inspirationally inked arms to snare running backs. One of the tattoos reads "Believe." "When a person says, 'I think,' I feel that leaves room for doubt," he said. "If I want to do something, I want to believe I can do it—not just think."

Willis believed in himself early, and his actions helped protect his siblings. As *The New York Times* recounted in 2012, Willis was 17 when he had enough of his father, Ernest Willis. When the boy saw his father striking his younger sister, Ernicka, he stood up to his father and alerted his counselors at Central High about what was happening at home. Willis and his three siblings moved out shortly thereafter. Patrick and Orey stayed with Chris and Julie Finley, who helped point the young linebacker toward stardom. Ernicka and another brother, Detris, lived with another foster family and then bounced between homes.

On the day he was drafted, Willis was asked about the adversity he faced growing up. "Oh, I would have to say it was a good thing," he said. "It hasn't slowed me down. It's only helped me throughout my process—on the field, in the classroom, or just life in general."

20 Run The Hill Like Jerry Rice

To understand how Roger Craig and Jerry Rice could dig deep when the game was on the line, grab a pair of running shoes and head for the Edgewood Park and Natural Preserve in Redwood City, California.

Don't be fooled by the beauty. This idyllic little county park is home to a four-mile trail that became the 49ers' offseason torturing grounds for much of the 1980s and '90s. Craig, Rice, and several other players of that era did endurance work here, charging up the steep inclines so fast you'd think they were being chased by a mountain lion—or Lawrence Taylor.

The training ground became known simply as The Hill. "That hill was pretty much the fourth quarter for me," said Rice, who continued to run the trail even after turning 50. "It taught me how to be able to endure—in pain—and still perform at a very high level. You have to challenge yourself. And that's what I did in the offseason."

As usual when it came to 49ers fitness, Craig led the charge. The late Walter Payton, the Hall of Fame running back from the Chicago Bears, had told Craig that the key to thriving in their position was endurance, and that the key to endurance was training on the steepest hill he could find.

At first Craig trained on a nondescript stretch of mountainside just off Highway 280 not far from the 49ers' Redwood City headquarters. The terrain was steep, which was good, but the footing was treacherous. Arthur Ting, a noted Bay Area orthopedic surgeon, happened to drive by one day and spotted Craig tramping down the rocky pathway. "You can blow your knee out here," he told the running back. "Come with me."

Ting, an avid runner, introduced Craig to Edgewood Park. And it was all uphill from there.

"It was the toughest thing I ever did in my life," Craig said. "I threw up a couple of times going up this trail. I was a football player. I'd never run that far. I was only good for 100 yards. I ran track and stuff, but as far as running four miles, that was unheard of. [Ting] said, 'Just hang in there…So I did it for a few weeks with him. And I started loving it. I could feel it. I was getting in great shape. So I introduced it to some of my teammates. I said, 'Man, you guys need to come out here and run this trail.'"

As Craig and Rice became disciples, The Hill soon went from training ground to proving ground, an initiation to show what it took to become a champion. Are you tough enough? Are you dedicated enough? How much are you willing to suffer? Craig said they eventually had a group of up to 15 players running the hill three times a week. To this day the tradition endures. On May 7, 2012, not long after the 49ers drafted receiver A. J. Jenkins, Rice tweeted him: "I'm getting in top shape to get you up that Hill." (Jenkins never took Rice up on his offer; he had zero catches as a rookie.)

Rice points to this training regimen as a reason he was able to remain productive even into his early 40s. He may have been old, but he was never over The Hill.

He takes pride in scoring more touchdowns in the fourth quarter than any player in NFL history. "That's when I was at my best. I was in such great shape," Rice said. "The defensive backs were breathing hard, and I was bouncing around saying, 'Okay, I'm ready to play football. Let's go!' That was exciting to me."

Among the challenges of running The Hill is finding it in the first place. It's tucked away at the corner of Edgewood Drive and Old Stage Coach Road in Redwood City. Craig, now a veteran of several marathons and half-marathons, has run the trail so many times that he does it by memory, not maps, so his directions tend to be esoteric. *Watch for this tree…there'll be a little slope to the left…Don't take any of the switchbacks.*

In researching this book, I ran The Hill three times to make sure I got it right. I'd periodically check back with Craig to describe what I saw, and he'd talk me through it again: "Did you see the bench? *No?* Then you didn't go high enough."

When I became confident I was in the right place, I ran The Hill with a pen in one hand and a notebook in the other. Here's the four-mile path to glory:

1. Use the parking lot at 10 Old Stage Coach Road just off Edgewood Road.

2. As you walk from the parking lot toward the park, stay toward the left. Your starting point is the sign marked "Sylvan Trail Exercise Loop," which runs parallel with a private road for about 30 yards.
3. It's a steady, gradual climb from the start. There's a sign at the one-mile mark, and just beyond that, the trail forks. Follow the sign to the left that points toward Live Oak Trail.
4. Follow the sign to the right toward Scenic View.
5. After a few hundred yards, you'll see that the peak of the hill is to the left. There's a trail but no sign. Trust your instincts.
6. You've reached the summit. The telltale sign is a bench with a plaque that says "In Memory of James and Margaret Hutchison." Enjoy the view. You're in the footsteps of Roger Craig and Jerry Rice.
7. Retrace your steps back down toward the main trail. Look for the sign that says "Ridgeview Loop Trail" and follow it left (to the west).
8. The Ridgeview trail takes you back down the mountain. You should be able to see the I-280 freeway in the distance.
9. A little less than a half-mile (0.4 miles) down the Ridgeview Loop Trail, there's a fork with a high road to the right and a low road to the left. Take the low road (Franciscan Trail).
10. After just a quarter-mile, follow the sign to the right. From this sign it's 2.04 miles back to the parking lot. It can be tough to tell whether you're on Edgewood Trail or the Serpentine Loop trail, but the key is just to follow every arrow toward the Old Stage Picnic Area.
11. The finish line is the parking lot. If you've been carrying a football, spike it here.

Got it? You're ready for training camp. If you approach the trails like a cross country runner at a steady pace, The Hill is mildly strenuous. The key to making it a workout worthy of the 49ers dynasty is to attack the toughest parts of the course by sprinting up the inclines.

If you have a hard time at first, don't worry. You'll be in good company. "When you first start out the trail, everything is new," Craig says. "There are all these switchbacks. So you have to run it a few times to feel comfortable."

21 Charles Haley

Charles Haley's disdain for quarterbacks was not limited to opponents. In 1991 he wanted to fight teammate Steve Young in the locker room after the 49ers lost a game to the Raiders. Haley's rage was so out of control, that Ronnie Lott—a Raider at the time—was summoned from the opposing locker room to help restore the peace.

But Haley's goal in the NFL was all about rings: He retired with the distinction as the only player in history to play in and win five Super Bowls, two with the 49ers and three with the Cowboys. He, though, won zero Mr. Congeniality trophies. "Man, I don't worry about how people perceive me," Haley said. "I'm not here to be everybody's friend."

At his best the linebacker/defensive end was the enemy of passers everywhere. After the 49ers selected him in the fourth round out of James Madison, he stormed onto the scene with 12 sacks as a rookie in 1986. And even when he didn't get the sack, the five-time Pro Bowl selection was an intimidating force. "An offensive lineman, if you get somebody that's not too mature," former coach George Seifert said, "he can psyche himself out before the game even starts because of Charles' ability."

The problem was that Haley was too often psyching out his own teammates. He was such a volatile, divisive presence in the

49ers locker room that he wore out his welcome despite five astonishing seasons. "He was such a great player but such a difficult person," former general manager Carmen Policy recalled. "Charles got along with Eddie (DeBartolo)…but I can't fault our coaches for saying, 'We just can't deal with him anymore.' Unfortunately, we lost his talent. We tried to do everything to make it work, but Charles was so hard-headed about how he needed to be respected. Even if you bent over backward, it would be an admission of guilt to him."

In Jeff Pearlman's book, *Boys Will Be Boys*, he wrote that Haley threw used toilet paper at a coach and exposed himself to teammates during meetings. The last straw came when Haley reportedly urinated on teammate Tim Harris' car. As one 49ers player of that era put it: "You never knew when he was going to go off. Other guys still tease and kid around, but Charles was different…He was mean. I didn't like him."

As those glittering trophies attest, though, the 6'5", 252-pound menace was often worth the trouble. Haley had 11.5 sacks in 1988 when the 49ers won the Super Bowl. He had 10.5 more the next season when the 49ers won the Super Bowl again.

By the end of the 1991 season, the internal pressure he put on the team proved to be so much that the 49ers traded him to their rival and main threat to the Super Bowl, the Dallas Cowboys, for second- and third-round draft picks. Although the 49ers rid themselves of a divisive player, the move proved costly. Haley went on to win three more championships (and ruffle plenty more feathers) in Dallas. He was a Pro Bowl selection in '94 and '95 before a bad back forced him into retirement after the 1996 season.

The 49ers, meanwhile, struggled to replace his terrorizing ways at defensive end. They tried filling the void with other veterans (Harris, Chris Doleman) and whiffed with some young players (Todd Kelly). No one brought the ferocity or threat that Haley did in his prime.

Their defensive line was so overmatched and shorthanded that by the 1998 playoffs, they decided Haley wasn't such a bad guy after all. "I thought, *Jeez, when you're a pass-rush guy, you don't forget to do that*," said 49ers defensive assistant Bill McPherson. So the team signed the two-time All-Pro in the nick of time to face the Green Bay Packers in the wild-card round.

Almost 35 years old and out of football for two years, Haley harassed quarterback Brett Favre all day, forcing an interception and deflecting a pass. "In my heart," he said, "I wanted to go out a winner. When I got hurt, my back was out, and there was just a void in me. I wanted to walk out of the game saying, 'Hey, I gave it all I had and I don't want no more,' not that other people could say, 'He can't give no more.' I wanted to be able to say that."

Haley played in all 16 games of the 1999 regular season before retiring—this time for good—with 100.5 career sacks.

22 Young Wins the Big One

Steve Young had a nickname for Mike Shanahan, his offensive coordinator in 1994. The quarterback called him "Let's Go Over It Again Shanahan" in honor of the coach's favorite phrase. Shanahan wanted Young to go over it again at practice. And over it again at meetings. And again on the sideline before games.

But when Shanahan approached him on January 29, 1995 before the biggest game of his life, Young waved him off. "Mike, I can't go over it again," Young told him.

Shanahan understood. "Well, you're ready," the coordinator replied. "You're going to throw more touchdowns than you've ever thrown in your life."

Let's go over that game again: The 49ers crushed the San Diego Chargers 49–26 in Super Bowl XXIX as Young completed 24-of-36 passes for 325 yards. Not only did he throw more touchdowns than he ever had in his life—six—he threw more touchdown passes than anyone had in Super Bowl history. The previous record belonged to some guy named Joe Montana.

The rout was an all-around team performance: Jerry Rice and Ricky Watters each scored three touchdowns. The offense generated seven touchdowns, 28 first downs, and 455 total yards. But there was no mistaking the man at the center of the action. Young had spent his career obscured by Montana's mighty shadow, and after the game, he wrapped his arms around the Lombardi Trophy and hugged it to his chest like a firstborn child.

Young had finally won the big one. The biggest one. "Yeah, I think this one is different," offensive tackle Harris Barton said in the locker room after the 49ers' fifth championship. "This is Steve's Super Bowl. And that's good."

The high-voltage ending was a fitting way for the '94 Niners to cap their season. They rolled to a 13–3 mark during the regular season, outscoring opponents 505–296 along the way. They walloped the Chicago Bears in the divisional round (44–15) and toppled their NFC nemesis, the Dallas Cowboys, in the conference title game (38–28), meaning that a date with San Diego was the only thing still tethering the monkey to Young's back.

After all those years of waiting, the suspense was gone in an instant. With smoke from the pregame firework display still wafting across the field, Young set up after a play-action fake and waited for Rice to break clear from safeties Stanley Richard and Darren Carrington. Young launched a perfectly thrown pass into Rice's arms. Just 1:24 into the game, the 49ers led 7–0.

The 49ers scored three more times in the first half to assume a commanding 28–10 lead, with Young hitting 17-of-23 passes for 239 yards and four touchdowns. In the halftime locker room,

After throwing six touchdown passes to defeat the Chargers 49–26 in Super Bowl XXIX, quarterback Steve Young, who played in Joe Montana's shadow, celebrates the redemptive victory.

Young and Shanahan had another one of their perfectionist conversations. "I'd just thrown four touchdown passes, and he looked me straight in the eye and said, 'I want eight,'" Young said. "After the game I came in with six, and he was really upset. He wanted eight."

That hardly seemed necessary. The 49ers defense made sure the Chargers never got closer than 18 points in the second half. Rice matched his own Super Bowl high with three touchdown catches while hauling in 10 passes for 149 yards. "When we scored early, I think the Chargers said, 'Oh, God,'" guard Jesse Sapolu said. "And then when we scored again and again, I think they realized that maybe they're a couple of years away."

San Diego running back Natrone Means, who had rushed for 1,350 yards during the regular season, managed just 33 yards on 13 attempts against the 49ers.

For Young it was a fitting conclusion to a season in which he topped Montana's team record for completion percentage, broke his NFL mark for passer rating and—once and for all—stuck it to critics who thought he couldn't win the big one.

Toward the end of the game, Young was heard on the sideline yelling, "Somebody take the monkey off my back!" Linebacker Gary Plummer reached toward his back as if he were completing the symbolic gesture.

As he had after beating Dallas in the NFC Championship Game, Young took a victory lap. He ran through the end zone and basked in chants of "Steve! Steve! Steve!" The quarterback was about to duck into the tunnel, but before he got there, Barton stopped him and told him to look back at the field. "You did this," Barton told him. "It's yours."

Young would further display the emotions of having officially crawled out from under the imposing shadow cast by Montana. During a passionate speech captured on the postgame telecast, Young held the Super Bowl trophy and declared: "No one—no one—can ever take this away from us! No one ever! It's ours!"

23 Steve's 49ers vs. Joe's Chiefs

Leading up to a September 11, 1994 49ers-Chiefs contest at Arrowhead Stadium, players from both sides insisted it was merely another game, just one of 16. There was a lot of lying going on that week.

The obvious truth was that this was one of the all-time most emotional, personal, operatic regular season showdowns: Joe Montana vs. Steve Young, Master vs. Student, the Quarterback with Four Super Bowl Rings vs. the Quarterback Still Trying to Win the Big One. "This is one of those situations," Hall of Fame quarterback Dan Fouts said in advance of the game, "where, if you're a 49ers fan, you hope for Joe Montana to throw for six touchdowns, 900 yards, and still lose and for Young to have an equally impressive game and win. Maybe the best thing is to have Steve win anyway, because if he doesn't, people will say, 'Well, he's no Joe Montana,' which he isn't, but he's pretty damn good."

In this corner was Montana, who spent 14 years with the 49ers and was facing them for the first time since his awkward 1993 trade. And in *this* corner was Young, who suffered through a strained dynamic with Montana before succeeding him and who had back-to-back passer titles but no Super Bowl rings to show for it. This one had the air of something personal—no matter how mightily the participants argued otherwise. "Basically, it's the San Francisco 49ers against the Kansas City Chiefs," 49ers coach George Seifert said. "Otherwise we'd just put two guys out there and let them go at it. But that's called boxing or kick fighting or whatever they do on pay-per-view."

There was no less fervor in Kansas City. For a typical regular season game, the Chiefs media relations staff usually fielded up to 40 credential requests for cameras and video. This time the list topped 200. And here's what all those cameras saw. The Chiefs beat the 49ers 24–17 as 38-year-old Montana completed 19-of-31 passes for 203 yards, two touchdowns, and no interceptions. Young completed 24-of-34 passes for 288 yards, a touchdown, and two interceptions. "I learned from Joe, from the master," Young said. "Today the master had a little more to teach the student."

To understand how the game really unfolded, though, all it took was one look at Young as he headed for the postgame shower. There was a purple bruise on his right side and a nasty scrape down his back. His torso looked as if he'd gone 12 rounds with a sledge-hammer. "Look at Steve," tight end Brent Jones said, pained by the sight. "He looks like he got whipped."

Young played gamely, but there was only so much he could do as his injured, makeshift offensive line barely slowed down an elite pass rush led by Derrick Thomas and Neil Smith and aided by the raucous Arrowhead Stadium crowd. Young was sacked four times and spent much of the rest of the day scrambling for dear life. It got worse as the game went on. By halftime left guard Jesse Sapolu was out with a pulled hamstring. In the third quarter, right guard Derrick Deese was on the bench with a mild concussion. After absorbing blow after blow from Thomas, Young bent over the bench late in the game and vomited repeatedly.

Suffice it to say, Young took his lumps. But in a weird way, the drubbing didn't undermine Young's status in the locker room; it enhanced it. Teammates saw the way the quarterback stood up to the pressure and the pounding and managed to keep the game within reach. "People need to stick by Steve," running back Dexter Carter said that day. "Steve did everything Steve could do under adverse circumstances. You can't run for your life for four quarters and expect him to have a good game." Tackle Steve Wallace said: "I think personally he's going to win the big one. And I want to be there when he does."

Wallace got his wish. Young capped that season by guiding the 49ers to a victory against the San Diego Chargers in Super Bowl XXIX, throwing six touchdown passes and becoming the game's MVP.

This day, though, clearly belonged to Montana. With plenty of protection—he was sacked just once—the former 49ers quarterback was as accurate as ever. In a sight that looked familiar to 49ers fans, Montana kept connecting on the short, maddening stuff, mostly to his backs and underneath receivers. Montana's longest pass of the day was a 38-yarder to running back Marcus Allen, who ran an up pattern. That play was a reminder of how Montana could dissect the field like no other: Allen was the fourth man on his read.

After the game Montana looked fresh and relaxed. He even carried around a bag of burgers and handed them out to some of his teammates in the locker room. Someone asked him how he was feeling. "How do I feel?" Montana said. "I'm glad it's all over."

24 T.O.

There's a hilariously off-base newspaper clipping that annually makes its rounds among the 49ers press corps. It's a 1996 *Oakland Tribune* article about a polite newcomer from Alexander City, Alabama, a rookie receiver who responded to coaches with a "yes, sir" or a "no, sir" and had all the makings of a perfect Southern gentleman.

The polite rookie grew up to be Terrell Owens. And by the time he left San Francisco in 2003, he had managed to thrill, annoy, enthrall, aggravate, entertain, and alienate—sometimes all in the span of four quarters.

Was it ever boring? No, sir.

Based on raw numbers, Terrell Eldorado Owens is the second greatest receiver in franchise history, trailing only Jerry Rice in total touchdowns, receiving yards, and catches on the 49ers' all-time lists. On the unofficial lists, he was the 49ers' runaway leader in the categories of outrageous antics, nutty quotes, and self-serving touchdown celebrations. The Owens soap opera ran for eight seasons in San Francisco (1996 to 2003) before being renewed in Philadelphia (2004 to 2005), Dallas (2006 to 2008), Buffalo (2009), and Cincinnati (2010).

Drafted in 1996 in the third round from the University of Tennessee at Chattanooga, the sleek and powerfully built receiver was a breakout star by his second NFL season. Jerry Rice sustained a torn ACL in the '97 season opener, so Owens stepped in—and flourished—as Steve Young's new go-to receiver. Owens finished that season with 936 yards and eight touchdowns.

One of the best ever in churning out additional yards after the catch, he became a full-fledged star in '98, catching 67 passes for 1,097 yards and 14 touchdowns. Owens capped that season with an incredible game-winning touchdown catch against the Green Bay Packers in the playoffs. The famous play was coined "The Catch II" following Dwight Clark's historic grab.

The receptions were never a problem. But there was always a catch. Owens' disruptive behavior began to overshadow his talent, raising the question about whether his production was worth the distraction.

If he was a TV show, you could say Owens jumped the shark on September 24, 2000. That's the day he celebrated a touchdown by sprinting back to midfield and frolicking upon the Dallas Cowboys' iconic star logo. Then he did it again after another touchdown. This time he was blindsided by Cowboys safety George Teague, who secured a spot in Cowboys lore by decking Owens to protect the Dallas honor.

Even in a 49ers-Cowboys rivalry that was often bitter and hard fought, the receiver's celebrations crossed a line, and the 49ers said so. Coach Steve Mariucci promptly suspended Owens for one game and fined him a week's pay. "This decision is based on how we intend to conduct ourselves," Mariucci said a day after the Cowboys game. "It disturbs me when the integrity of the game is compromised in any way, shape, or form."

Owens, who by the end of his tenure rarely granted interviews to local media, told *The New York Times* that he had no regrets about the controversial Dallas incident. "When I ran the first time to the star, I was just being creative and having fun. There was the star below me and the opening in the roof above me. My intentions were not bad ones. But then after Emmitt Smith did it after Dallas scored, I felt I had to go back a second time after I scored. The second time I did do it out of spite. But I didn't expect it to create such a stir. I guess I'll never live that down."

A year later after the 49ers blew a 19-point lead in Chicago and lost 37–31 in overtime on October 28, 2001, Owens accused Mariucci of letting up in the game against good friend Dick Jauron, the head coach of the Bears who once served on the Packers staff with Mariucci. The comments created a stir, and the receiver was unrepentant. "Everybody is criticizing me for standing up and just wanting to win," he said. "If wanting to win real bad is wrong, then I don't even want to be right."

In addition to Mariucci, Owens repeatedly criticized his quarterback, Jeff Garcia. That continued after both moved on to new franchises. In 2004 he told *Playboy* magazine that Garcia was gay. "Like my boy tells me," he said, "'If it looks like a rat and smells like a rat, by golly, it is a rat.'"

With the 49ers franchise starting to falter by 2003, Owens was eager to leave. He triggered a complicated trade in which the Eagles gave up a fifth-round draft pick to the Baltimore Ravens and defensive lineman Brandon Whiting to San Francisco. An earlier trade, in which Owens went from the 49ers to the Ravens, was voided. After landing in Philly, Owens signed a seven-year, $42 million contract.

The name of that once-shy kid from Alabama still peppers the 49ers record book: 83 touchdowns (second to Rice's 147), 592 catches (Rice had 1,281), five 1,000-yard seasons (12), and 25 100-yard games (66). As for the controversies, *The Times* asked him if he would do it all the same way. "Yes, I would," Owens said. "Maybe I'm too honest, brutally honest. I'm not a politically correct guy. I didn't do anything to try to embarrass or hurt anyone. I just tried to be honest to others and myself, and that's something I'm not going to change."

25 R.C. Owens

When it came to one of the most famous plays in franchise history, Y.A. Tittle had the easy part. All the quarterback had to do was chuck a high-arching pass in the general direction of the end zone. "Do you know any teenagers? Even they could throw that pass," Tittle said. "You just throw it up in the air and hope."

R.C. Owens would take it from there. The 6'3" receiver would soar over hapless defenders, pluck the ball from the clouds, and land back on planet Earth for another touchdown. Sound simple? Try stopping it. The play so confounded opponents during the magical fall of 1957 that the 49ers play earned a spot in the record books— and in the reference books. *The Oxford English Dictionary* credits the Tittle-to-Owens touchdown pass as the first "alley-oop" in sports.

Though the phrase is more often associated with basketball, it originated not with NBA star Elgin Baylor but with Owens, who happened to have been Baylor's roommate at the College of Idaho. "Today they'd say I have 'great hops,'" Owens joked late in life.

Raleigh Climon Owens was born in Shreveport, Louisiana, on November 12, 1934 and grew up in Southern California. He starred in football, basketball, and track at Santa Monica High, earning a scholarship in football and basketball at the College of Idaho. The 49ers took him in the 14th round (160th pick overall) in the 1956 draft. He blossomed immediately in '57 with 27 catches for 395 yards and five touchdowns. Owens would go on to become the 49ers' first 1,000-yard receiver in 1961 when he had five more touchdown catches and averaged 18.8 yards per catch.

Along the way he made one giant leap into 49ers lore. Accounts of the birth of the alley-oop vary, which only adds to the legend. In honor of the 50th anniversary of the play in 2007, Tittle and Owens provided their versions of its origins.

The way they told it, they connected on a throw-and-leap touchdown play as early as the 49ers' fourth exhibition game in 1957. Tittle, facing a ferocious rush from the Chicago Cardinals, tried to throw the ball away by heaving it over the end zone. But he was jostled as he let go of the ball, and it came out of his hand awkwardly. The ball fluttered toward the goal line where Owens soared over a cluster of defenders to make the catch. "Gee whiz, you made me look good," Tittle said.

"I can do it every time," Owens replied.

It looked like a happy accident and quickly vanished from conversation. It wasn't until weeks later during practice at the 49ers' training facility in Redwood City that they realized the power they had in Owens' outstretched fingertips. While bracing for the high-flying Los Angeles Rams in the second game of the season, the coaching staff instructed Tittle to mimic Rams quarterback Norm Van Brocklin, who specialized in deep passes. Coach Frankie Albert and top assistant Red Hickey wanted Tittle to give his defensive players "a picture of the play."

The trouble was, Tittle was reluctant to let it fly—even in a drill—and Owens was so well covered downfield that he figured no quarterback would make such an idiotic pass. Tittle's reluctance made Hickey increasingly infuriated. "He said, 'I don't care if they're covering the play, dammit, throw the ball down there and give them a picture of the play!'" Owens said.

So Tittle let one fly, unleashing a 40-yard rainbow toward the end zone. Owens jumped into the stratosphere to snag the ball. Then he did it again. And again.

The 49ers unwrapped their new toy on October 6, 1957 in front of a Kezar Stadium crowd of 59,637. Just before halftime Tittle launched a pass down the sideline despite tight coverage on Owens by defensive back Don Burroughs. Both players jumped. Owens jumped higher, bringing down the ball for a 46-yard score and a 16–7 halftime lead.

The 49ers did it again with about three minutes to play in the game. From the Rams' 11-yard line, Tittle lofted a change-up into the sky, and Owens flew over Jesse Castete for another touchdown. This one won the game 23–20. "I remember going to Colonel—that was one of Y.A.'s nicknames—and saying, 'Colonel, just put a little wobble on the ball. That way I can catch either end,'" Owens said. "Y.A. said, 'I've spent my whole life trying to rifle the ball on a line, and you want me to wobble it?'"

On October 13 Owens caught a touchdown pass with 27 seconds on the clock to defeat the Chicago Bears 21–17 at Wrigley Field. Owens was knocked down in the end zone while running his route and crawled to his knees to make the catch. Owens called it "an alley-down."

Against the Detroit Lions on November 3, Owens caught a game-winning 41-yarder, leaping over defensive backs Jim David and Jack Christiansen to give the 49ers a 35–31 victory with 11 seconds remaining. By then opposing teams were expecting Owens to be the go-to player. That only made it better. The 49ers had no desire to keep their play a secret.

"No, no, no," Hall of Famer Tittle said. "If they knew it was coming, that only made it better…I used to try to make a big production when we called it. I'd wave my arms for R.C. to move farther out, then farther, then farther. Then I'd say, 'Now! Perfect!' You wanted the defense to know: There he is."

26 Dwight Hicks and His Hot Licks

Dwight Hicks and His Hot Licks were never a band, but they had a string of memorable hits. And their debut shot straight to No. 1. The front man, of course, was Dwight Hicks, a shutdown safety who made four consecutive Pro Bowls starting in 1981. That was the season he was joined by rookies Carlton Williamson, Ronnie Lott, and Eric Wright.

The fab four helped capture Super Bowl XVI in their first season together. By 1984 all of them would make the Pro Bowl in the same season. "We had one of the best secondaries in NFL history," Hicks told the *San Francisco Chronicle* in 2002. "Seeing the guys I worked with every day—Eric, Ronnie, and Carlton—it gave me goose bumps. I stood back and said, 'Yes!' I don't think it will ever happen again."

Before he began collecting interceptions, however, Hicks had been passed over a few times himself. The Detroit Lions drafted the 6'1", 190-pounder out of Michigan in the sixth round of the 1978 draft. But he failed to make an impression and was cut during the

How the 'Hot Licks' Were Born

Never discount the value of goofing off.

In 1981 a few members of the 49ers media relations staff were shooting the bull in the boss's office one day when the conversation steered toward country music.

Public relations director George Heddleston had worked in Dallas and grown to love the names of great country music songs. He threw out a favorite, "Don't Cry on My Shoulders Cause You're Rusting My Spurs."

Then the staff began trying to outdo each other. Delia Martin countered with: "Thank God and Greyhound (You're Gone!)" Jerry Walker nominated "If the Phone Don't Ring, You'll Know It's Me." And then Walker mentioned another: "How Can I Miss You When You Won't Go Away?"

Heddleston howled with laughter. He knew that song, which was by a band called Dan Hicks & His Hot Licks. Still laughing, Heddleston quipped, "That would be a great name for our defensive backfield, huh?"

The P.R. staff looked at each other and realized this was no joke. Walker recalled someone in the room saying, "Let's run with it!"

preseason. Hicks played for a while with the Toronto Argonauts before signing with the Philadelphia Eagles in December 1978. The Pennsauken, New Jersey, native was thrilled: He would be playing right down the road from where he grew up.

But the Eagles cut him, too.

This time Hicks was so distraught that he considered giving up football for good. He wound up working at a health food store in Southfield, Michigan. He was between shifts there one day when the 49ers tracked him down and said they wanted him to participate in a workout with a few other defensive backs, receivers, and quarterbacks. Suffice it to say, the future leader of the Hot Licks passed the audition. "We were in shorts and cleats," said Hicks in *The Game of My Life: San Francisco 49ers*. "We had to cover the wide receivers and do some drills. I remember these guys were diving and jumping all over the place, just trying to make an impression. I wasn't diving. I'd just close in on the wide receivers and I think I showed them I could make a play."

The 49ers signed him three weeks later.

As opposing receivers can attest, this time Hicks was an instant smash. In his first extended playing time at safety, he snuffed a Broncos drive by intercepting a Craig Morton pass in the end zone on November 18, 1979 in Denver. By 1980 Hicks was entrenched at the position, starting all 16 games and recording four interceptions.

And then a strong draft blew in: The 49ers selected Lott from USC in the first round (eighth overall), Wright from Missouri in the second (40th), and Williamson from Pittsburgh in the third (65th). (The team also took Lynn Thomas, who proved to be a valuable nickel back, out of Pittsburgh in the fifth round and 121st overall.)

It didn't take opposing receivers long to catch on. Lott recalled how Williamson "laid out" two Steelers receivers in that 1981 season. "First he knocked John Stallworth right out of the game, then he cracked one of Calvin Sweeney's ribs," Lott said.

That young, hard-hitting group would become known as "Dwight Hicks and His Hot Licks." In their first season together, the 49ers had the NFL's second-ranked pass defense. The 49ers won the Super Bowl again in 1984—with Wright delivering one last lick. His stunning interception of a pass from Dan Marino to Mark Clayton deprived Miami of a touchdown. Many have called it the best play of Super Bowl XIX.

That was the year that the entire starting defensive backfield made the Pro Bowl, the only time in history that a team's entire secondary earned the honor. "I'm telling you," Hicks said then, "it's like we can almost read each other's minds out there."

27 George Seifert

During George Seifert's two seasons as Cornell University's head coach from 1975 to 1976, the Big Red went 3–15. At .167 it remains the worst winning percentage in the history of the school's football program, which began in 1887. Suffice it to say, Seifert's second head coaching gig went a little better.

Under his leadership, the 49ers went 98–30–1, won six NFC West titles, and captured two Super Bowl championships over an eight-season span. Including his time as an assistant, Seifert's career spanned all five Super Bowl victories. But because Seifert happened to succeed Bill Walsh, some people thought he was simply the lucky guy who inherited the winning formula. "He hasn't gotten the credit he deserves," former quarterback Joe Montana said.

Seifert is one of only 13 head coaches with more than one Super Bowl victory.

Then again, Seifert never wanted the spotlight. Though a relentlessly influential force behind the scenes of the 49ers dynasty as the defensive backs coach (1980 to 1982), defensive coordinator 1983 to 1988), and head coach (1989 to 1996), Seifert deflected attention. "Fans come to see the players on the field and not the coaches on the sidelines," he said. "Once we're on the field, it's their game. My excitement is coaching and watching the intelligence of Montana and the way [Roger] Craig runs and the grace of a [Jerry] Rice and the other marvelous athletes we have."

A San Francisco native born January 22, 1940, Seifert grew up like any other kid in the Mission District of that era. He worshipped Frankie Albert and Y.A. Tittle and died a thousand deaths when the team blew a 20-point lead to the Detroit Lions in the 1957 playoffs. Seifert spent his teen years as a linebacker at

Mooch Takes Over

Steve Mariucci had only one year of head coaching experience at any level when the 49ers put him in charge before the 1997 season. Big shoes to fill? At his introductory press conference, he took the podium flanked by Bill Walsh (three Super Bowl wins) and George Seifert (two). "I am in awe of those two coaches," Mariucci said that day. "I understand what I'm getting into. This has been the most successful franchise in professional football over the last 15 years."

Mariucci, 41, was the third head coach for the 49ers in 18 years. He took over from Seifert, who was stepping down while holding the record as the team's winningest coach. (The team's owner, Eddie DeBartolo, and top executive, Carmen Policy, said Seifert's decision to leave was strictly his own.)

The move worked well for a while. Engaging and charismatic with a sharp offensive mind, Mariucci went 13–3 as a rookie coach and 12–4 in his second year. Those 25 wins represent the second best total in NFL history for a coach over his first two seasons. Only Seifert had done better with 28. And not even Jim Harbaugh could match them; he won 24 over his first two years. Moreover, Mariucci's first season included an 11–0 start, topped only by Jim Caldwell's 14–0 start with the Indianapolis Colts in 2009.

Unfortunately he could never reach the postseason success of his glittering predecessors. The 49ers fired him after the 2002 season despite a 60–43 record (including playoffs) and four playoff berths over six seasons. He had back-to-back losing seasons in 1999 and 2000, but that was due in part to salary cap considerations that prompted a roster shakeup.

Terry Donahue, the team's general manager at the time of Mariucci's firing, cited "philosophical differences" between coach and owner John York. York later told *the San Francisco Chronicle* that he blamed Mariucci for a disconnect between the coaching staff and the front office. "Even with differences and arguments, there needs to be an agreement that we're going to play on the same team," York said, "and I don't think Steve was on that team."

After a less successful coaching stint with the Detroit Lions, Mariucci became a distinguished broadcaster with the NFL Network.

Polytechnic High across the street from Kezar Stadium. He was an usher at 49ers home games, which he admitted was basically a ploy to get to watch the games for free. If he wasn't working a game, he'd climb aboard the rooftop of a classmate's house and watch from there. That's how in 1957 he watched R.C. Owens make the first alley-oop catch in NFL history.

Seifert attended the University of Utah on a football scholarship. He immersed himself in school where he majored in zoology and he envisioned a career in teaching or wildlife management. "We called him 'Lonesome George,'" said Lynn Stiles, Seifert's college roommate and later an assistant on Seifert's coaching staff with the 49ers. "He was always in his room studying bugs."

His scientist's demeanor—analytical, detail-oriented—served him well in his approach to football, much to the initial chagrin of players like Ronnie Lott. When Seifert joined Walsh's staff as the defensive backs coach in 1980, he began tormenting members of the secondary by making them study for games as if cramming for a final exam. "God, how we despised him," Lott wrote in his autobiography, *Total Impact*. "He constantly rode us. He demanded we watch game film during our lunch break. He forced us to stay on the field at least half an hour after practice for more drills and then he ushered us into the meeting room for a few hours of extra film work. Many a night the janitorial crew would arrive before we would leave for dinner."

Defensive players thought his coaching was too meticulous, too time consuming, even too demanding. But by the time Seifert was done, no one was complaining. "It's humbling to be around George," former 49ers president Carmen Policy said. "To know what he's capable of and what he's accomplished but to see how unassuming he is."

By January 1989 Seifert's success as an assistant put him in high demand as a head coach. He scheduled a flight to interview with the Cleveland Browns but never made it: By the time of his layover in Dallas, he got word to turn around. The 49ers wanted him as head coach.

In his first season, Seifert responded to the pressure of following in Walsh's footsteps by doing the only thing that would satisfy a fan base: He guided the team to a 17–2 overall finish (including playoffs) and a record-setting 55–10 victory against the Denver Broncos in Super Bowl XXIV. As if to prove that was no fluke, he won another Super Bowl in 1994—this time with a 49–26 victory against the San Diego Chargers that was unmistakably his own.

Steve Mariucci stepped in when Seifert resigned following the 1996 season, but Seifert finished his 49ers career as the winningest coach in franchise history both in terms of total victories—98 and just ahead of Walsh's 92—and winning percentage—.766 ahead of Buck Shaw's .645.

He still ranks the lowest on the all-time ego list. "I've been around a lot of head coaches, but George is the first one who was ever this way: Every Monday morning after a big win, George's first words to the team were, 'Men, congratulations on your win,'" former offensive line coach Bobb McKittrick told *The New York Times*. "Not 'my' win or even 'our' win but 'your win.' It's an easy thing to say, but I'd never heard it said. It kind of sums up his ways."

28 Super Bowl XIX

As the minutes ticked down toward kickoff at Stanford Stadium on January 20, 1985, coach Bill Walsh plopped down on the floor of an otherwise quiet 49ers locker room. With his legs outstretched and his hands behind his head like a man staring up at the clouds,

Walsh began to fret—loudly and sarcastically: "How are we ever going to stop Dan Marino?…Miami's offense is so great…And that 'Killer B' defense, how are we ever going to get a first down?…How are we even going to get one yard?"

Typically and brilliantly, Walsh managed to both break the tension and drive home the motivational message. Like everyone else in the room, Walsh was sick of hearing a week's worth of questions about Mighty Marino and the unstoppable Dolphins. After all, the 49ers had a quarterback who wasn't too shabby either.

As if responding to their coach's rhetorical questions, the 49ers answered in the most emphatic way possible. They demolished the Dolphins 38–16 before 84,059 fans at Super Bowl XIX. Joe Montana, that *other* quarterback, completed 24-of-35 passes and established a new Super Bowl passing record with 331 yards. Montana also threw three touchdown passes to capture the game's MVP honors for his second time. In all, the 49ers outgained Miami 537–314 in total yards. "All we heard all week long was Miami's offense: 'How you going to stop them?'" Montana said at the postgame podium. "Deep inside we knew we had a great offense, too. Nobody was thinking about how to stop us."

The victory capped an incredible 49ers season—18–1, including playoffs—and answered any questions about the best quarterback in the game. "They played us better than any team played us defensively this year," said Marino, 23, who would never get another Super Bowl opportunity. "I didn't make the plays on some occasions when I had a chance."

The hype machine naturally focused on the quarterback showdown between Montana and Marino, two gunslingers from Western Pennsylvania: Montana was from New Eagle; Marino was from Pittsburgh. But the 49ers felt insulted that Montana was getting the short shrift. A headline for a story by noted sports columnist Mitch Albom read: "NFC finds its king in Wimpy Montana." Montana was even asked during the week whether he

After besting Dan Marino and the Dolphins, quarterback and Super Bowl XIX MVP Joe Montana poses with the Vince Lombardi Trophy and Bill Walsh (left) and Eddie DeBartolo Jr. (right). (AP Images)

was jealous of Marino's stardom. "Everybody has their time. And this is his right now," Montana replied calmly. "He's had a great year. I didn't expect anything less for him. I think this is great what's happening to him."

A less diplomatic response came on gameday. Montana proved that playing quarterback required more than a bazooka right arm. He scrambled away from trouble (59 rushing yards), made accurate throws from out of the pocket, and tormented the Dolphins with his high-percentage passes.

With the Dolphins leading 10–7 after the first quarter, Montana directed three successive touchdown drives and kept rolling from there. The 49ers' 38 points tied the Super Bowl record established by the Los Angeles Raiders a year prior. Montana had help from running back Roger Craig, who scored a pair of rushing touchdowns (of eight and two yards) and also had a touchdown catch (16 yards). In doing so Craig became the first player to score three touchdowns in a single Super Bowl.

Marino, meanwhile, completed 29-of-50 passes for 318 yards, one touchdown, and two interceptions. Many of the passing yards came late in the game with the score out of reach. The best-protected quarterback in the NFL during the regular season was sacked four times in one afternoon. "They were hitting his ass," former defensive back Dwight Hicks told NFL Films years later. "And you start doing that to a quarterback in the NFL, I don't care who you are, it'll make you look very ordinary."

The 49ers became the first defense to hold the Dolphins to under 21 points that season. And in the end, there were no more questions, sarcastic or otherwise. "Montana is the greatest quarterback in this league—maybe of all time," Walsh said. "This was his year."

29 Y.A. Tittle

Even Lou Cordileone was surprised. "What? Me even up for Y.A. Tittle? You're kidding?" he reportedly said in reaction to the 1961 trade that swapped the New York Giants guard/linebacker for the 49ers star quarterback.

The deal appeared lopsided at first and only looked worse over time. Tittle, a top-shelf performer during 10 seasons (1951 to 1960) with the 49ers, would go on to win the NFL MVP award in 1962 and 1963 with the Giants. In '62 he threw for 33 touchdown passes and 3,224 yards. Tittle helped the Giants reach three consecutive title games en route to his enshrinement in the Pro Football Hall of Fame. Meanwhile, Cordileone lasted only one season in San Francisco, and his NFL career consisted of 75 games.

Even up for Y.A. Tittle? You're kidding?

To the 49ers the move made sense at the time. They traded away Tittle, their star who was approaching his 35th birthday, to clear the path for quarterback John Brodie, the third overall pick of the 1957 draft, who was ready to be a starter. Coach Red Hickey was committed to a new shotgun offense, and Tittle was a proud member of the classic drop-back fraternity. Tittle once joked that he "couldn't run his way out of a wet paper sack."

Tittle already understood that quarterback transitions were inescapably awkward. He had been on the other end of it in 1951 when he was the emerging young hotshot who challenged veteran Frankie Albert.

Born on October 24, 1926, Yelberton Abraham Tittle was known by a lot of names. But *Yelberton* was never one of them. He was always Y.A. growing up. His football nicknames included "Ya-Ya," "Colonel," and "The Bald Eagle." On the day he got married, the preacher even messed up and called him "Wayne."

Whatever the name, it was on the lips of a lot of football executives for a stretch of the late 1940s. The Cleveland Browns of the All-America Football Conference and the Detroit Lions of the NFL each used a first-round pick on him in 1948. Tittle signed with the Browns but didn't stick. Cleveland was already a powerhouse with Otto Graham at quarterback, so the AAFC commissioner awarded Tittle to the Baltimore Colts in an attempt to give the league some parity.

Coming off a stellar LSU career, Tittle was an instant hit in Baltimore. He passed for 346 yards, threw four touchdown passes, and scored a rushing touchdown in a 45–28 victory in the Colts' season opener against the New York Yankees. But that incarnation of the Baltimore Colts would soon crumble. Low attendance and dysfunctional leadership combined to doom the franchise even after the AAFC was absorbed for the 1950 season by the NFL. When the Colts folded, Tittle was dispersed via draft in 1951, and the 49ers snatched him up.

Upon arriving in San Francisco, Tittle quickly recognized that Albert was the heart of the franchise. At his first training camp in Menlo Park, California, Tittle noticed how Albert's carefree confidence set the tone for the entire team. On the other hand, Tittle later wrote, "There was one man Frank had no intention of keeping loose—me. When I came to the 49ers camp, he wasn't about to help anyone take his job away from him. He let me know that early. I asked him to explain something about one of our plays, and he grinned at me. 'You forget you're after my job,' he said and walked away."

Tittle described that exchange in a remarkably candid first-person series for *Sports Illustrated* in 1965. His "My Life in Football" co-written with Tex Maule is available at si.com/vault and is a must-read for 49ers fans.

Tittle played sparingly in 1951 but began divvying up snaps with Albert almost evenly by 1952. "It is not a system I recommend," Tittle wrote. "It is impossible to split the responsibility of quarterbacking without splitting the loyalties of fans, writers, and, most important, players. It may be subconscious on the part of the players, but it has to be there."

By 1953 Albert retired, leaving Tittle as the unquestioned starter. He responded by making the first of his seven career Pro Bowls and went on to spend the decade surrounded by Million

Dollar Backfield mates Joe Perry, Hugh McElhenny, and John Henry Johnson. Tittle also developed a wonderful rapport with receiver R.C. Owens as the two teamed up for the legendary alley-oop pass.

Tittle still ranks among the 49ers' all-time leaders in most quarterback categories, including games (fourth), yards (fifth), and touchdown passes (sixth).

30 Jim Harbaugh

On the day he was introduced as the 49ers' new head coach in 2011, Jim Harbaugh settled in for a press conference at the Palace Hotel's posh Gold Ballroom in downtown San Francisco. Cameras clicked. Writers scribbled. Tributes flowed. And Harbaugh couldn't wait to leave. "I want to get out of here so I can get to work," he said.

As it turned out, Harbaugh really was in a rush. While his immediate predecessors often pleaded for more patience, Harbaugh needed none. The former quarterback ran the coaching equivalent of the hurry-up offense, needing two seasons to reach the Super Bowl. In Harbaugh's rookie coaching campaign, the team went 13–3 and reached the NFC Championship Game. Ronnie Lott marveled that it was "one of the greatest coaching jobs in the history of coaching."

That was just a warm up for his second season when he became the eighth coach in NFL history to win a division title in each of his first two seasons. Harbaugh was the third to do so after inheriting a team with a losing record, joining Chuck Knox (who led the

Harbaugh and the "Say Hey Kid"

Jim Harbaugh got to meet the guy who made "The Catch."
No, not Dwight Clark. That other guy: Willie Mays. "It was neat as hell," the 49ers head coach said. "I want to remember everything about it."

Harbaugh arranged for the "Say Hey Kid" to attend a 49ers practice in Santa Clara on October 4, 2012. The coach is a big believer that greatness is contagious, so he arranges for the 49ers players to be around people distinguished in their field—any field—as often as possible. Harbaugh often asks decorated members of the military to address his team. He welcomed actors and noted *Wedding Crashers* Owen Wilson and Vince Vaughn into the locker room after a game. Poker champion Phil Hellmuth has given a pep talk.

But in the eyes of the Harbaugh family, no one can match Mays. Jack Harbaugh, the father of Jim, John, and Joani, was a huge fan of the Giants slugger who hit 660 home runs and made the most famous grab in baseball history—an over-the-shoulder catch of a ball hit by Cleveland Indian Vic Wertz at the Polo Grounds in the 1954 World Series.

So when Mays came to meet the 49ers, Jim Harbaugh made sure his dad was invited, too. "My dad and Willie had great conversations about the Indians and the Giants," Harbaugh said. "My dad knew all of the names and the positions, and Willie told a story about each guy."

Once upon a time, Mays had been a football star himself in Fairfield, Alabama. "I've never seen clips of him playing football, but I could visualize that he would have been a heck of a quarterback," Harbaugh said.

Los Angeles Rams to five straight titles starting in 1973) and Ted Marchibroda (three straight for the Baltimore Colts starting in 1975).

Harbaugh not only changed the 49ers record, but he also changed their culture. He kicked open the doors at 4949 Centennial Boulevard with an intense confidence that bordered on lunacy, and his players followed merrily along. By the bye week of that first season, when tight end Vernon Davis returned to his native

Washington, D.C., friends kept asking him the same question: Is Jim Harbaugh out of his mind? "The first thing they said to me was, 'Your coach is crazy,'" Davis said with a laugh.

The tight end assured them that Harbaugh was sane. But the perception that the coach had a screw loose was understandable. It took less than half a season for Harbaugh to nearly come to blows with Detroit Lions coach Jim Schwartz during a postgame handshake. On the day the final roster was announced in September 2012, he left auto mechanic work shirts in every player's locker, meaning millionaires like Frank Gore walked around with a circular nametag that read "Frank." Harbaugh also taught his players a call-and-response routine he'd break out at any moment. He'd shout, "Who's got it better than us?" And players would yell back, "NO-BODY!"

One last hint at insanity: Harbaugh warned players to be on the lookout for a four-inch-tall man who likes to sit atop shoulder pads and whisper messages of complacency. Harbaugh even had a name—Frederick P. Soft—for that mythical man. Defensive coordinator Vic Fangio played along, too, telling the press: "There's word that he's been lurking here in the Bay Area. So we're on guard. Our security people out front have been given a description. We're trying to keep him out of the facility."

The craziest thing of all? Harbaugh made the 49ers relevant again.

Inheriting a team that hadn't been to the playoffs in nine seasons, Harbaugh reinvigorated the franchise by unearthing some long lost Xs and Os. Harbaugh had been a longtime NFL quarterback, making the Pro Bowl in 1994, and his offensive acumen was a welcome change for a team that had stalled under defensive-minded coaches Mike Nolan and Mike Singletary.

Harbaugh coaxed a new level of play from quarterback Alex Smith, who had been all but abandoned by other coaches (not to mention a disgruntled fan base). He was able to find what Smith did best and tailored an offense that suited his strengths. And no player better exemplified the creativity of Harbaugh's staff than backup tight end Delanie Walker, who lined up in 15 different spots during that 2011 season. "Harbaugh makes everyone feel, like Bill Walsh used to say, 'like they're an extension of each other,'" former running back Roger Craig said. "He's got the secret sauce."

In some ways Harbaugh had been preparing for coaching since the crib. His father, Jack Harbaugh, was a longtime college coach who would win an NCAA Division I-AA national championship. Jim also grew up with a competitive mother (Jackie), a driven brother John (later the coach of the Baltimore Ravens), and a savvy sister Joani (who would marry Indiana basketball coach Tom Crean). That oft-repeated 49ers question—"Who's got it better than us?"—was actually a family credo. Joani recalled that her dad would use it even when she didn't want to go to school. "My dad would say, 'Who's got it better than us? You get to go to school! You get to have a recess! You get to learn a little math!'"

Jim Harbaugh would put those head coaching genes to good work, establishing himself first at the University of San Diego before reviving Stanford. The Cardinal went 29–21 during his four seasons there, including a 12–1 mark in 2010 with Andrew Luck at the helm. That's when the 49ers decided to make a big splash, luring Harbaugh to the NFL with a five-year, $25-million deal. He paid dividends in that rookie season, winning the Coach of the Year award.

But first Harbaugh had to get through that opening press conference. Among his first words: "Losing is not an option."

31 Steve Young's Crazy Touchdown Run

To understand the way Steve Young could confound a defense with his legs, track down the clip of his crazy, zigzagging touchdown run against the Minnesota Vikings on October 30, 1988.

But take some Dramamine first.

Young whirled around the turf that day like a cat at a dog kennel—half terrified, half crazed, and entirely uncatchable.

Joe Montana, injured and watching from the sidelines, was laughing by the time Young tumbled into the end zone. "I know I couldn't have made it," Montana said. "I would have passed out long before that."

Young's touchdown run was staggering—in every sense of the word. It was the game winner, a 49-yard romp with less than two minutes remaining to catapult the 49ers to a 24–21 victory against the NFL's top defense. (It stood as the longest run by a 49ers quarterback until 2012 when Colin Kaepernick blazed in from 50.) In terms of style points? Well…

"It was ugly," linebacker Michael Walter said that day. "But it was beautiful." In fact fullback Harry Sydney ran up to Young after the play and told him, "A hell of a run, Steve. Next time open your eyes."

As it turns out, Young's wide eyes were the keys to the whole nutty thing. The play was designed as a curl to Mike Wilson. When the quarterback saw that the receiver was covered, he began searching for tight end Brent Jones. Instead, the next thing he saw was the hand of ferocious Vikings defensive end (and a future 49er) Chris Doleman. "That's when I just rolled," Young said.

At least five Vikings had a shot at Young. Safety Joey Browner and linebacker Jesse Solomon missed him at midfield. Cornerback

Kaepernick's Run

Heading into his first career playoff game on January 12, 2013, there were still questions about whether untested quarterback Colin Kaepernick could handle the big-game pressure. He left those questions in the dust—along with a slew of Green Bay Packers defenders.

By the time Kaepernick finished his record-setting 56-yard touchdown bolt, the only remaining question was: How did he just do that? "Man, he's fast," 49ers linebacker Patrick Willis said. "To see a guy come across the field at an angle, and he eats up the angle, man, that's fast."

Kaepernick's big play came in a 45–31 victory in a divisional round game at Candlestick Park, moving the 49ers into a new era. After that play the 49ers clearly would have to follow him—at a high rate of speed.

Kaepernick had an early run for a 20-yard score on his way to topping the NFL record for most rushing yards by a quarterback. His 181 yards bested the mark of 173 set by the Atlanta Falcons' Michael Vick in 2002. "I didn't know how fast he was," Packers defensive back Charles Woodson admitted after the game. "Coming in, I really never paid attention to it. But he is fast."

Woodson, and the rest of the football world, found out for sure with the score tied at 24 in the third quarter. Lined up in the Pistol formation, Kaepernick faked a handoff to LaMichael James, turned around the right side, got a couple of blocks, and then was gone for a 56-yard score that made Green Bay players look like statues. Woodson looked like he had a clear angle to chase down Kaepernick. But he never came close to catching the 6'5", 230-pound express train.

Watching at home was a huge 49ers fan who just happened to be a former Olympic sprinting medalist. Ato Boldon's scouting report on Kaepernick? "He's a freak in the same way that Usain Bolt is a freak," Boldon said.

Carl Lee missed him at the 40. Browner missed him again. Near the 30, Young delivered a stiff arm to Solomon. But his toughest defender was gravity, which seemed intent on stopping him for those final five yards.

Young looked as if he'd blown a tire, wobbling...sputtering...collapsing...and finally tumbling into the safe arms of the end zone. "I always laughed when I used to see guys stumble like that," Young said that day, once he'd caught his breath. "I couldn't get my legs out in front of me. My legs died. I'm glad I was only on the 5."

Steve Young wasn't the only man out of breath by the end of his 49-yard touchdown run. Broadcaster Lon Simmons had to keep up with his play call.

"Young back to throw. In trouble. He's going to be sacked. No! Gets away. He runs. Gets away again! Goes to the 40. Gets away again! To the 35. Cuts back at the 30! To the 20! To the 15! To the 10! Young is exhausted. He dives. Touchdown 49ers!"

The play gained further attention when Burger King introduced a nationally televised commercial in 2006, superimposing the Burger King mascot on Steve Young's body as the mascot ran for the dramatic—and stumbling—score.

32 The De-Cleating Fullback

Before earning the glamorous role as the do-everything fullback in Bill Walsh's innovative West Coast Offense, Tom Rathman made his mark on special teams.

The bruises he administered to opponents while blocking on kickoffs and punt return units might still be under an ice pack somewhere. The Nebraska-tough, 230-pounder blasted players so hard that opponents' feet wound up over their heads. Rathman called those blocks "de-cleators."

It didn't take the 49ers coaches long to notice the human rubble being left in Rathman's wake. Midway through his second season in 1987, Rathman was promoted to the starting fullback job. Doing so allowed the 49ers to shift Roger Craig from fullback to halfback, a move that paid off for everyone—except opposing defenses.

As part of the 49ers backfield from 1986 until 1993, Thomas Dean Rathman was an integral part of some potent offenses. Though his blocking got the third-round pick on the radar, he proved to be more than just a wrecking ball. Rathman could be a shifty runner. (He'd averaged 6.4 yards per carry while in college at Nebraska.) And under Walsh he blossomed as a pass catcher. In 1989 Rathman led NFC running backs with 73 catches for 616 yards.

All along, though, he never lost his first love: de-cleating opponents. It's just that he learned to do it with the ball in his hands. As Rathman once explained to the *San Francisco Chronicle*: "I most like to take a pass in the flat and turn up field on a defensive back. It's always nice when you find those 190-pound DBs trying to take on a guy who is 235 pounds and in full stride. I don't try to put a move on them. I just try to go right through them."

Born on October 7, 1962, Rathman grew up in Grand Island, Nebraska, where he learned an appreciation for doing the dirty work. As a teenager his summers were full of tedious, demanding labor in the cornfields. He also helped his father and uncle on a construction crew, pouring cement under a blazing Midwestern sun.

Rathman took that hard-nosed work ethic to college at Nebraska, where he first demonstrated his knack for separating opponents from their footwear. He once described his style of play to sportswriter Dennis Georgatos: "My forte was the block, running into that wall. Don't blink. Go as hard as you can and

Fullback Tom Rathman, a crushing blocker and nifty receiver, carries the ball during a 1993 playoff game versus the Giants.

don't pull up because something is going to give, and it wasn't going to be me."

Upon sizing up the country kid from Nebraska, Joe Montana gave Rathman the nickname "Woody" after the naïve bumpkin on *Cheers*. But Rathman was incredibly sophisticated when it came to football, handling whatever role Walsh threw his way.

In his eight seasons with the team, Rathman helped the 49ers win seven division titles and two Super Bowls (XXIII and XXIV). He played his final NFL season with the Raiders in 1994, closing out his career with 2,020 rushing yards and 34 total touchdowns.

Rathman launched a second career as a running backs coach, including two distinguished stints with the 49ers. He worked for the team from 1997 to 2002 (guiding the likes of Garrison Hearst and Charlie Garner) before returning in 2009.

Frank Gore, one of his disciples, has learned to embrace the idea of becoming a complete back. Thanks to constant one-on-one mentoring, Gore has improved as a power runner, receiver, and— of course—a blocker. "If you can't block" Gore said, "then you can't play for Coach Rathman."

33 Visit the Canyon Inn Restaurant

If you want a Hacksaw Burger the way Hacksaw Reynolds ate his, you've got to douse your double-cheeseburger with Tabasco sauce. If you want a burger the way Bob St. Clair liked 'em, make sure the chef doesn't actually cook it. St. Clair preferred raw meat.

And those of you who have delicate stomachs—or simply good sense—can still enjoy the Canyon Inn Restaurant, an eclectic family-style joint in Redwood City where Joe Montana, Dwight Clark, and other stars from the 1980s dynasty would come for a post-victory meal.

The Canyon Inn is part eatery, part time machine: Walls are speckled with snapshots, autographs, newspaper clippings, and letters from some of football's most famous names. It's the kind of place where you might find an old NFL contract autographed by Paul Brown tucked under the counter by the pizza oven.

And if the vintage photos aren't enough to bring memories to life, there's a reasonable chance a former 49ers player will be there in the flesh. On the day I visited with former 49ers public relations director Jerry Walker to do research for this book, Tim Anderson, the team's first-round draft pick from 1971, happened to stop by. So did Alyn Beals Jr., whose father led the All-America Football Conference in receptions as a member of the original 1946 49ers.

The Canyon Inn was established in 1973. But the restaurant, like the team, really took off in 1981. Shortly before training camp that season, 49ers executive John McVay stopped by for lunch. Owner and founder Tim Harrison introduced himself and told McVay he wanted to host a season kickoff rally for the team. McVay directed him to former 49ers star R.C. Owens, who by then was working in the team's community relations department. Owens told Harrison that players would come to the restaurant for a rally—but only if they got something in return.

So Harrison came up with a promotional deal for the players: Win a game, get a voucher for a free meal. It hardly seemed like a financial risk. The 49ers had gone 2–14, 2–14, and 6–10 during the previous three seasons.

But Harrison got an inkling of what was to come almost immediately. He was listening to a Week 2 game on the radio when the 49ers walloped the Chicago Bears 28–17.

Harrison turned to his girlfriend and asked, "Do you think anybody will show up?" The next day, players were lined up out the door, still in their practice sweatpants, and waiting for their burgers.

The 49ers would go on to finish 16–3 (including the play-offs) that season and worked up quite an appetite along the way. Offensive linemen would come in and gorge on burgers, hot dogs, sandwiches, and maybe even the occasional salad. But they weren't the worst. Harrison still remembers a low-level assistant coach who turned the Canyon Inn into his personal all-you-can-eat buffet.

Let's do the math. Sixteen victories multiplied by more than 50 players equals?

"I bet it was about $10,000," Harrison said. "And that was 30-years-ago money."

Harrison didn't mind, though. For one thing he had made a commitment and never thought about backing out. For another the payoff to the Canyon Inn has been priceless. On the day after The Catch, for example, Clark came in for a burger. He used those famous fingertips—fresh off hauling in Montana's pass—to sign a *San Francisco Chronicle* sports page that now hangs above one of the booths.

Harrison kept his offer in place until the 49ers relocated their headquarters to Santa Clara in 1988. The restaurant remains located at 587 Canyon Road in Redwood City (www.canyoninn.com). In fact, it's just a stone's throw away from The Hill, the famous Roger Craig–Jerry Rice training ground detailed in Chapter 20 and the perfect place to go burn off those Hacksaw Burgers.

34 Brent Jones

Brent Jones' path to greatness began with a bad route. Five days after the Pittsburgh Steelers selected the tight end in the fifth round of the 1986 draft, Jones and his future wife, Dana, were in a car accident near their San Jose, California, home. The vehicle was struck by a drunk driver. Jones sustained a herniated disk in his neck and was sidelined for several months.

Tired of waiting for Jones' return to health, the Steelers cut him about a month into the '86 season. That allowed Bill Walsh to strike gold by taking a flier on the promising pass catcher from Santa Clara University. As the *Los Angeles Times* later put it: "49er fans caught a break—between the fourth and fifth vertebrae."

"It was the best thing that could have happened," Jones said, looking back in 2003. "You don't think it at the time, but it changed my whole life for the positive." Jones went on to become one of the most prolific tight ends of his era, a four-time Pro Bowl selection and three-time Super Bowl player for the 49ers from 1987 to 1997. He was a reliable target for Joe Montana and Steve Young and played more games at tight end than anyone in franchise history (143).

Tempting as it is to poke fun at the Steelers for letting a 6'4", 230-pound future Pro Bowler slip away so easily, their concerns about his injuries were well justified. After being cut, a frustrated Jones returned to San Jose wondering whether he would ever get a chance to play again. Even after the 49ers signed him to a free-agent deal and invited him to training camp in 1987, there was no guarantee he would make the team. Jones remembers reporting to Rocklin, California, as the eighth-string tight end. (Russ Francis and John Frank were among the notable names ahead of him.)

But Jones, like his roommate Young, who was waiting behind some guy named Joe Montana, combined patience with persistence and eventually got his chance. It took until 1989 for his first start, but he promptly made up for the lost time. Jones caught 40 passes for 500 yards that year, including a seven-yard touchdown pass in Super Bowl XXIV against the Denver Broncos.

Soon Jones was making his mark as a secret weapon in the West Coast Offense. He was the guy who slipped into the open spot against zone defenses or made teams pay when they were too focused on Jerry Rice or John Taylor. There were times when nobody even covered him. "It's kind of a weird feeling," Jones said in 2013. "It happened to me a few times over the years, and you kind of look around and think, 'Uh, I'm not going to fall for this.' You kind of do a double-take while you're running. *Seriously? Nobody is covering me? Am I not going to miss somebody who is going to lay me out?*"

Consistently productive, Jones set his career high for yards in 1990 (747), catches in 1993 (68), and touchdowns in 1994 (nine). All those marks stood as team records for tight ends until Vernon Davis came along years later. Among 49ers the only players to appear in more playoff games than Jones (21) are Jerry Rice (23) and Jesse Sapolu (22).

Jones went on to a second career as a top executive for the Northgate Capital management company. But as successful as he's been in business, it's been difficult to replace the thrill of running wide open through a soft spot in the opponent's defense—and the camaraderie of being part of a team. "You do miss it. You miss the thrill of coming out of the locker room. But what you miss most is the relationships in that tight-knit locker room," Jones said. "You still have the highlights and the trophies and the memories, but you miss the bond you had with your fellow players and your coaches."

35 Bobb McKittrick

In a business where 275 pounds could be considered puny, the 49ers blockers were often undersized. But they were never under-prepared. That's because Bobb McKittrick, one of the premier offensive line coaches of all-time, specialized in teaching the techniques that paved the way for Joe Montana, Steve Young, and the dazzling offense of a dynasty.

McKittrick coaxed the best out of a generation of otherwise unheralded linemen. Too small? McKittrick taught the likes of Guy McIntyre and Jesse Sapolu to rely on quickness and precision to outwit defensive behemoths. Bill Walsh said that McKittrick "has developed more offensive line knowledge than anyone ever. His men have played longer, with better technique, more production, fewer injuries. In every possible category you can measure, he's right at the top."

Said McIntyre: "Playing for Bobb, you always knew where you stood. He didn't really mince his words. There wasn't a lot of praise. But he was always honest and straightforward."

McKittrick, who died at 64 on March 15, 2000, remains a beloved figure in the franchise. Every year the 49ers salute the offensive lineman "who best exemplifies the dedication, excellence, and commitment of offensive line coach Bobb McKittrick" with an award that bears his name.

And that first name alone tells you plenty about the man. As a seventh-grader in Baker, Oregon, he added an extra 'b' to his name. "I just wanted to be different," Bobb explained. Indeed, there was no one like him. The 49ers offensive line coach from 1979 to 1999 ran drills with the precision of a drill sergeant (McKittrick had spent three years as an officer in the U.S. Marine Corps.)

The Thomas Herrion Award

Thomas Herrion was with the 49ers only briefly. But his NFL dream will live on forever.

The relentlessly positive lineman collapsed and died of a heart attack in the locker room moments after an August 20, 2005 preseason game in Denver. "It's a day of mourning for the 49er family," then-coach Mike Nolan said. "We lost a teammate and a very good friend as well."

He suffered from hypertrophic cardiomyopathy (HCM), a condition where the muscles of the chamber of the heart thicken and enlarge. Herrion, who was 23, was so beloved by teammates that the York family established a tribute in the player's honor. The Thomas Herrion Award goes annually to the rookie or first-year player who, in the words of the team, "best represents the dream of Thomas Herrion. The award will go to a player, like Thomas, who has taken advantage of every opportunity, turned it into a positive situation, and made their dream turn into a reality."

An undrafted player from the University of Utah, the 6'3", 310-pounder's time with the 49ers lasted less than a year, but the lineman found time to leave a tremendous impact. As his last act, Herrion helped the 49ers finish the game against the Broncos with a 14-play touchdown drive.

For years after his death, the 49ers left his locker intact—behind protective glass. "It reminds me of how important the team was to Thomas and how hard he had worked to get there," former teammate Justin Smiley said. "And he would have made it, too. Thomas was a pro."

Thomas Herrion Award Winners

2005—OT Thomas Herrion
2006—OT Harvey Dahl
2007—CB Tarell Brown
2008—WR Dominique Zeigler
2009—FB Brit Miller
2010—RB Anthony Dixon and DT Will Tukuafu
2011—CB Cory Nelms
2012—WR Kyle Williams

By focusing on precision footwork, he coached relatively smaller players to gargantuan feats. McIntyre (275 pounds) was a five-time Pro Bowl selection. Sapolu (a 271-pounder taken in the 11th round) made it to two Pro Bowls. *Sports Illustrated* described McKittrick as perhaps "the most successful position coach of his era (because) few coaches have done so much with so little."

Opponents, however, weren't always so amused. "We had a bad reputation," McIntyre said. "[Opponents] said we were dirty because we would cut block. But that's what Bobb told us to do. We were only doing what Bobb told us to do. Because if we didn't, he'd say, 'You could have cut here. That would have made this play better. You need to get the guy down on the ground.'"

Known for his toughness, McKittrick was famous for his refusal to wear a jacket no matter how cold or snowy. The only exception anyone can remember came during a 1989 playoff game at Soldier Field in Chicago. He relented and wore a windbreaker; it was minus-26 degrees with the windchill factor.

Never, however, did he show more courage than he did at the end of his career. McKittrick was diagnosed with cancer of the bile duct and faced it head-on. Teckla McKittrick, his wife for more than 40 years, once recalled how doctors inserted stents down his throat to open his bile duct. She watched doctors, unable to use anesthesia, turn away at the thought of the pain they were about to inflict, and she barely saw her husband wince.

The 49ers saluted their longtime mastermind at halftime of a game during his final season. Teckla and Walsh had trouble making sure the guest of honor showed up at the ceremony. "He was very embarrassed, not wanting all of this fuss about him," his wife said. "I told him, 'Bobb, it's your turn to be gracious. You've done so many things for other people. Now it's your turn.'"

36 The Million Dollar Backfield

The answer to the question is no.

The Million Dollar Backfield did not actually make a million bucks. Not collectively and certainly not individually. Dave Newhouse, the esteemed writer who authored an entire book on football's famous quartet, estimates that the Million Dollar Backfield combined to make about $70,000 a year.

NFL stars did not get rich in the 1950s, not even Y.A. Tittle, Joe "the Jet" Perry, Hugh McElhenny, or John Henry Johnson. Each of those players wound up in Canton, Ohio, making the Million Dollar Backfield the only full-house backfield in which all of its members were enshrined in the Pro Football Hall of Fame. The nickname, alas, was simply a metaphor. Dan McGuire, the 49ers' early public relations man, came up with the sobriquet to describe the astounding talent that shared the same field from 1954 to 1956.

In reality all of the future Hall of Famers had offseason jobs (or even in-season jobs) to supplement their incomes. Newhouse's book, *The Million Dollar Backfield: The San Francisco 49ers in the 1950s,* recounts how McElhenny would finish 49ers practice and then head off to his other job as a salesman for Granny Goose potato chips.

Tittle launched an insurance business in 1958 and eventually *did* become a wealthy man, thanks to Y.A. Tittle & Associates. The quarterback is also the only player in professional football history to be drafted in the first round three times: by the Cleveland Browns of the AAFC (1948), Detroit Lions of the NFL (also '48), and the 49ers after Baltimore Colts disbanded ('51 NFL Draft). But he still needed offseason employment. "Oh yeah, we all had to get

Million Dollar Plaques

In honor of the four enshrined members, here's a glimpse at each man's Hall of Fame plaque:

JOE "THE JET" PERRY: Class of 1969

Fullback. 6'0", 200
(Compton Junior College)
1948 to 1960, 1963 San Francisco 49ers (AAFC/NFL), 1961 to 1962 Baltimore Colts
Fletcher Joseph Perry...Spotted playing service football by pro scouts... Signed as free agent by 49ers...Extremely quick runner who earned nickname "The Jet"...First to gain over 1,000 yards two straight years, 1953 to 1954...Career record: 12,532 combined net yards, 9,723 yards rushing, 260 receptions, 513 points...Played in three Pro Bowls...Born January 22, 1927, in Stevens, Arkansas...Died April 25, 2011 at the age of 84.

HUGH McELHENNY: Class of 1970

Halfback. 6'1", 195
(Washington, Compton Junior College) 1952 to 1960 San Francisco 49ers, 1961 to 1962 Minnesota Vikings, 1963 New York Giants, 1964 Detroit Lions
Hugh Edward McElhenny Jr....Washington All-America...49ers' No. 1 draft pick, 1952...Scored 40-yard TD on first pro play...Had phenomenal first season, winning All-NFL, Rookie of Year honors... Played in six Pro Bowls...MVP of 1958 Pro Bowl...Gained 11,375 combined net yards in 13 years...Record includes 5,281 yards rushing, 264 pass receptions, 360 points...Nicknamed "The King"... Born December 31, 1928 in Los Angeles, California.

Y.A. TITTLE: Class of 1971

Quarterback. 6'0", 192
(Louisiana State) 1948 to 1950 Baltimore Colts (AAFC/NFL), 1951 to 1960 San Francisco 49ers, 1961 to 1964 New York Giants.
Yelberton Abraham Tittle...AAFC Rookie of Year, 1948...Joined 49ers in 1951 after Colts disbanded...Career record: 2,427 completions, 33,070 yards, 242 TDs, 13 games over 300 yards passing...Paced 1961, 1962, 1963 Giants to division titles...Threw 33 TD passes in

1962, 36 in 1963...NFL's Most Valuable Player/Player of the Year, 1961, 1962, 1963...All-NFL, 1957, 1961, 1962, 1963...Elected to seven Pro Bowls...Born October 24, 1926, in Marshall, Texas.

JOHN HENRY JOHNSON: Class of 1987
Fullback. 6'2", 210
(St. Mary's, Arizona State) 1954 to 1956 San Francisco 49ers, 1957 to 1959 Detroit Lions, 1960 to 1965 Pittsburgh Steelers, 1966 Houston Oilers
John Henry Johnson...Steelers No. 2 draft pick, 1953...Joined 49ers in 1954 after year in Canada...Completed "Million Dollar Backfield" with McElhenny, Perry, Tittle in San Francisco...Powerful runner, superior blocker...Had best years in Pittsburgh, surpassing 1,000 yards rushing in 1962, 1964...Career stats: 6,803 yards, 48 touchdowns rushing; 186 receptions for 1,478 yards, 7 TDs...Born November 24, 1929, in Waterproof, Louisiana...Died June 3, 2011, at age of 81.

another job in those years," Tittle told writer Matt Maoicco for *San Francisco 49ers: Where Have You Gone* (2005). "They paid us with blue chip stamps, so it was tough to live on our football salary."

Even the folks in Canton still marvel at the 49ers' long ago riches. Pete Fierle, the Pro Football Hall of Fame's manager of digital media, wrote an essay in 2011 in which he continued to scratch his head in disbelief. "There's fact and there's folklore...Were they really that highly touted when they were playing or has the legend grown over the years? The answer is yes, the Million Dollar Backfield was really that spectacular, especially during the first season the four greats were together...Today the literal meaning of a Million Dollar Backfield is commonplace for all NFL teams. But even in the age of free agency, it's hard to imagine any team ever having a backfield like the 49ers had for that brief moment in time."

37 Jimmy Johnson

Jimmy Johnson spent much of his early life known as Rafer Johnson's little brother. He was proud of that. Rafer was a world decathlon champion. But he always wanted something of his own. And by the time he finished tormenting opposing quarterbacks for nearly two decades, Jimmy Johnson had another name to go by: Pro Football Hall of Famer.

The 49ers cornerback was a four-time first-team All-Pro during a career spanning 1961 to 1976. Using the speed that ran—and ran and ran—in his family, Jimmy Johnson racked up 47 interceptions (second in team history to Ronnie Lott's 51) and returned them 615 yards (second to Lott's 643). "I'm a defensive-minded back first," Johnson told *The Sporting News*. "My job is to keep the receiver from catching the ball. I don't start thinking about interceptions until I'm sure the receiver can't get the ball. Some cornerbacks are always thinking about interceptions, and that can get you in trouble when you play the ball instead of the man."

In retrospect Johnson seemed born to play the position. But he took an indirect route to Canton. The 6'2", 187-pounder considered giving up football while at UCLA. Johnson wanted to focus on basketball and track. He was a 13.9-second high hurdler and a 25-foot broad jumper. But he was just good enough as a football player to stick it out with the Bruins, serving as a wingback and defensive back.

Johnson had no designs on a pro football career. Even when several NFL teams sent him pre-draft questionnaires, he filled them out only so he could tell his kids about it someday. It wasn't until he started getting invites to college All-Star Games that he truly believed he'd soon be working on Sundays. His future in football was obvious to everybody else. The San Diego Chargers of the AFL drafted him, as did the 49ers, who took Johnson with the sixth overall pick 1961. Johnson chose San Francisco over San Diego in part because 49ers halfback John Henry Johnson (no relation) was his favorite player.

But before Johnson became entrenched as one of the greatest defensive backs in team history, the 49ers tinkered with him on offense. During the 1962 season, coaches moved him to flanker in order to take advantage of his athleticism. Despite being hampered by injuries for part of the season, Johnson finished second on the team in receiving with 34 catches for 627 yards for an 18.4-yard average and four touchdowns. Against the Detroit Lions, he caught 11 passes for 181 yards, including a 73-yard reception.

The future Hall of Famer didn't move into the secondary for good until 1963, his third full season. At last he'd found his home. Johnson wound up playing 213 games for the 49ers—second in team history to Jerry Rice (238). Johnson's impact, though, was hard to measure in statistics. His Hall of Fame plaque notes that "Johnson's reputation was so great that opposition quarterbacks threw only rarely into his defensive territory." Former 49ers coach Dick Nolan once called him "the best defensive back I have ever seen."

Unlike so many cornerbacks who thrived on cockiness (see Sanders, Deion), Johnson said the key to his own success was humility. It was a lesson learned the hard way when he dismissed Los Angeles Rams receiver "Red" Phillips as slow and easy to cover. In two matchups against the 49ers in 1963, Phillips totaled nine catches for 172 yards. "He made me look real bad. I'll never forget that," Johnson told *The Sporting News*. "Whenever I see a receiver who is small or slow, I remember Phillips and try even harder."

38 The Catch II

There were no wild gyrations from Terrell Owens after the biggest catch of his 49ers career. No dances, no Sharpies, and no popcorn. He was too busy crying tears of joy under an avalanche of giddy teammates. "At the bottom of the pile," Owens said, "I was just saying, 'Thank you Jesus.'"

His touchdown against the Green Bay Packers on January 3, 1999 came to be known as The Catch II because the last-gasp effort shared some elements of Dwight Clark's miracle from a generation earlier. Both catches came at Candlestick Park against a dreaded playoff nemesis.

This time Owens caught a 25-yard pass from Steve Young with three seconds left for an improbable 30–27 victory in an NFC wild-card game. And while The Catch II had a nice ring to it, Owens had another name in mind. "Redemption," he said after the game. "I guess it's 'The Redemption Catch.'"

Indeed, Owens needed atonement in those final seconds because the other 59:57 of his performance had been miserable. Owens had fumbled on the game's third offensive play, setting up a Packers field goal. He also dropped four passes, including a third-quarter debacle when he was wide open in the end zone but lost the ball in the sun. He also had a drop on a third-and-10 late in the game, killing a 49ers drive and sending the Packers on their way to a go-ahead touchdown. "I kept walking by him, saying, 'You're going to make plays. You're going to make plays,'" 49ers wide receiver J. J. Stokes said. "Lo and behold, he made the biggest play of the year."

Owens erased every mistake with one play that crushed the Packers, a team that had beaten the 49ers five consecutive times

On the last play of the 1999 playoff game against the Packers, wide receiver Terrell Owens hauls in a pass between defensive backs Pat Terrell (40) and Darren Sharper. Known as The Catch II, the play not only won the game, but also symbolized the nearing conclusion of the 49ers' dynasty.

and had killed their Super Bowl hopes for three years running. "I just knew I had to make a play for this team," Owens said. "All year I'd been doing it. I didn't want to come into a big game and choke up."

With the victory safely entrenched in the books, the 49ers now might be willing to acknowledge they caught a break. Their winning drive—a nine-play, 76 yarder in 1:53—stayed alive with a little help from the referees. Jerry Rice appeared to fumble with 39 seconds remaining, and Packers linebacker Bernardo Harris recovered the ball. But line judge Jeff Bergman ruled that Rice hadn't fumbled the ball, and field judge Kevin Mack declined to overrule him.

Given a new life, the 49ers capitalized. Facing a third-and-3 from the 25-yard line, Coach Steve Mariucci ordered up an "all go," a five-man pattern in which Rice and backup running back Chuck Levy lined up to the left, and Owens and receiver J.J. Stokes lined up to the right. Terry Kirby ran his pattern out of the backfield.

Young took the snap from center, lost his footing, and looked as if he would trip to the ground. Instead, he somehow launched a pass toward the middle of the end zone. Owens had a Packer to the left of him, a Packer to the right, and two more chasing him from behind—"a red dot in a sea of white and yellow" wrote *San Jose Mercury News* columnist Mark Purdy—but somehow Young's pass found Owens' hands.

"Two things actually helped set up the touchdown play," Young said after the game. "First I stumbled pulling out from center and I believe I may have disappeared for a second, which made the defense unsure. And secondly I looked [outside first, then inside] and saw Terrell was there. Actually, there was a bigger hole down the middle than I expected."

Packers coach Mike Holmgren said: "There were a lot of people right in the middle there. When the ball goes down the middle like that, you don't think the ball's going to be caught ever."

As is often the case with sequels, this one did not live up to the original. Instead of catapulting the 49ers toward a Super Bowl victory, The Catch II merely led to a 20–18 playoff loss the next week in Atlanta. Things would unravel from there. The 49ers would go 4–12 the next season when a concussion ended Young's career, which is why some see The Catch as beginning an era—and The Catch II ending it.

For an idea of just how crazy that latter finish was, consider radioman Joe Starkey's legendary play call:

So Rice goes out to the left. If you want to take one crack, maybe he's the guy you should go for...Young almost falls down...throws to the end zone...Owens! Owens! Owens! Owens! Owens! Owens! Caught it! He caught it! He caught it! He caught it! Twenty-five yard touchdown pass! Terrell Owens! He hasn't held on to anything, including his fingers, all day and he makes the winning touchdown catch. I don't believe it! One of the greatest finishes in 49er history! Somehow, someway, Owens right down the middle. The coverage was there. He had very little room. The ball had to be perfect. It was! He caught it. Niners will win it! Niners will win it!

39 Leo the Lion

In its October 27, 2000 obituary of Leo "the Lion" Nomellini, *The New York Times* also included a tribute to the 49ers' dearly departed muscle-measuring machine.

The machine's cause of death was murder. It seems somebody made the mistake of telling young Leo Nomellini to give it a try in 1955. The device had been designed by Dr. Jay Bender of Southern Illinois University, whose contraption of two-by-fours, pulleys, and wires were designed to measure the size of a muscle above the ankle.

Nomellini put his leg in the machine and was instructed to pull as hard as he could. "The two-by-fours started flying, the wires broke, the scales fell off, and the doctor's eyes popped out," Lou Spadia, a former 49ers general manager, recalled in *The New York Times* account. "I remember having to duck pieces of flying wood. Leo just exploded the machine, blew it apart. Bender had to start it all over again with six-by-sixes instead of two-by-fours and thicker wires."

There was no need for science to intervene. Nomellini spent 14 seasons in the NFL, playing every game for the 49ers from 1950 to 1963, and opponents on both sides of the ball would attest that Nomellini's muscles were large and powerful. He was inducted into the Pro Football Hall of Fame in 1969.

Versatile? Nomellini was a first-time All-Pro on defense and an All-Pro twice on offense. And if that wasn't enough, he wrestled professionally in the off-season as "the Lion." Asked which sport was tougher, the Lion responded: "Oh, wrestling is much tougher. Every night you have to drive a lot of miles to another arena."

In retrospect, it's no wonder Nomellini stayed so busy. He was making up for lost time. Born in Lucca, Italy, in 1924, the Lion was just a cub when his family arrived in Chicago. Even as a kid, he had to work to help his family make ends meet. High school football was not an option. The first game Nomellini ever saw was one he played in as a member of the Cherry Point, North Carolina, Marines team.

After World War II, Nomellini blossomed as a star at the University of Minnesota. He was 6'3" and 264 pounds—huge for that era—and was also fast, aggressive, and dedicated to conditioning. The 49ers made him their first-round draft pick (11th overall) in 1950, their first season in the NFL. He was the last of the 49ers' two-way players, an all-league offensive tackle in 1951 and 1952 and an All-NFL selection in '53, '54, '57, and '59.

He was a terrific wrestler, too, once winning an AWA World Tag Team Championship with partner Wilbur Snyder. Anybody who snickered at that line on his resume risked the same fate as the muscle-testing machine. "There was one thing old Leo was really sensitive about, and that was his wrestling," former 49ers quarterback Bob Waters told *Sports Illustrated*. "He couldn't stand for anyone to make fun of that sport.

"The rest of us, we had sense enough to keep our mouths shut, but there was this rookie offensive lineman in camp one year—I can't even remember his name—who walked right up to Leo and said, 'Hey, Leo, that rasslin' is all a big fake, isn't it?' I guess you can imagine what kind of practice that kid had playing opposite Leo Nomellini that afternoon.

"I don't believe we ever saw him again."

40 Bob St. Clair

Bob St. Clair was a rare specimen who liked his meat even rarer—as in raw. He developed that peculiar culinary preference as early as five years old when his grandmother, a Yaqui Indian from Mexico, would flip him scraps while she was preparing dinner. "She'd be chopping pieces of chicken or meat and she'd throw pieces to me and the dog, and we would fight over it," he told 49ers.com in 2010.

Could there possibly be a more fitting training ground for life as an NFL offensive lineman?

A 49ers tackle from 1953 to 1963, the San Francisco native started in five Pro Bowls and blocked for the likes of Joe Perry and Hugh McElhenny. At 6'9" and 263 pounds, he is the tallest player ever inducted into the Pro Football Hall of Fame. "I guess after a few years they looked and saw the 49ers had the Million Dollar

Retired Jersey Numbers

You won't see a 49ers player wear No. 79. That's because Bob St. Clair is one of 12 49ers who have had their jersey numbers retired by the franchise.

8: Steve Young
12: John Brodie
16: Joe Montana
34: Joe Perry
37: Jimmy Johnson
39: Hugh McElhenny
42: Ronnie Lott
70: Charlie Krueger
73: Leo Nomellini
79: Bob St. Clair
80: Jerry Rice
87: Dwight Clark

Backfield in the Hall of Fame," St. Clair, a 1990 inductee, joked to 49ers.com. "And all of a sudden a light went off, and they realized somebody had to be blocking for them all those years."

Considering all the years he spent mauling opponents, it can be hard to believe that young Bob St. Clair was something of a pipsqueak. Born February 18, 1931, St. Clair spent his childhood in San Francisco, attending Polytechnic High School right across the street from Kezar Stadium. He stayed in town to attend college at the University of San Francisco. But as he later told the audience at his induction into the West Coast Conference Hall of Fame, USF was rolling the dice on the kid who was a mere 5'9", 160 pounds while in high school. St. Clair recalled one of his early coaches telling him to "go home and try to grow a little." "I was very conscientious in those days, so I went home and gave it a hell of an effort," St. Clair quipped. "I grew six inches and put on 60 pounds in one season."

After the 1951 season when the Dons abandoned their football program for a lack of funding, St. Clair transferred to the University of Tulsa where he was an All–Missouri Valley Conference star. The 49ers took him with their third-round draft pick in 1953. With his size, speed, and intelligence, St. Clair thrived as both a run and pass blocker. He excelled on special teams, too and was credited with blocking 10 field goals in 1956.

St. Clair pulled off that trick largely because of his height. But there was also an art to it, which hinged on not-so-subtle mind games. "The first couple of times, I would duck my head and plow through the center and run over the top of him with my cleats," he told 49ers.com. "The next time I looked at the snapper, and instead of him getting turned over backward again and having my cleats running over his chest, he'd go down automatically on all fours. Once they did that, I'd leapfrog over the top of them and I could jump straight up and usually I could block the field goal, extra point, or punt."

Such a freakish skill set, combined with a lust for raw steak, prompted teammate Bruno Banducci to start calling him "the Geek." That was a nod to the Tyrone Powers movie *Nightmare Alley* in which the hero was locked in a cage at the circus. "They used to throw live chickens in there, and that's where it came from," St. Clair told the Pro Football Hall of Fame. "However, I only let my friends call me that!"

This Geek, though, was no sideshow. He was a ferocious blocker with power and strength. St. Clair was the 49ers team captain from 1957 to 1959 and was named first or second-team All-NFL nine times. St. Clair always listed Baltimore's Gino Marchetti, his former USF teammate, as the toughest competitor he ever faced, and the respect was mutual. Marchetti wrote the forward for St. Clair's 2005 biography, *I'll Take It Raw!*

A diplomat off the field, St. Clair dabbled in politics even during his playing days. He served as the mayor of Daly City,

California, from 1961 to 1962. And in honor of his contributions to Bay Area football, the city of San Francisco renamed Kezar's playing surface "Bob St. Clair Field." "When you're still alive and they name a field after you," he said, "it doesn't get any better than that."

41 The Goal-Line Stand

A franchise defined mostly by its glittering offensive plays owes plenty to the defense, too. Just ask the Cincinnati Bengals. In Super Bowl XVI on January 24, 1982, the 49ers stuffed the Bengals four straight times at close range for the most famous goal-line stand in Super Bowl history. To this day the mere mention of "Dan Bunz" can send Bengals fans buckling at the knees.

The Goal-Line Stand—yes, it deserves capital letters, just like The Catch—came in the dying minutes of the third quarter. The 49ers led 20–7, but quarterback Ken Anderson had the Bengals pounding at the door.

What followed were four game-saving tackles: the stuffs of legend.

First-and-goal from the 3: The 49ers had to be brilliant because they had made an error one play prior. On a fourth-and-short from the 5, linebacker Keena Turner didn't hear the play call and remained on the sideline as Pete Johnson banged his way for a first down against a 10-man defense.

The Bengals did the reasonable thing, handing the ball to Johnson again. But this time the 49ers goal-line defense had 11 players on the field—six linemen, four linebackers, and Ronnie

Lott in the secondary—and they bunched in to stop the thrusts of the 249-pounder out of the backfield. Defensive tackle John Choma was left unblocked and had a clean shot at Johnson. With help from Bunz, Choma stopped Johnson for a two-yard gain.

Second-and-goal from the 1: When center Blair Bush snapped the ball, he leapt off the line in an attempt to wipe out inside linebacker Jack "Hacksaw" Reynolds. Instead, Reynolds anticipated that Johnson would be coming to his right and charged in to bury him at the line for no gain.

Bush's wasted leap was just one of two Bengals miscues on the play. Anderson had called a blocking audible at the line of scrimmage, which meant that David Verser, the receiver in motion, was supposed to engage linebacker Craig Puki. But Verser whiffed, allowing Puki to help make the stop.

Third-and-goal from the 1: Since the two runs didn't work, the Bengals took a shot with a high-percentage pass—Anderson swinging the ball quickly to running back Charles Alexander in the right flat. The problem for Cincinnati was that Bunz had spent his week scrutinizing game film and sniffed out the play. "In one crazy moment, I thought, *I should just sprint forward and go for the pick*," he told KPIX television in 2013. "But when I'd done that in practice, [running back] Bill Ring tipped the ball and caught it in the end zone. So I chickened out and went for just a really good tackle."

Bunz later told me that blasting Alexander felt exactly like when he hit a blocking sled just right: He hit and he drove through.

This is how John Madden described the slow-motion replay during the broadcast that day: "This should have been a touchdown. When this is completed here, Alexander turns, and Bunz is right there. Boom!"

Fourth-and-goal from 1 foot: On the game's official play-by-play summary, the credit for the tackle goes "to the entire middle of the line." Defensive lineman Archie Reese was there. (In replays you can see him pumping his arms in giddy celebration.) Reynolds was there. So was Bunz, even if he doesn't remember—his helmet-to-helmet collision was hard enough to loosen the screws in his facemask. "I knew that we stopped them," he said. "But I didn't know what stadium we were in. I couldn't even tell you what town we were in."

The 49ers held on to win 26–21. And a dynasty was born. "We're a team of character," Bill Walsh said. "You could see it in our Goal-Line Stand."

42 The Goose Is Loose

Should Billy Wilson be in the Pro Football Hall of Fame? At least one prominent offensive mind thought so. Bill Walsh, late in his life, spearheaded a campaign for the 1950s-era 49ers star to come join him in Canton. "He was the top pass receiver of his time and one of the finest blockers, just a great all-around end," Walsh told the *San Francisco Chronicle* in 2004. "As I've seen the men inducted into the Hall, including myself, I've thought that Billy certainly should have been enshrined some years ago."

Instead, Wilson might have to settle for being one of football's most underappreciated players. Listed as an end and flanker, the fleet-footed receiver made six Pro Bowls during the 1950s—and was the MVP of the '55 game. Wilson also led the NFL in catches three times and in touchdown catches once. The flanker/end caught 407 passes for 5,902 yards and 49 touchdowns over 10 seasons, all with the 49ers.

The Olympian Wide Receiver

There are players who face metaphorical hurdles in their careers—injuries, family hardships, and other setbacks. And then there is Renaldo Nehemiah, who faced actual hurdles.

The one-time world record holder in the 100-meter high hurdles tried to make a go of it as a 49ers receiver from 1982 to 1984. And while his success was elusive—43 catches for 754 yards and four touchdowns over three seasons—his 49ers career demonstrates the depths of Bill Walsh's risk-taking creativity.

Nehemiah was an experiment, a chemistry set in a helmet and pads. He had made his name as the planet's top hurdler from 1978 to 1981, setting the world 110-meter record three times during that span. In the summer of 1981, he became the first hurdler to break the 13-second barrier (12.93). He was the world's No. 1-ranked hurdler for four consecutive years.

Envisioning how those nimble legs might translate as an open field runner, the 49ers signed Renaldo "Skeets" Nehemiah in April 1982. He had worked out for several teams—the Pittsburgh Steelers were among the other interested suitors—before the 49ers inked him to a four-year deal worth up to $1.5 million. Never mind that Nehemiah had zero college football experience.

The 49ers' young aggressive defensive backs were in no mood to show him much hospitality during training camp. Walsh, in fact, had to intervene to make sure Nehemiah wasn't targeted. "He had to keep us away from him," safety Dwight Hicks said. "We would have destroyed him." Nehemiah had a sense of humor about being a fish-out-of-water as a 23-year-old rookie. "They say this team hits hard, or that team hits hard," he told *Sports Illustrated*. "I'm 177 pounds. To me they all hit hard."

Ultimately, one player hit harder than the rest: Atlanta Falcons defensive back Kenny Johnson walloped him in 1983, knocking Nehemiah unconscious. After that, Walsh was less prone to send his experiment across the middle. Nehemiah actually felt the coach became too protective, saying Walsh's caution "stymied my ability to run wild out there and do what I do best."

Released in 1985, Nehemiah returned to the track and field circuit and went on to earn world rankings four more times before retiring from athletics. Did the experiment work? A resounding no. Nehemiah dropped a lot of passes and rarely provided the big-play threat Walsh had in mind. Apparently, the 49ers were on the wrong track.

Long before the likes of Jerry Rice and Terrell Owens, the lanky kid nicknamed Goose was one of the 49ers' first star pass catchers. At 6'3", 190 pounds and quick, he was one of the toughest players in the league to cover especially on the button hook route.

At the time of his retirement in 1960, Goose was second only to Don Hutson in career pass receptions. In fact his total still ranks among the best in franchise history: The only wideouts with more receiving yards in a San Francisco uniform are Rice (19,247), Owens (8,572), Dwight Clark (6,750), and Gene Washington (6,664). "He was one of the fiercest competitors I ever played with," quarterback Y.A. Tittle said. "He was our No. 1 receiver. Whenever we needed a big catch, I went to him because I knew he would make the play." Tittle discussed Wilson after the receiver's death at age 81 in 2009.

Another teammate further praised Wilson's abilities. "Billy had hands like glue," offensive tackle Bob St. Clair told the Associated Press. "His ability to run after the catch was amazing. He is probably one of the most underrated players in NFL history."

Wilson was born in Sayre, Oklahoma, on February 3, 1927. Three years later his family headed west to escape the Dust Bowl. He grew up to become a fixture in the Bay Area, attending high school at Campbell High School, and after a stint in the U.S. Navy during World War II, returning to attend San Jose State.

The 1950 NFL draft, the 49ers' first after four seasons in the All-America Football Conference, foreshadowed a career in which Wilson would be criminally overlooked. He was the 283rd player selected and the seventh—seventh!—offensive end taken by the 49ers that year. The six taken ahead of him combined for 19 career NFL catches, 388 fewer than Wilson had all by himself.

Wilson promptly became the team's top target for the next decade, a receiving threat to complement a run-oriented team featuring the Million Dollar Backfield of Tittle, Hugh McElhenny,

John Henry Johnson, and Joe Perry. Never a speedster, Wilson simply understood the art of getting open. The Goose could get loose.

Colts receiver Raymond Berry, who *is* in the Hall of Fame, authored a story for *Sports Illustrated* in 1959, hoping to explain to fans the nuances of the position. He wrote admiringly of Wilson, calling him "the best end in the league at getting away from a linebacker playing head-up on him. He's real good at a head-and-step fake, and the maneuvers shown here on evading a linebacker are Wilson's…This fake right followed by a complete spin to the left is one of Billy Wilson's favorite ways to avoid linebackers. The spin helps because the linebacker can't grab you as easily when you spin."

43 Super Bowl XXIV

Joe Montana was in his first season in Kansas City in 1993 when offensive coordinator Paul Hackett, his former 49ers quarterbacks coach, decided to show his Chiefs players the blueprint for how to attack the Denver Broncos. Hackett popped in game film of Montana carving up the Denver defense in Super Bowl XXIV. But the opening scenes failed to impress. Montana misfired badly on two of his first three throws, skipping passes intended for Brent Jones and Roger Craig. In the Chiefs meeting room, backup quarterback Dave Krieg leaned forward and whispered skeptically into Montana's ear. "You were the MVP of this game?" he asked.

"Just hang on, buddy," Montana said. "It gets better."

As the film kept rolling, so did the 49ers. Montana wound up with five touchdown passes—three of them to Jerry Rice—as San

Francisco demolished Denver 55–10 at New Orleans' Superdome on January 28, 1990. The onslaught set Super Bowl records for most points scored by one team and for largest margin of victory. "This was so lopsided I'm surprised the stadium didn't tip over," wrote Mitch Albom of the *Detroit Free Press*.

Montana, playing in his fourth and final Super Bowl, became the first player to win three game MVP awards. He did so by connecting on 22-of-29 passes for 297 yards, hitting on 13 consecutive attempts at one point. Montana had 189 passing yards in the first half, which is 81 more than Denver quarterback John Elway had in the entire game.

Rice, who made seven catches for 148 yards and three touchdowns, still takes pride in setting the tone for the barrage. As Montana regrouped quickly on that opening drive, he spotted his No. 1 receiver cruising across the field. Rice caught the ball and ran headlong into safety Steve Atwater, who outweighed the receiver by 17 pounds. Atwater ended up on the ground; Rice ended up with a 20-yard touchdown catch just 4:54 into the game. "I remember catching the ball over the middle and I knew I was going to take a shot from Atwater and [Dennis] Smith," Rice said in 2013. "I was happy to be able to bounce off that and get into the end zone because I knew how important it was to score early. That's something we prided ourselves on."

The 49ers pounded Denver on the ground, too. Craig and fullback Tom Rathman combined for three touchdowns, 107 yards rushing, and 77 yards receiving—or 17 more yards of total offense than the entire Broncos team. "It was fairly easy," Rathman said after the game. "We hadn't even used all of the plays in the game plan by halftime. Every time we came off the field, we kept saying, 'They can't stop us. They can't stop us.'"

Apparently nobody could. The 49ers treated Denver just as roughly as they had their previous playoff opponents. San Francisco had ousted the Minnesota Vikings 41–13 and the Los Angeles Rams 30–3 en route to a postseason run in which they outscored their opponents 126–26.

And that was on the heels of a 14–2 regular season.

It was the most emphatic way for rookie coach George Seifert to sprint from the shadow of Bill Walsh, who had retired after the team's Super Bowl XXIII victory a year earlier. Seifert became only the second coach to win a Super Bowl title in his first season.

He had already won three Super Bowl rings as an assistant/coordinator under Walsh, so he knew the 49ers' demanding culture would not allow him to savor the victory for long. "A doctor doesn't do one great operation and then slack off," Seifert said within minutes of winning the crown.

At least he could breathe easy for a few non-stressful hours against Denver. Montana threw three first-half touchdowns, and Rathman scored on a one-yard run as the 49ers took a 27–3 lead at intermission. By the time Craig's one-yard touchdown run in the fourth quarter pushed it to 55–10, the broadcasters were struggling to fill the air. "Not much left to analyze," Pat Summerall mused to CBS partner John Madden.

The 49ers remain the only team to score at least eight touchdowns in a Super Bowl, and they did it with at least two touchdowns in each quarter. Montana became the third player in league history to win the Super Bowl MVP and the AP regular season MVP award in the same season, joining Bart Starr (1966) and Terry Bradshaw (1978). "The 49ers had an incredible performance," Broncos cornerback Wymon Henderson said after the game. "They were as good as I expected them to be."

44 Charlie Krueger

After the 1971 NFC title game against the 49ers, *Sports Illustrated* pointed out that the Dallas Cowboys ran 90 percent of their plays away from left defensive tackle Charlie Krueger. "No one is able to gain running at Charlie Krueger," Cowboys coach Tom Landry said, "and we were not about to experiment."

Not all opposing ball carriers had the good fortune to avoid the 49ers' defensive wrecking ball. Krueger spent 16 seasons in San Francisco, clogging up running lanes with such dependable dominance that he was too often taken for granted. For younger fans the best comparison is Justin Smith. Krueger was the rugged, no-nonsense lineman who did the dirty work of occupying double teams so that other players could swoop in and get the glory.

Among defensive tackles only Bryant Young ever played more games for the 49ers. Krueger was selected to Pro Bowls in 1960 and 1964. Other talented tackles of that era—Big Daddy Lipscomb, Merlin Olsen, Alex Karras, Bob Lilly, and Alan Page—overshadowed Krueger because of their camera-ready personalities. Krueger? Heck, he barely even talked to other players on gamedays not even when stars like Johnny Unitas and Bart Starr tried to strike up a conversation. "Starr and Unitas were as wily as they were good, and from my standpoint, they could be the best," Krueger said in that 1973 *SI* profile. "It's an old trick trying to distract a rusher. They'll say, 'Good move,' or 'How did you get here?' Sometimes they'll flat-out hit you with a compliment. Then you go away thinking what good folks they are and lose your concentration."

Krueger had grown up learning football on the dusty, rutted fields of his hometown of Caldwell, Texas. It showed. He was 6'4", 256 pounds of grit, which made him an ideal pupil for his college coach: the legendary Bear Bryant. Krueger played for Bear at Texas A&M, and the lessons he learned there lasted throughout his career, including how to endure. He later said that players who thrived under Bryant were like him—rugged workers from small towns who grew up toiling in farms and factories.

The 49ers' first-round draft pick (ninth overall) in 1958, he kept banging bodies until 1973. But his lunch-pail approach came at a price. Doctors kept telling him he could play through pain— pain that only intensified once his NFL days were over. Only later did he discover that the root of his anguish was unnecessary and that 49ers doctors had mismanaged his knee injury.

In 1988 a California Superior Court judge in San Francisco ordered the 49ers to pay Krueger $66,000 in special damages and $2.3 million in general damages. "It's like I worked 20 years in a slaughterhouse," Krueger told *The Boston Globe*. "The environment in pro football is such that you play with injuries. If I had an injury, I always went to the doctors…If they said I could play, I played. I played because it was my job. I relied on them to tell me not to play. I relied on the wrong people."

45 Visit Kezar Stadium

When you visit the hallowed ground of Kezar Stadium, enjoy looking back. Just don't look up. "Those birds were lethal," Hall of Fame quarterback Dan Fouts, a San Francisco native, told *The New York Times*.

Seagull droppings were just one of the many hazards at the 49ers' home from 1946 to 1970. There were also unruly fans, cramped seats, elusive parking spaces, and player accommodations more befitting a high school team. But boy, wasn't it great? "It had a real homey feeling to it," former receiver Gene Washington told *The New York Times*, "nothing like the big huge stadiums with the big huge parking lots that came after."

Kezar Stadium opened in 1925, was demolished after sustaining earthquake damage in 1989, and rebuilt as a smaller venue in 1990. The stadium itself is still known as Kezar, but the playing surface is now Bob St. Clair Field in honor of the legendary 49ers lineman who played more games at the stadium than anyone else. The field hosts the annual "Turkey Bowl," the city championship for high school football, and recreation league games.

You can take a walk there alongside the ghosts of 49ers past at 755 Stanyan Street, San Francisco. It stands at the southeast corner of Golden Gate Park in the Haight-Ashbury neighborhood. Located amid lush green lawns in a tree-speckled landscape, Kezar is quite lovely now. You can stroll along with no worry about flying beer cans as John Brodie once did.

In one of the great Kezar Stadium tales told in Brodie's autobiography *Open Field*, the quarterback once approached Baltimore star Johnny Unitas to congratulate him after a Colts victory. As the two passers approached the tunnel that led back toward the locker rooms, Brodie warned Unitas to strap on his helmet.

Unitas shrugged it off, so Brodie tried again. "Once you get near that group, it's a little active," he said.

"It can't be that bad," Unitas replied.

As they neared the end of their walk, a 15-foot railing was teeming with disgruntled 49ers fans. One of them fired a beer bottle at Brodie, but it clipped Johnny U instead. "They *mean* it!" Unitas said.

"You're damn right they mean it," Brodie said, but Unitas didn't hear him. He had already sprinted toward the locker room.

Mary Kezar effectively launched the stadium in 1922 when her estate gifted $100,000 to the San Francisco Park Commission.

Mary wanted the city to build something that would honor her mother and uncles who had been so influential in San Francisco. The local government poured another $200,000 into the project, and the stadium was christened on May 2, 1925.

Kezar's first event was a two-mile race featuring legendary Finnish runners Ville Ritola and Paavo Nurmi. But the stadium wasn't truly off and running until 1946 when the 49ers football team was founded and adopted Kezar as its home stadium. The first game was September 8, 1946 when 35,000 spectators watched the New York Yankees triumph 21–7.

The 49ers would go on to play 25 seasons at Kezar before moving into Candlestick Park in 1971. The team's first home wasn't exactly luxurious. At Kezar only 19,000 of the 60,000 seats were between the goal lines. The seats were cramped, offering only about 16 inches of space for a patron's posterior. The puny locker rooms wouldn't be big enough today to fit a single star's entourage. "Kezar Stadium was maybe not the most comfortable stadium from a spectator point of view, but it was a good place to play," former star Gordy Soltau said. "The playing surface was usually a wreck by the time we played on it. All of the high schools would play there. The field got all torn up between the hash marks, on the dirt."

Still, it was hallowed ground. The alley-oop took flight at Kezar with Y.A. Tittle launching cloud-scraping passes to R.C. Owens. Joe "the Jet" Perry blazed around the green grass here. Vikings defensive end Jim Marshall ran a long way, too—albeit in the wrong direction, taking a fumble recovery 66 yards into his own end zone. Kezar is also the source of film lore: Clint Eastwood's *Dirty Harry*, released in 1971, features several scenes at the venerable stadium, including one in its infamous late night fog.

The last NFL game played at Kezar was a 17–10 defeat at the hands of Dallas Cowboys in the 1970 NFC Championship Game. Recognizing that this was farewell to their beloved stadium, fans promptly began tearing the place apart. The frenzy for souvenirs resulted in 22 arrests and 13 people sent for medical attention.

The memories proved tougher to tear down. Future 49ers coach George Seifert, who played high school football across the street at the now-defunct Polytechnic High, worked at Kezar as an usher. There he collected chin straps from his heroes like Owens, Billy Wilson, and Matt Hazeltine. Mike Nolan, another future 49ers coach, also worked as a ball boy. The kid had connections— his father, Dick Nolan, coached the 49ers from 1968 to 1975.

Fouts spent his childhood there, too before his distinguished career with the San Diego Chargers. His father, Bob Fouts, was a 49ers longtime broadcaster, and Dan served as a ball boy, dodging seagull droppings the way that Brodie dodged beer bottles. "You always wore a hat at Kezar," Fouts told *The Times*. "If you didn't have a hat, you put a program or a newspaper on your head."

Today you can find safe haven across the street from the 49ers' former home at Kezar Pub, a cozy sports bar at 770 Stanyan Street. For a proper salute, cram a few people into the tightest possible space and raise a glass to the great old days.

46 Frankie Albert

Frankie Albert, the first marcher in the 49ers' dazzling parade of quarterbacks, was a mere 5'10", 165 pounds. To defenders, however, he was a big pain in the neck. Albert was the starting quarterback for the 49ers' debut game, September 8, 1946 when he threw a 40-yard touchdown pass to Len Eshmont for the first score in franchise history. Albert would go on to play seven seasons with the team and was one of the big stars of the All-America Football

Conference that lasted from 1946 to 1949. Albert shared MVP honors with Browns great Otto Graham in 1948.

Along the way, the left-handed passer bamboozled opposing defenses with his ball-handling skills. Albert is credited with popularizing the bootleg play, in which he faked a handoff and then took off running with the ball on his hip. His running skills were terrific. At Stanford he had been the first T-formation quarterback in college football, but what made Albert harder to defend was his knack for deception.

Comparing Albert to fellow running quarterback Fran Tarkenton, former Rams linebacker Don Paul told the *Los Angeles Times*, "At least with Tarkenton, those guys knew Francis had the ball. With Frankie Albert, you weren't always sure. Then he would stand there and laugh at you."

Clark Shaughnessy, Albert's coach at Stanford, put it more directly in a 1943 interview with *Esquire*. "He was neither strong nor fast," Shaughnessy said. "His talents were primarily those of a faker."

Albert twice led the AAFC in touchdown passes and completion percentage. Had quarterback rating been invented yet, Albert would have led the league in that, too, with a 102.9 mark in 1948. He was a Pro Bowl selection in 1950, the 49ers' first season in the NFL.

When former teammates talk about Albert, however, they have no need for statistics. They recall him as a swashbuckling leader, the player who took charge both on the field and in the locker room.

49ers wide receiver Gordy Soltau shared the story about how Albert once got the better of his boss. In the early days of the NFL, players didn't get paid for exhibition games. (They also paid their own way to training camp. And if they got cut, they paid their own way home.)

So during a 49ers preseason road trip to Syracuse, New York, Albert caught owner Tony Morabito at the pregame meal. "He

After initially serving as the first in a long line of star quarterbacks for the 49ers, Frankie Albert coaches San Francisco during a 27–20 win against the Packers in 1957. (AP Images)

said, 'Tony, the team has decided that we're going to bet you $25 to a man that we score the first time we have the ball,'" Soltau recalled. "'And if we do, you have to give us the $25.'"

"So we're all looking at Frankie thinking, 'Where are we going to find $25 to give to the owner?'"

Morabito agreed, and when the game started, the 49ers received the kickoff. Soltau said that on the first play from scrimmage, "We ran a sweep to the right, and I think we knocked down every Pittsburgh Steeler three or four times. We had an 80-yard run for a touchdown. The next thing you know, Albert was standing in front of the press box and yelling, 'Okay, Tony, get the money out!'"

Morabito indeed paid up, but the mischievous Albert eventually grew into an authority figure himself after his own playing career. He was the 49ers' coach from 1956 to 1958, compiling a 19–16–1 mark.

47 The Smiths from Mizzou

Because both Justin Smith and Aldon Smith came to the NFL via the University of Missouri, the 49ers owe the good people of Columbia, Missouri, a thank you note. Opposing quarterbacks, meanwhile, might want to send a different type of letter, one that says "cease and desist."

The two Smiths began terrorizing passers from the instant the 49ers selected Aldon with the seventh overall pick in 2011. Justin, who had been with the 49ers since 2008, hardly needed the help—he had long established himself as one-man wrecking ball. But with his fellow Mizzou Tiger aboard, quarterbacks didn't stand a chance.

In fact most of them didn't stand at all. With Justin playing Mr. Inside and Aldon playing Mr. Outside, passers usually became Mr. Backside.

During 2011, their first season paired together, the duo combined for 21.5 sacks as the 49ers advanced to the NFC title game. In their second season together, they combined for 22.5 sacks as the 49ers advanced to the Super Bowl. "Anytime you work with a great player, it makes it that much easier," Justin Smith said. "We play well together. We work well together."

Though they will be long linked together, let's start with a few differences. Justin Smith, originally the fourth overall pick in 2001, spent his early career being underappreciated for a mostly lousy Cincinnati Bengals outfit. The Bengals made the playoffs just once during his seven seasons there. During that time Smith was viewed as a solid player with a strong work ethic but nothing more. He never made a Pro Bowl—let alone merited consideration for a Defensive Player of the Year.

But his career began to take flight with a helicopter ride: During a free-agent visit to San Francisco in 2008, then-coach Mike Nolan arranged to take the 6'4", 285 pounder for a whirlybird tour of Bay Area attractions like Alcatraz and the Golden Gate Bridge. Along the ride Smith spotted something that really impressed him: a 49ers coaching staff that would know how to use him properly. Justin Smith promptly canceled scheduled visits to Minnesota and Jacksonville and signed his name to a six-year contract with $20 million in guarantees right there on the spot. "Why go on another visit if you're just going to come back here?" he explained.

It didn't take long for San Francisco to embrace what Justin Smith was all about. The kid who grew up on a cattle ranch in Holts Summit, Missouri, had no desire for glitz, glamour, or gabbing. Nicknamed "Cowboy" for his blue-collar, Midwestern approach to football, Smith was happy to do the dirty work. He would occupy multiple blockers so that someone else could swoop in and make the tackle or the sack. He cemented his tough guy legend by returning from a partially torn triceps late in the 2012 season and helping the team advance to Super Bowl XLVII. "Justin Smith is a great player," New England Patriots quarterback Tom Brady said. "He's got a great motor. He's big. He's powerful. He takes up two guys and allows those other guys some one-on-one matchups. He's in there every play and he plays to the end of every play."

With that Smith happy to pave the way, Aldon Smith was more than ready to do the rest. He had already broken Justin's single-season sack record while at Missouri and he arrived in the NFL with a freakish blend of skills. His wingspan measured in at almost 84 inches, which prompted Justin to joke: "He doesn't have to bend over to tie his shoes. That's for sure."

Aldon Smith was supposed to be a project, someone who needed a few years to develop. He was a defensive end at Missouri converting into a 3-4 outside linebacker in the NFL. To make matters more difficult, he was drafted at a time when a prolonged labor dispute wiped out rookie camps and minicamps. Luckily for him another Smith was there to help him. "He has made my transition a lot easier," Aldon Smith said a few days before Super Bowl XLVII against the Baltimore Ravens. "We came from the same college and are from the same area. I know it's a hard transition to the league, but he has made mine easy and he's been a great help since I've been here."

Aldon Smith promptly became one of the NFL's most feared pass rushers, setting a rookie franchise record with 14 sacks and finishing second in voting for the AP Defensive Rookie of the Year. In his second season, he was on pace to challenge Michael Strahan's single-season sack record of 22.5 (set in 2001) before injuries slowed him over the final month and he settled for 19.5.

Using those long arms to fend off blocks and his speed to get around burly linemen, the 6'4", 258-pounder had a total of 33.5 sacks over his first two seasons. That was the most in history by a player over his first two years, surpassing Hall of Famer Reggie White (31). "When [opposing coaches] sit down, the first thing they say is, 'How do we slow 99 down?'" Justin Smith said. "That brings a lot of attention over there. Teams change their scheme up when they play us. That's pretty noticeable."

48 Jeff Garcia

There was a time when the NFL fan club for future four-time Pro Bowl quarterback Jeff Garcia consisted of one guy. Luckily for him, it was the right guy.

Bill Walsh knew all about the scrappy, hyper-footed, red-haired wonder, having tried in vain to slow the kid down when Garcia played for San Jose State. Walsh was the head coach at Stanford in 1993 when Garcia nearly led San Jose State to an upset.

Stanford had to score twice in the fourth quarter to win 31–28 and overcome Garcia's 380 passing yards and three touchdowns (two running, one passing). When it was over, Walsh chased down Garcia—not SJSU coach John Ralston. "Bill came straight over to Jeff and shook his hand," Ralston said. "I thought it was kind of strange he didn't even look at me. But he was paying tribute to a great performance."

Walsh said: "Jeff almost won that game by himself. We won, but it took an interception at the end of the game for us to win it. He just played superbly. He reminded me so much of Joe Montana."

The rest of the NFL, however, viewed him more like Joe Shmoe. Listed at 6'1", 195 pounds and without the prototypical arm strength, he went undrafted in 1994. No NFL team even signed him as an undrafted free agent.

Grbac: "Embarrassment to Humankind"

San Francisco mayor Willie Brown was on a business trip to Paris in November of 1996 when a reporter jokingly asked if the French might invest in a new 49ers stadium. "Well, I'm trying to get the French to invest in a new quarterback," the mayor answered. "This guy, [Elvis] Grbac, is an embarrassment to humankind."

Ouch. But Brown was just getting warmed up. "After that interception and that bonehead intellectual breakdown in the last game against Dallas, and we lost 20–17," he said, "he can't play in any stadium that I'm going to assist to build."

Brown was a skilled politician, but going negative on a beloved institution like the 49ers did not play well with the masses. Fans besieged city hall and talk radio with complaints. Steve Young, Grbac's teammate, said of Brown: "He needs to stay in politics and not in sports."

What Brown did not know about Grbac's two interceptions in relief of an injured Young was that the backup quarterback had other things on his mind. Grbac and his wife were more concerned with the condition of their nine-month-old son, Jack, who was battling spina bifida and had recently undergone surgery to alleviate pressure on his spinal column.

Four days after his comments, Brown called Grbac to say he was sorry. "He apologized to me and my family," the quarterback said. "He understands he made stupid remarks."

In his next game, Grbac completed 26-of-31 passes for 268 yards, with one touchdown passing and one rushing, in a 38–20 victory against the Baltimore Ravens.

One 49ers fan held up a banner that said: "Keep Elvis, Trade Willie."

But Walsh remained an enthusiastic booster. Four months after that first meeting at Stanford, the Hall of Fame coach got another glimpse of him at the East-West Shrine Game. Garcia took over in the fourth quarter and threw three touchdown passes, including the game-winning, two-point conversion with 47 seconds left, to earn MVP honors. So Walsh, who knew a little something about quarterbacks, responded to Garcia's draft snub by writing letters to about a dozen of his NFL colleagues urging them to extend a camp invite. Improbably, nobody listened to Bill Walsh.

Instead Garcia went to Canada where he rocketed to fame as the man who replaced another undersized dynamo, Doug Flutie. Garcia capped his five-season career with the Calgary Stampeders by leading them to the 1998 Grey Cup championship, the CFL's version of the Super Bowl.

By 1999, however, Walsh was back as the 49ers general manager. He called Garcia and told him that the team needed a backup for Steve Young. The Niners' other candidates heading into the '99 season were Steve Stenstrom and Jim Druckenmiller. "The impression I get is, there's really not a set No. 2 guy," Garcia said, shortly upon signing. "Jim is returning, and I'm sure he will get an opportunity. But I don't think anything is set in concrete. The door is relatively open. I don't know how wide, but it's open. I can come in and compete for that No. 2 job, and that's all I can ask. I could have stayed in Canada and been comfortable in my lifestyle there. I like Calgary and I feel the city and I responded to each other well. But I've worked every year in football to get this kind of opportunity, and it's finally here."

A month into that '99 season, Young's career ended when Arizona cornerback Aeneas Williams blasted him for a devastating concussion. That awful injury gave Garcia his chance. As a lifelong 49ers fan who grew up in Gilroy, California, he well understood the daunting task of following in the footsteps of Montana and Young. And the pressure got to him during the first few weeks.

One of his early starts was a 27–6 loss to the Pittsburgh Steelers in which he threw for a mere 39 yards. After that one, even Garcia began to question his ability to play in the NFL. Eventually, though, it only strengthened his resolve. Four weeks after the Pittsburgh debacle, he threw for 437 yards and three touchdowns.

Even though the 49ers lost that game 44–30 to Cincinnati, Garcia felt like he belonged.

"When Steve Young first came into the 49ers, I don't think he was thrown into the fire as quickly as I was," Garcia said. "People are always talking about how difficult the 49ers' system is, how difficult it is to learn, and how you need time in it. But all of a sudden, I'm thrown in there after three games, and it's like, 'Well, what's wrong with him? Why can't he do this?' It was just a learning stage I had to go through."

Garcia certainly figured things out. He threw for 4,278 yards in 2000, a single-season franchise record that still stands. (Young held the previous mark with 4,170 in 1998). Garcia was a Pro Bowl selection in 2001 and 2002 as well.

But in 2004 general manager Terry Donahue exiled Garcia as part of a salary cap purge. "You lose stars; you don't worry about it," Donahue said. "You create new stars." The 49ers promptly went 25–55 over the next five seasons.

49 The Intimidator

Dave Wilcox came from a different era of 49ers football, an era he often describes as the time "before Joe and money." The linebacker made $12,500 in his first year, 1964, and his teams never got a whiff of that Montana-esque glory.

But as his Hall of Fame enshrinement reminded a generation of younger fans, 49ers history did not begin in 1981. He happened to be in the same Canton class as Montana and Ronnie Lott, but the highlight film of Wilcox's bone-rattling tackles that aired during the ceremony earned wild cheers from his new fans in the crowd.

Wilcox played for the 49ers from 1964 to 1974 and was a seven-time Pro Bowl selection. Nicknamed "the Intimidator," he stopped ball carriers in their tracks. His former coach, Dick Nolan, recalled how Miami's Larry Csonka tried to bowl Wilcox over. "Csonka stumbled to the sideline out on his feet," Nolan said.

Niners coaches of that era would issue each player an effectiveness score at the end of the season. The average linebacker got 750; one year, Wilcox got 1,306. "About every third guy, he'd just throw them into the ground," said cornerback Jimmy Johnson, who roamed the left side with Wilcox. "It wasn't like he'd get a big hit every now and then. The big hits were a thing of regularity."

While his other teammates on the defense would be bent over gasping for air, Wilcox occasionally stood ramrod straight, palms on his hips, and crossed one leg over the other. Was it a stance of intimidation? Yoga? Not quite. Former *San Jose Mercury News* writer Sam Farmer, discovered the answer years later while visiting Wilcox's tiny hometown in Oregon. "I'm from a family of eight kids, and we didn't have indoor plumbing until my sophomore year of high school" Wilcox explained. "It can get pretty painful waiting in line for the outhouse. That's how I learned to stand that way."

That wasn't the only lingering effect of Wilcox's upbringing in Vale, Oregon. The star linebacker never abandoned his small-town roots. During the interview, Farmer also discovered that Wilcox continued to drive around his muddy Jeep pickup truck while the rest of his NFL teammates tooled around in Cadillacs and Lincolns. On a drive from Oregon to San Francisco, his sheepdog got overheated riding in the bed of the truck. Dave's solution? His human passenger rode in back while the sheepdog moved up to the air-conditioned cab.

Selected in the third round (29th overall) of the 1964 NFL draft, Wilcox finished his career with 14 interceptions and 12 fumble recoveries. When he went into the Hall of Fame with the rest of the class of 2000, it marked the first time since 1965 that three players from one team entered the Hall of Fame in the same year. Chicago Bears guard Dan Fortmann and quarterbacks Sid Luckman and Paddy Driscoll entered the Hall together in '65.

There was, however, at least one player from Wilcox's era who could hit just as hard. While playing against the Baltimore Colts as a rookie, the linebacker intercepted a Johnny Unitas pass around the 49ers 5-yard line and had visions of cruising 95 yards with the return. "I got about three steps, and Unitas just nailed me," Wilcox said with a laugh, "knocked me about 12 yards behind our bench."

50 Jed York

Jed York took his first major step toward resuscitating the 49ers on a day he was so sick with the flu he could hardly speak. The breaking point came December 26, 2010 when coach Mike Singletary had just blundered through another atrocious loss. "Our objective is to win the Super Bowl year in and year out," York fumed in a somber St. Louis locker room. "We're going to make sure we get this right." Singletary was fired by nightfall. And suffice to say, both the kid and the franchise were feeling better soon.

Angered by the team's 6–10 finish that season, York cranked up the dial on his overhaul project. He hired a mastermind head coach away from Stanford, spent wisely, demanded excellence, and banished losing from the premises. In short, he followed in the footsteps of his uncle, Eddie DeBartolo Jr., who created the blueprint during his own 49ers ownership from 1977 to 2000. Even players from that dynasty's teams weren't afraid to compare York's ownership to the old one. "I see a lot of Eddie D in him," former running back Roger Craig said.

How did he do it? York was in his late 20s when he was anointed the 49ers CEO in 2008. He took the reins from his parents, John York and Denise DeBartolo York (Eddie's sister), who stayed on as the 49ers co-chairmen. But as it turned out, that was no silver spoon in Jed's mouth. It was a shovel.

By 2009 York had launched an ambitious renovation project, adding 9,000 square feet of space for players and office employees. The team also expanded the players lounge, built an expansive outdoor weightlifting facility, and knocked down walls to give meeting rooms more square footage. Even the Niners cafeteria was upgraded complete with first-rate chefs. "What Jed shows—and what his uncle showed—is a passion for excellence," said former Pro Bowl offensive lineman Harris Barton, who played for the 49ers from 1987 to 1996. "Players come out here and realize, 'You know what? I'm going to play hurt and I'm going to play hard because I know I'm going to be taken care of here much better than any other place. The owner cares.'"

Like his uncle, who struck gold in hiring Bill Walsh, York found the key to the 49ers' turnaround a few miles away at Stanford University. He was able to outmaneuver several other suitors to land Jim Harbaugh's services. "That was absolutely the move that put the 49ers in a different category," said tight end Brent Jones, who made four Pro Bowls for the 49ers from 1987 to 1997.

York set the tone for the future while also embracing the past. Born and raised in Youngstown, Ohio, his roots in the organization ran deep. He ordered a redesign of the 49ers uniforms to incorporate echoes of the classic look from the dynasty years. But he also took modern inspiration from Silicon Valley innovation. York hired Gideon Yu, the former CFO of both Facebook and YouTube, in 2012 and turned him loose on the 49ers' long-stalled stadium project. Yu promptly led an effort to secure an $850 million stadium construction loan, the largest ever in professional sports, and a $200 million financing package from the NFL. "I've worked for a lot of guys in the past that have audacious, big visions," Yu, now the team's president and co-owner, told *San Jose Mercury News* columnist Tim Kawakami. "Jed ranks up there with those guys that were set to change the world."

York wasn't afraid to spend big, but he mostly invested in players already on the premises. Turning up their nose at top-tier free agents, the 49ers identified players worth keeping for the long haul and locked them up with multiyear extensions. Among the players sticking around to form the nucleus are linebacker NaVorro Bowman (signed through 2018), left tackle Joe Staley (2017), linebacker Patrick Willis (2016), tight end Vernon Davis (2015), and running back Frank Gore (2014). To Barton the work of the owners carries echoes of the DeBartolo days. "Players stay with the 49ers because they know they're in a first-class organization. That all starts at the top," Barton said. "If the top is not leading the charge, then you're going to get mediocrity. The quality of ownership means a ton in pro football. It means a ton."

51 John Henry Johnson

John Henry Johnson was fast enough to be elusive, but he was also powerful. Rather than run around defenders, he could knock them on their backsides. "He was one of the few runners who would look for somebody to hit," former offensive lineman Bob St. Clair, his fellow Hall of Famer, told the *San Francisco Chronicle*.

Johnson played just three seasons for the 49ers (1954 to 1956), but he left a lasting impact. As the hardest coin in the Million Dollar Backfield, the 6"2", 210-pound fullback was one of the league's toughest players during a rough-and-tumble era of NFL history. Teaming with quarterback Y.A. Tittle and running backs Hugh McElhenny and Joe Perry, the hard-nosed runner relished contact with defenders whether he had the ball or was just paving the way for a teammate. "Football was like a combat zone," Johnson said. "I was always told that you carry the impact to the opponent. If you wait for it, the impact will be on you."

At the time of Johnson's death at age 81 on June 3, 2011, *The Washington Post* listed one of Johnson's unofficial career stats: The runner "broke the jaws of at least two players, including one teammate in an intrasquad scrimmage. 'What do you want me to do?' an unapologetic Johnson asked. 'Kiss the guy or tackle him?'"

Born on November 24, 1929, Johnson began establishing his legend on the Bay Area athletic fields by the time he was at Pittsburgh High School. He led the Pirates to league titles in football and baseball in his senior season and also won titles in the high jump, hurdles, shot put, and discus. Johnson went on to play football at nearby St. Mary's College, transferring to Arizona State after the Gaels dropped the sport.

The Pittsburgh Steelers took him in the second round of the 1953 draft, but Johnson signed instead with the Canadian Football League where he played with former 49ers quarterback Frankie Albert. Johnson returned to the United States to play for the 49ers starting with the 1954 season and was an immediate sensation, finishing second in the league in rushing with 681 yards. He spent the next two seasons as an integral part of the Million Dollar Backfield.

As for his running style? "He was a wild man, legs, arms, and elbows, and knees going every which way when he was running," Perry said in 2006. "And John was tenacious at all times. If you wanted to [label] him, you would say he was one of the meanest SOBs to go on the football field."

In an exhibition game against Chicago in 1955, Johnson smashed into Cardinals star Charley Trippi so hard that Trippi sustained multiple face fractures. Plays like that earned him the rep as a dirty player in some people's eyes. The *Chronicle* ventured that his style might have prolonged his wait for the Pro Football Hall of Fame: Perry, McElhenny, and Tittle received induction shortly after their retirements in the 1960s; Johnson had to wait until 1987. "I was confident someday I would be here, but then on the other hand, I thought I might be dead since it had taken so long," Johnson said during his acceptance speech in Canton, Ohio. "Today I feel that I finally have that respect and I want to tell you—it makes me feel damn good."

Johnson's best years as a runner came elsewhere. He was part of the 1957 Detroit Lions that defeated the 49ers in the playoffs en route to the NFL championship. While with Pittsburgh in 1962, he became the first Steeler to rush for 1,000 yards. Johnson was a four-time Pro Bowler. At the time of his retirement in 1966, Johnson's 6,803 career rushing yards trailed only Jim Brown, Jim Taylor, and Perry on the all-time list.

52 Len Rohde

For 15 years offensive lineman Len Rohde was the 49ers' iron man. Neither rain nor snow nor Deacon Jones could get him off the field. He played through minor pain and through an agonizing knee injury on his way to 208 consecutive games—a franchise record for regulars that still stands.

Rohde may still be standing out there at left tackle if coach Dick Nolan didn't pull him aside one day during training camp of 1975. Rohde was trying to gut his way through a painful back injury and thought he was playing pretty well. That's when Nolan

49ers Consecutive Games Streaks

49ers Most Consecutive Games Played

Rank	Name	Position	Years	Games
1.	Len Rohde	OT	1960 to 1974	208
2.	Brian Jennings	TE/LS	2000 to 2012	208*
3.	Jerry Rice	WR	1985 to 2000	189
4.	Leo Nomellini	OT/DT	1950 to 1963	174

Still Active

Most Consecutive Games by 49ers Offensive Linemen

Rank	Name	Position	Years	Games
1.	Len Rohde	OT	1960 to 1974	208
2.	Keith Fahnhorst	OT	1974 to 1987	193
3.	Randy Cross	OG/C	1976 to 1988	185
4.	Jesse Sapolu	OG/C	1983 to 1997	182
5.	Steve Wallace	OT	1986 to 1996	166
6.	Bruce Bosley	OG/C	1956 to 1968	163
7.	John Ayers	OG	1977 to 1986	148
8.	Guy McIntyre	OG	1984 to 1993	145
9.	Fred Quillan	C	1978 to 1987	143
10.	Harris Barton	OT	1987 to 1996	138

made a proposal. "You've always been a team player and you could really help us out," Nolan told him.

"How's that?" Rohde said.

"You could retire," Nolan said.

The conversation may not have been quite that blunt—Rohde can't remember the exact phrasing—but the message was beyond clear. Rohde took the suggestion and bowed out gracefully after one of the most distinguished careers of any 49ers lineman.

Retirement might have been the only way to get him off the field. Those 208 games from 1960 to 1974 have been matched only by long snapper Brian Jennings (who tied the record in the final regular-season game of 2012). The only non-special-teamer to come close is Jerry Rice, who played in 189 straight. "[The record's] one of those things that just creeps up on you, and you don't realize," Rohde told 49ers.com.

The guy who couldn't stop playing had a hard time getting started. Rohde grew up on a dairy farm outside of Palatine, Illinois, where chores were his concern, not sports. It took relentless nudging by his English teacher, Charles Feutz, just for the farm-strong kid to give football a try.

Rohde was a natural and went on to a standout career as a two-way lineman at Utah State. The 49ers took him in the fifth round of the 1960 NFL draft, but it would be a few seasons before Rohde cracked the lineup he would never leave. Coach Red Hickey experimented with Rohde, who was listed at 6'4", 247 pounds, by trying him as a defensive end. But Rohde played so poorly during the 1962 exhibition season that he was unceremoniously punted to the offense. "At that point I figured I'd wait out the season and if the 49ers didn't want me, I'd go play defense for somebody somewhere," Rohde said.

Instead, he caught a break. Right tackle Bob St. Clair sustained a season-ending Achilles tendon injury during a game against the Los Angeles Rams on November 18, 1962, which opened the door for Rohde. In desperation the coaches thrust him into action as St. Clair's replacement, and the kid played well enough in emergency duty—against a young Deacon Jones, no less—that he got another chance. And another. And another.

By 1970 Rohde had blossomed into a Pro Bowl left tackle. And under the guidance of offensive line coach Ernie Zwahlen, the 49ers allowed only eight sacks in 383 pass attempts that year to establish an NFL record for fewest sacks allowed. Rohde played 15 seasons with the 49ers and helped the team win its first three NFC Western Division titles.

When he retired, after Nolan's not-so-subtle suggestion, Rohde's streak was still intact. "You don't set out to do something like that," he told 49ers.com. "You take things one at a time and all of a sudden you realize you've got a string going. And then you hope you can hang on."

53 Gordy Soltau

Gordy Soltau spent his entire nine-year NFL career with the 49ers. But to understand what he was about, you only need one game. On October 28, 1951, the 49ers defeated the Los Angeles Rams 44–17 at Kezar Stadium. Soltau caught three touchdown passes, drilled a 23-yard field goal, and made five point-after attempts.

One man. Twenty-six points. "The Rams never forgave me for that," Soltau said with a wry smile, more than 50 years later, at age 88.

The game underscored his dazzling all-around skills and demonstrated how Soltau was often a one-man scoreboard. He led the 49ers in points during eight of his nine seasons with the team and by the time he retired in 1958 he owned the franchise scoring record with 644 points. Players in the modern era of specialization might find it hard to believe just how busy Soltau was on gamedays. For a stretch he was a three-way player as a kicker, receiver, and defensive end.

In that regard NFL stadiums felt a lot like his neighborhood back in Duluth, Minnesota. Born on January 25, 1925, Soltau spent his childhood playing every sport imaginable: baseball, basketball, hockey, skiing—and football, of course. "That was long before there was Pop Warner and youth league teams," Soltau said. "We played what was called 'sandlot football.' The neighborhood kids would gather up, choose up sides, and start playing.

Sometimes you had a football and sometimes you didn't, but you still played. I guess somebody had to kick the ball. I said I'd do it. And I just kept doing it."

Before the 49ers made use of Soltau's remarkable versatility, the U.S. military did. Soltau enlisted in the Navy in June of 1943 and served in an elite branch, the Office of Strategic Services (OSS), a precursor to the CIA. As part of the original class of "Frogmen," only a last-minute decision spared him from a potential suicide mission in conjunction with D-Day. The plan called for Soltau's eight-man unit to sabotage German submarine pens on the coast of Nazi-occupied France. As Soltau detailed in *The Game of My Life* with writer Dennis Georgatos, the plan was scrapped because no one could figure out an escape. "It was a very risky program to start with, and there was no plan to get us out," Soltau said in the book. "We would be on our own in France once we completed the mission, and hopefully, D-Day operations would take care of the Germans. We were a little dubious of that. Fortunately for us it never happened."

When the war ended, Soltau was relieved to be back on the playing fields. He attended the University of Minnesota where his teammates included future 49er star Leo Nomellini and future Hall of Fame coach Bud Grant. The Green Bay Packers drafted him in the third round (29th overall pick) in 1950 but immediately shipped him to Cleveland, an odd deal for the Browns, considering they already had a kicker, Lou Groza, and talented ends named Dante Lavelli and Mac Speedie. "So Paul Brown called me in and said, 'Look, I think you can make this team, but I'm damned if I know how much playing you'll do,'" Soltau said in *San Francisco 49ers*. "'We can deal you to San Francisco, and I have an idea you'll do a lot of playing there.' So I went out to San Francisco, talked with Buck Shaw, and made the move. It's something I've never been sorry for."

The 49ers acquired him by sending the Browns their 1951 fourth-round pick (a choice used on end Bob Oristaglio). Soltau, meanwhile, found his coveted playing time in San Francisco. Soltau became known as one of best trades the 49ers ever made. He caught 249 passes for 3,487 yards and 25 touchdowns. In the kicking game, Soltau converted 70-of-139 field goals and added 284 extra points for 494 points. He was a three-time All-Pro (1951 to 1953) and led the NFL in points in both 1952 and 1953.

After a half century of retrospect, Soltau says he could have had more. "Buck Shaw was our coach and Buck didn't believe in field goals," he said. "He believed in touchdowns. No matter where we were on fourth down—even if we were in field goal range—he was going for a first down.

"He just didn't believe in field goals. You had to make touchdowns." Soltau was more than happy to provide those, too.

54 Ray Wersching

Ray Wersching never looked at the goal posts before a kick. But not long after Wersching arrived on the roster, the fortunes of the 49ers started looking up.

Wersching would go on to establish himself as one of the most important kickers in 49ers history, a scoring machine for a team on the brink of a dynasty. His career highlights included a record-tying four field goals in the 49ers' first Super Bowl victory, a 26–21 triumph against the Cincinnati Bengals. "Put it this way," coach Bill Walsh said. "Had we had an average kicker or a good kicker, we might not have won. But we had a great kicker. We had Ray."

Wersching provided eight more points in a 38–16 victory against the Miami Dolphins in Super Bowl XIX. By the time he retired, he held the team's regular-season records for points, field goals, and extra points. In short Wersching provided exactly what the team was looking for when they called him in 1977. Hard as it is to believe, considering the years that followed, but at that time the franchise was desperate for points.

The low point that season came on October 9 when the Atlanta Falcons beat the 49ers 7–0 at Candlestick Park. The home shutout was even worse than it looked. "We were a walking refund request," offensive lineman Randy Cross said. "We set football back 50 years." Said wide receiver Gene Washington: "It had to be one of the most boring games I've ever been in."

Determined to get at least some points on the board, the 49ers decided to give a tryout to a veteran kicker released by the San Diego Chargers a few weeks earlier. The 49ers summoned Wersching, who was then 27 and working as an accountant, to their Redwood City practice facility. (Wersching called in sick to his auditing job.)

Wersching already had taken an unusual route to the NFL. In *Game of My Life: San Francisco 49ers*, Wersching recounted how his father, Wendell Wersching, had been part of the German army and spent much of World War II in a POW camp in Great Britain. Released in 1946, Wendell was reunited with his wife, Theresa, and they moved to a refugee camp in Austria. That's where Wersching was born in 1950. At the age of two, he and his family were permitted to come to the United States.

A 1972 University of California at Berkeley graduate, he clearly felt comfortable upon his return to the Bay Area. Under the watchful eyes of coach Ken Meyer, Wersching put on a show during that fateful 1977 tryout. He made every field goal the 49ers asked him to try and blasted every kickoff five yards deep in the end zone. "It

David Akers Blasts One

David Akers owns a place in NFL history. He booted a record-tying 63-yard field goal on September 9, 2012.

And no one was more surprised than the man himself. Akers watched the ball sail through the air with a sense of resignation. For one thing he didn't think he'd struck it hard enough. For another he could see it was destined to hit the crossbar. "I'm like, 'All right that's going to be great, you have a chance from 63 and you came up an inch short,'" Akers remembered, his voice thick with sarcasm. "And then it was the opposite—it went in. It was my own little miracle."

Akers tied the NFL field goal record just before halftime of a season-opening 30–22 victory against the Green Bay Packers at Lambeau Field. The three other kickers to hit 63-yarders were New Orleans Saint Tom Dempsey in 1970, Denver Bronco Jason Elam in 1998, and Oakland Raider Sebastian Janikowski in 2011.

Akers, 37 and in his 14th season at the time of his kick, was an unlikely candidate to join the exclusive club. Once upon a time, he found it difficult just to stay employed in the NFL. From 1997 to 1998, he worked as a substitute teacher at Westport Middle School in Louisiana between stints with the Carolina Panthers and Atlanta Falcons. Released again in 1999—this time by the Washington Redskins—he found a part-time job as a waiter at Longhorn Steakhouse in Lawrenceville, Georgia. Finally, after hitting the waiver wire three times, Akers was signed by the Philadelphia Eagles in 1999 and began putting his best foot (the left one) forward. By the time he signed with the 49ers in 2011, Akers had five Pro Bowls on his resume and had been named to the NFL's All-Decade team for the 2000s.

It all culminated on that surprisingly balmy 72-degree day in Green Bay with the wind blowing out of the northwest at 11 miles per hour. That's when the one-time steakhouse waiter got something that was both rare and well done. The ball bonked off the crossbar and sailed into the record books. "When you hit the goal post at any part, it usually makes that horrific noise and then it usually bounces back," Akers said, shaking his head and smiling. "This time it got there. It was a sweet bounce. It was definitely a once-in-a-lifetime type of a deal."

was the strangest thing," Wersching told me years later, still sporting his trademark mustache. "I didn't miss anything. At the end of the tryout, they walked up and said, 'Where have you been?'"

In the 49ers' next game, against the New York Giants, Wersching opened the scoring with a 50-yard field goal. After that the points just kept coming. Behind Wersching and the soon-to-be arriving cavalry of Bill Walsh, Joe Montana, Jerry Rice and Co., the 49ers would go an NFL-record 420 games without being shut out again. "Bill was going to score, somewhere somehow," Wersching said. "There's no way a Bill Walsh team is going to go scoreless."

Wersching led the NFL in points in 1984 and in extra points in 1985 and 1987. He nailed 11 career game-winners. Even one of his misses was memorable. In the "Snowball Game" on November 11, 1985 in Denver, Wersching geared up for a chip shot 19-yard field goal on the 49ers' final possession of the first half.

But as the snap was being delivered from center, a fan at Mile High Stadium launched a snowball that struck just to the right of holder Matt Cavanaugh. Distracted, Cavanaugh bobbled the snap, pulled the plug on the field-goal attempt, and instead tried a desperate pass over the middle of the field. Cavanaugh's pass, like the snowball, thudded to the turf. The 49ers lost that game 17–16, so the failed field goal was extra painful.

Wersching had some rotten luck after his playing days, too, when he became entangled in an embezzlement case that focused on his business partner in the Ray Wersching Insurance Agency. Charges against the kicker were dismissed, but Wersching had to work hard to repair his reputation. He told the *San Francisco Chronicle* in 2009 that he was embarrassed to be "snookered" into a business deal gone wrong. "I'm always beating myself up," he said. "'How could you be so stupid?'" He rebounded by making use of his business administration degree from Cal and working at a bookkeeping job in San Francisco's financial district.

Wersching still approaches life the same way he did on the football field. "I put my head down and go," he said.

55 Gene Washington

Before Jerry Rice arrived and ended all discussion, you could ignite a lively debate by asking fans to name the best receiver in 49ers history. Billy Wilson and Dwight Clark were popular nominations as was an elegant gamebreaker from the 1970s named Gene Washington. No less an authority than John Madden once compared Washington to Hall of Fame receiver Lance Alworth. "He has the same fluidity, the ability to go long or catch the short ones," Madden said in 1970. "That's pretty good, comparing a guy to Lance Alworth."

Washington made four Pro Bowls during his nine seasons in San Francisco (1969 to 1977) and was a first-team All-Pro in '69, '70, and '72. Intelligent and Stanford-educated, Washington spent much of the early '70s breaking loose from defensive backs and hauling in long passes from John Brodie. To this day no 49ers receiver has topped Washington's career average of 18 yards per catch.

Not John Taylor (16.1). Not even Jerry Rice (15).

"We saw eye to eye a whole bunch when it came to football," Brodie wrote of Washington in *Open Field*. "His experience as a quarterback gave him a valuable perspective as a receiver. He knew how the field looked from where I was standing, and that helped him explain to me how the field looked to him, and what worked best for him."

The first black quarterback to play for Stanford, Washington had been a trailblazer in high school, too: He was the first black

160

student body president in the history of Long Beach Poly High School, an institution founded in 1915. Washington played quarterback as a sophomore at Stanford but switched to receiver for his junior season. He promptly earned All-America honors. The 49ers drafted Washington in the first round (16th overall) in 1969, and he made an immediate impact with six catches for 92 yards in his NFL debut against the Atlanta Falcons. Washington went on to catch 51 passes that season, earning Pro Bowl honors as a rookie.

That was just a warm-up act. By 1970 Washington led the NFL in receiving yards with 1,100. By 1972 he led the league with 12 touchdown catches. "He was a very smart receiver and he had great speed," the late Dick Nolan said. Only five times in 49ers history has a receiver averaged more than 20 yards per catch in a season—and Washington represents three of those. He did it in 1970, 1972, and 1974 while Freddie Solomon did it in 1983 and Rice in 1988.

Washington spent a final season with the Detroit Lions in 1979 before retiring to a colorful post-playing career. The receiver dabbled in Hollywood, even while still with the 49ers, and had a role in *The Black Six*, a low-budget 1974 film about a group of black bikers who cruise the West fighting crime. Washington played a character named Bubba Daniels. "You just laugh your head off," Washington later told Michael Martinez of the *San Jose Mercury News*. "We made the movie in two weeks. It's forgettable, and if you look at it, you crack up and say, 'Did we really do that?' But we got two weeks in California and got to learn how to ride motorcycles."

Washington also spent five years as a game analyst for NBC before a stint with the Los Angeles ABC affiliate as a sports reporter and weekend sports anchor. His post-playing days are best remembered for his tenure as the NFL's director of football development. One of his duties was fining players for on-field infractions. "The first year or so was gut-wrenching," Washington said. "After that

I learned that as long as you're consistent and interpret the rules properly, people may not like it, but they'll accept it."

56 Freddie Solomon

Freddie Solomon rose to fame as a receiver, but he'll be better remembered as a giver. "I have never met a man who cared so much about the human race," former owner Eddie DeBartolo said. "There will never be another Freddie."

Solomon, who died on February 13, 2012 after a nine-month fight with cancer, had amazing hands—and an All-Pro heart. In an early 1980s locker room full of strong-willed leaders like Ronnie Lott, Roger Craig, and Joe Montana, players say it was Solomon who set the tone. "There was no one who gave more on and off the field than Freddie," said Montana on the day Solomon passed. "The kindness he demonstrated was inspirational to all that knew him."

Originally a second-round pick by the Dolphins in 1975, Solomon spent three uneventful seasons in Miami. Suffice it to say, things picked up in San Francisco. Acquired in a trade with the Dolphins in 1978, the 49ers found a long list of uses for the 5'11", 185-pound burner from the University of Tampa.

How versatile was Solomon? With quarterbacks Steve DeBerg and Scott Bull both injured in the 1978 season finale, the receiver wound up behind center. In that game the 49ers first turned to defensive back Bruce Threadgill, who had played quarterback in Canada, but he was trying to gut his way through a broken hand, and it showed. So in desperation, coach Fred O'Connor turned to Solomon, who had been an option quarterback at Tampa.

Solomon completed 5-of-9 passes for 85 yards and ran for 42 more. He even contributed an 11-yard touchdown run.

Luckily for Solomon—and for 49ers history—a new quarterback arrived the next season by the name of Joe Montana. The two had a terrific chemistry, on field and off the field. Then again Solomon had a rapport with anybody who came his way. "Freddie took me under his wing," said Lott, a rookie in 1981. "He told me right from the start, 'Hey, I'm going to help you be the best you can be.' He was always special in terms of his character because he was always there for you. He was there to provide wisdom and to provide guidance. The thing that people forget about Freddie Solomon is the impact he had on players like Jerry Rice and Dwight Clark. Freddie Solomon's fingerprints were all over those players. His fingerprints were on me."

Solomon was more than just a cheerleader. He helped launch the 49ers dynasty as a major contributor for the franchise's first Super Bowl win. "Freddie was essential to the success," Dan Audick, the starting left tackle on that team, wrote in an e-mail. "Words cannot say enough about the key role Freddie played."

Audick pointed to Solomon's overlooked performance in the landmark 1981 NFC Championship victory against the Dallas Cowboys. Solomon caught an eight-yard touchdown pass in the game and later provided three first downs (two catches and a reverse) on the 89-yard drive that led to The Catch—the signature play in 49ers history.

On that play Montana first looked to Solomon (who slipped) before connecting with Clark in the back of the end zone for the winning touchdown. At a public appearance in November 2012, Montana joked, "The Catch would have never happened if I'd hit Freddie Solomon, who was wide open on the play before…I threw it three feet over his head."

In 1983 Solomon averaged 21.4 yards per catch, a team record that still stands. In that season's playoff opener, Solomon caught the winning touchdown pass with two minutes remaining in a 24–23 divisional triumph against the Detroit Lions.

Two seasons later, though, the 49ers began to ease Solomon out of the picture. They had high hopes for their first-round draft pick, some kid named Jerry Rice, and Solomon, 32, was staring at the end of his career. But Solomon did whatever he could to help Rice grow into the role of the 49ers' new go-to receiver, even though Rice's rookie season of 1985 proved to be Solomon's last. "Freddie would help him out with the mental side of the game, just believing in him," Craig said. "That was kind of an unusual situation because Freddie was 'the guy' at that time, and he knew that Jerry was there to replace him. But he still helped him as much as he could.

"It takes a special guy to do that. That was just him. He had the heart of a lion."

57 Visit the 49ers Hall of Fame

One of the most exhilarating days you'll ever spend at the 49ers' new stadium might come when there's no game at all. That's because the team's shrine to its glorious past will be open year round.

A 49ers Hall of Fame museum will be a highlight of Levi's Stadium, which is set to open in Santa Clara, California, in 2014. The hallowed halls—all 20,000 square feet of them—will display artifacts that range from the old (a Kezar Stadium seat) to the new (Frank Gore's record-setting cleats) to the just plain cool (Bill Walsh's coffee cup). Fans will also get an up close look at five Super Bowl trophies.

Think of it as the Taj Mahal of ball. The Louvre for leatherheads.

Jerry Walker, the team archivist, served as the 49ers' version of Indiana Jones, scouring the landscape for priceless artifacts. As the 49ers public relations ace during their glory years—he was there from 1981 to 1993—Walker was well-positioned to land the coolest stuff this side of Canton, Ohio. Walker's anecdotes alone are worthy of enshrinement. According to him, he stored Dwight Clark's ball from The Catch in his closet for nearly 10 years. (The hope is to have that ball, too, on display at the Hall of Fame.)

Among Walker's favorite items scheduled for display is a game jersey from wide receiver Gordy Soltau, who played for the 49ers from 1950 to 1958. As always with Walker, there's a funny story behind how he acquired that historic jersey.

Back in the Kezar days, the lockers were not at the stadium itself but up the tunnel inside Kezar Pavilion, along with the Kezar offices, a basketball court, and other amenities. During the week these facilities hosted city rec leagues, which is how in the late 1950s Robert Ervin unwittingly shared a locker with a three-time Pro Bowler.

Ervin was playing with his Standard Oil officemates on a Monday night when he discovered that someone had left behind a football uniform. Ervin slipped the jersey into his bag...then tossed it into his closet. It sat there for several decades before Robert's son, Michael, researched the No. 82 jersey and recognized the historical significance of what they had on their hands: a complete Soltau jersey remarkably preserved.

When Walker and the 49ers sent out a public plea asking fans to donate items to the new museum, Michael Ervin didn't hesitate. "When it's part of history—whether it's football, baseball, hockey, or anything—it has to be out there for the public to see," Ervin said. "You can't put a monetary value on it. The value is in having people see it, and there's no better place for it than at the museum."

49ers in the Pro Football Hall of Fame

Position	Player	Years on 49ers	Year Inducted
OG	Larry Allen	2006 to 2007	2013
DE	Fred Dean	1981 to 1985	2008
DE	Richard Dent	1994	2011
DE	Chris Doleman	1996 to 1998	2012
WR	Bob Hayes	1975	2009
LB	Rickey Jackson	1994 to 1995	2010
CB	Jimmy Johnson	1961 to 1976	1994
FB	John Henry Johnson	1954 to 1956	1987
DB	Ronnie Lott	1981 to 1990	2000
RB	Hugh McElhenny	1952 to 1960	1970
QB	Joe Montana	1979 to 1992	2000
DT	Leo Nomellini	1950 to 1963	1969
FB	Joe Perry	1946 to 1960, '63	1969
WR	Jerry Rice	1985 to 2000	2010
CB	Deion Sanders	1994	2011
RB	O.J. Simpson	1978 to 1979	1985
OT	Bob St. Clair	1953 to 1963	1990
QB	Y.A. Tittle	1951 to 1960	1971
Coach	Bill Walsh	1979 to 1988	1993
LB	Dave Wilcox	1964 to 1974	2000
DB	Rod Woodson	1997	2009
QB	Steve Young	1987 to 1999	2005

Listed in alphabetical order

A hard bargain? Hardly. Ervin never considered of asking for a penny. Instead, he only required that vintage Soltau jersey be displayed with a message from his family: "Robert, Michael and Devin Ervin—Three Generations of Football Fans."

Among the other items scheduled to be on display is the ball quarterback Alex Smith threw to tight end Vernon Davis for the game-winning touchdown pass in the January 14, 2012 playoff game against the New Orleans Saints (aka "The Grab"). You'll also be able to see Gore's shoes, gloves, and game ball from the day Gore

Leo Nomellini, a two-way player inducted into the Pro Football Hall of Fame in 1969, takes a rare break during a 1962 game at Kezar Stadium.

surpassed Joe Perry as the 49ers' all-time leading rusher. There'll be a ball from the Har-Bowl—the Thanksgiving game between Jim Harbaugh's 49ers and John Harbaugh's Baltimore Ravens, the first meeting between head-coaching brothers (and a prelude to Super Bowl XLVII).

To make sure everything looks just right, the team has hired Cambridge Seven Associates, Inc. and Cortina Productions to head the project. Those firms helped design a similarly sized Hall of Fame for the New England Patriots, which opened in 2006 and promptly began drawing 120,000 visitors a year. That museum included a brief film on the team's history and highlights. "I'm not a Patriots fan by any means," Walker said. "But what they did gave me goose bumps." So it should surprise no one that there are plans in the works for a 12-minute 49ers film at the Santa Clara site.

For those with more vintage tastes, it's likely there will also be some of the founding documents that launched the 49ers as a franchise in the All-America Football Conference starting in 1946. Donated by Bill Walsh's former personal assistant, Nicole Gisele, there will also be a hand-drawn play or two straight from Walsh's pen.

58 Harris Barton

After the 49ers selected offensive tackle Harris Barton in the first round of the 1987 draft, the kid called his parents with the happy news. Well, happy to him, anyway. Paul and Joan Barton had raised Harris in a kosher Orthodox Jewish home in Atlanta and had little understanding of NFL life. They envisioned their boy in a more suitable profession—one with a tie and briefcase. So when

Harris rang, his dad tried one last time to get his son to work at IBM. "And I said, 'Dad, the 49ers are going to pay me $150,000 a year, and IBM is going to pay me $30,000,'" Barton told me.

"And he said, 'You know what? You should go work for the 49ers.'"

Barton would eventually put his bachelor's degree in finance from the University of North Carolina to use. But first he would make his mark by protecting the 49ers' valuable investments of Joe Montana and Steve Young.

Barton spent 10 seasons as a right tackle for the 49ers, making the All-Pro team twice and winning three Super Bowl rings. When Montana famously spotted John Candy in the stands before leading the winning drive in Super Bowl XXIII, he was pointing him out to Barton. Along the way, his parents never quite learned to draw up Xs and Os, but they understood the important stuff. "They were Harris' biggest fans,'" Young said.

Barton started playing football in the fifth grade at the Hebrew Academy of Atlanta. Because of his size—he would play at 6'4", 286 for the 49ers—more than 100 colleges recruited him. He chose the campus at Chapel Hill where he would become the first Jewish player in 30 years to be selected as an AP All-American.

When he reached the NFL, Barton knew he would need more than size and strength. He said he viewed the head-to-head wrangling of monstrous physical specimens as a "chess match."

"He was obsessed with watching film," Brent Jones, a tight end who played alongside Barton, told Bloomberg News. "Harris was always a key player on our offensive line."

Barton's career essentially ended in August of 1988 at the age of 34 after a Miami Dolphins defensive player fell on him, breaking his left fibula and creating an uncertain future. At long last he got one of those white-collar jobs his parents had in mind, but there was no happy ending. Barton and Ronnie Lott co-founded HRJ Capital LLC. That investment firm collapsed in 2009 amid complaints by investors who say they were misled about the extent of its woes.

Barton has acknowledged that mistakes were made, saying the fall of HRJ hurt worse than anything he ever endured on the football field. "At the end of the day, my name was on the door," he told Bloomberg, "So I'll take the hit."

In the meantime his other venture with Lott has proved more rewarding. The two former 49ers teammates created Champions Charities, which raises money to fund brain tumor research at the University of California at San Francisco where Barton says his late parents got first-rate care after their own diagnoses.

In the summer of 2012, a star-studded fund-raiser brought together some of the most famous quarterbacks in Northern California history—Montana, Young, New England Patriot Tom Brady (from San Mateo, California), Green Bay Packer Aaron Rodgers (Chico, California), and former Oakland Raider Jim Plunkett (Stanford). Represented on one stage were 1,101 touchdown passes, 11 Super Bowl championships, and eight Super Bowl MVP awards. "Harris' ability to get us all together is incredible no matter what the circumstances," Young told me. "The fact it happens to be for a good cause, too, makes it that much better."

Organizing it, though, wasn't that difficult. Barton said the cast came together quickly in part because he enlisted recruiting help from his Hall of Fame friend. "When Ronnie Lott calls people, they tend to show up," Barton said with a laugh. Even so, it wouldn't have taken much cajoling. "These are guys who understand how important charity is," Barton said, referring to his quarterbacks. "These are guys who are willing to give up a morning for a great cause."

The guys generated more than $500,000 that day, a figure that would have made Paul Barton proud.

59 One Heck of a Guy

Guy McIntyre's favorite Super Bowl XXIII memory is captured on film. There's a photograph of the 49ers breaking their huddle before the final drive.

That's the moment he loves most—not Jerry Rice's 27-yard catch on that drive, not the 13-yard toss to Roger Craig, not even John Taylor's 10-yard touchdown catch to win it. Stepping out of that huddle marked the first step after a lifetime of preparation. "The intensity of the moment—this is it," McIntyre said. "You're down. You need to score. You need to give the greatest quarterback in the game the opportunity to do what he does. We're either going to do it or we're not going to do it. And I don't want to be the one who gives up a sack or gets called for a hold. Bill Walsh always said: 'Don't be that guy.' I didn't want to be that guy."

McIntyre was never "that guy." More like "the Man." The longtime left guard racked up five Pro Bowl appearances over the course of an NFL career that spanned from 1984 to 1996. In many ways he was the prototype offensive guard for Walsh's West Coast Offense. Though considered small (6'3", 275 pounds), he was quick, smart, and packed a powerful pound-for-pound punch that allowed him to take on much bigger defenders.

Because of his size, McIntyre was the kind of player other teams overlooked when he came out of Georgia in the 1984 draft. "There was some speculation about how long I would even last in the NFL because I had flat feet and bunions," McIntyre recalled with a laugh. But midway through the third round, Walsh gave offensive line coach Bobb McKittrick license to make his pick. McKittrick

A Large Fullback

Guy McIntyre opened the door for the Fridge.

A year before the thunderous William "the Refrigerator" Perry created a sensation as a 325-pound blocking fullback for the Chicago Bears, the 49ers used McIntyre in a similar role to aggravate the Bears.

McIntyre, a 275-pound rookie guard, remembered that Bill Walsh summoned him into his office before the 1984 NFC Championship Game against the Bears. That's when McIntyre was told to line up in the Angus short-yardage formation, serving as the blocking back instead of Roger Craig. "I'm a rookie third-round draft pick. Who was I to refuse to go in and block?" McIntyre said with a laugh. "I just do what I'm told."

The blocking worked. And the Bears coaches were so ticked off that they took the idea. The next year they used the Fridge, who became a Madison Avenue darling, especially after scoring on a 1-yard run in the Super Bowl. "And if anybody scores a touchdown in the Super Bowl and you win, you have some instant fame," McIntyre said, "especially if you weight 300-and-something."

wanted McIntyre so badly that the 49ers traded up to get him. "I was on the phone with the Detroit Lions at the time when my agent said, 'Hang up. The 49ers just took you,'" McIntyre said. The 49ers took him at No. 73. The Lions used No. 74 on running back Ernest Anderson, who never played in the NFL.

McIntyre would go on to spend 13 years in the league and lists Green Bay Packers/Philadelphia Eagles defensive lineman Reggie White, New York Giants linebacker Lawrence Taylor, Dallas Cowboys defensive lineman Leon Lett, and Eagles defensive lineman Jerome Brown among the most difficult defensive players he ever faced. But his toughest foe? "Michael Carter, my own teammate," McIntyre said, still shaking his head.

Carter, a defensive tackle, was taken in the fifth round in '84—the same draft class as McIntyre. The 6'2", 285-pounder was a three-time Pro Bowl selection. "There were times when Coach Walsh, especially my rookie year, would call from the other side of the field, 'I want to see McIntyre vs. Carter' during one-on-one passing drills," McIntyre said. "That puts you on center stage right there. And after you face Michael Carter—golly, man. He was nasty, nasty—unnecessarily nasty at times. He would pinch you, grab meat, and twist. And he had the grip because he was a shot putter. You had to fight through all of that."

McIntyre kept fighting, working his way up from a special teamer on the '84 champs to an offensive line mainstay on the 49ers teams that won back-to-back titles in '88 and '89. He earned the first of his five consecutive Pro Bowls in '89. "You know, after earning the first one, I can remember asking Ronnie Lott, 'How do I act?'" McIntyre said. "It's not that I didn't want it. My goal when I came here was to earn the respect of my peers, to work hard, and play whatever role I could to be a champion."

60 Lon Simmons

Listen up, all you aspiring broadcasters. No, seriously, *listen.*

Track down any of the plentiful Lon Simmons audio clips available on the Internet and study how it's possible to be funny without being a comedian, entertaining but not overwhelming, and informative but never dull.

Simmons spent 26 seasons as the voice of the 49ers, enthralling audiences with vivid descriptions and dry wit. With his baritone voice and natural gravitas, the broadcaster was a voice-of-God type like John Facenda—but with better punch lines.

Consider his deadpan farewell in 2002 when he retired from broadcasting after one last go-round with the San Francisco Giants. "To the people who have voiced the opinion that they enjoyed my work, I can only say, 'Thank you.' It's always pleasant to hear that they grew up enjoying listening to me," Simmons said. "To those that hated me—and believe me, there are a lot of them—I want to apologize for sticking around so long."

Simmons' original stint in the 49ers radio booth lasted from 1957 to 1980. For a broadcaster with an otherwise impeccable sense of timing, this seemed cruel: Simmons signed off from the 49ers just as things were about to get good. Even without championships, however, Simmons had his share of memorable calls. He was behind the microphone when Minnesota Vikings defensive end Jim Marshall picked up a 49ers fumble and returned it the wrong way for a safety. It was one of the wackiest plays in NFL history, but Simmons still managed to keep his audience abreast of exactly what was happening on October 25, 1964.

[George] Mira, straight back to pass…looking, now stops, throws…completes it to [Billy] Kilmer up at the 30-yard line, Kilmer driving for the first down, loses the football… it is picked up by Jim Marshall who is running the wrong way! Marshall is running the wrong way! And he's running it into the end zone the wrong way, thinks he has scored a touchdown! He has scored a safety! His teammates were running along the far side of the field, trying to tell him go back!

Born July 19, 1923, Simmons grew up in Burbank, California, dreaming of reaching the major leagues as a pitcher. The Philadelphia Phillies signed him shortly after he finished a stint in the U.S. Coast Guard, but the hard-throwing right-hander sustained a back injury in his first minor league game and was never the same. His first full-time sports broadcasting job was at KMJ in Fresno, California, before KSFO hired him as its sports director in July 1957. Simmons' big break arrived along with baseball's Giants in '58.

Despite his sustained popularity, Simmons shunned accolades. He was practically embarrassed by being honored by the Baseball Hall of Fame in 2004. "I had felt and still feel I don't rate up there with people like [Vin] Scully, [Ernie] Harwell, and Russ Hodges," Simmons said. "People can tell you things and make statements about how you do your job, and that's gratifying. But I'd finish broadcasts and be driving home and be really upset with myself because of something I didn't say or some mistake I made...I never thought of myself as being a polished announcer."

In his rookie year in the 49ers booth, Simmons served as the color man for play-by-play announcer Bob Fouts, the father of future Hall of Fame quarterback Dan Fouts. In 1958 Simmons took over as the play-by-play man and stayed in that role until 1980. Simmons returned to the 49ers broadcast booth for the 1987 and 1988 seasons and finally got to describe the action in a Super Bowl. His call of the 49ers' game-winning drive in Super Bowl XXIII against the Cincinnati Bengals—featuring Joe Montana to John Taylor—remains a staple on NFL Films. "Everybody felt they knew Lon," said the late broadcaster Bill King, another Bay Area broadcasting icon. "You always felt—here's another guy just like you. That's the way he always came across on the air."

61 The Crushing 1957 Playoff Loss

No matter how crowded San Francisco's trophy case gets, there will always be an empty spot for a title that never was. The 1957 49ers looked like such a shoo-in by halftime of its division playoff game that the printer got the green light to start cranking out tickets for the NFL Championship Game against the Cleveland Browns. The Pro Football Hall of Fame has one of those ill-fated stubs on display on its website, showing off a beauty for Section V, Row 13, Seat 8 for a mere $7.50.

Instead, 49ers fans were shortchanged. San Francisco blew a huge halftime lead as the Detroit Lions roared back to win 31–27 at Kezar Stadium on December 22, 1957. It remains among the most painful losses in franchise history.

The 49ers led 24–7 at halftime behind the exploits of players like Y.A. Tittle, R.C. Owens, and Hugh McElhenny. Legend has it that all of the 49ers' hooting and hollering at halftime echoed through the thin walls of the Kezar Stadium locker room. As the story goes, the Detroit players overheard the party and channeled their anger into a second-half comeback.

Wide receiver Gordy Soltau doesn't buy it. "That's a lot of hooey that the Lions made up," he responded with his disgust still tangible more than 50 years after the final whistle. "What they heard is this: Right before we went back out on the field after half-time, Buck Shaw got us all together, and we had a big cheer. It had nothing to do with the Lions."

Tittle agreed. "Guys might have been excited that we were playing well," the quarterback said. "But we were only up by 17 at halftime. That's not very much, and no one felt like we had won the game."

On the other hand, the pain from the end of the game was all too real. With their first ever trip to the championship game within their grasp, the 49ers pushed the lead to 27–7 with a field goal to open the second half. That's when the wheels started to wobble.

Lions fullback Tom "the Bomb" Tracy, who hadn't carried the ball in the previous four games, started gashing the defense up the middle. Tracy scored two touchdowns in the third quarter, including a 58-yarder.

Tittle, meanwhile, went cold as the Lions got hot. He threw three interceptions after halftime, and the 49ers committed four turnovers in all. "I'm still trying to forget that game," Tittle told sportswriter Dennis Georgatos years later. "But I was the one calling the plays. And I took full responsibility for booting it away. I didn't see how they could beat us, so I started trying to ride the clock out by running the ball. But their defense stiffened up and got tougher and, unfortunately, Detroit came back with some big plays."

The Lions went on to rout the Browns 59–14 in the title game, and the 49ers were left wondering what might have been. They didn't make the playoffs again until 1970. "What a blow that was to all of us," running back Joe Perry said. "I'm still not sure how or why our offense came to a standstill. All I do know is that the harder we tried to get going, the worse we got."

62 Hollywood Hardman

After his playing days were over, Cedrick Hardman dabbled in acting. His characters had names like Rock, Righteous, and, most notably, Big Mean in the movie *Stir Crazy*. To opposing quarterbacks, those names sound about right. Big Mean was a role

Hardman was born to play. "I don't like to have fun and frolic with the enemy until the battle is over," Hardman told *Sports Illustrated*. "If I need to slap him upside his head, I don't want friendship getting in the way."

With Hardman in a starring role, the 49ers defensive line was a formidable unit for the better part of a decade. It peaked with the 1976 front four that became known as the "Gold Rush." Quarterback hunters Hardman, Tommy Hart, Cleveland Elam, and Jimmy Webb helped the 49ers amass 61 sacks in '76, which still ranks as the team's single-season record. More impressively, the group did so in a 14-game season. (Sacks weren't an official NFL statistic until 1982; the 49ers reviewed game film of the '76 season and assigned sacks retroactively.)

The Gold Rush had more than brawn. It also had a terrific scheme engineered with help from defensive line coach Floyd Peters. The 49ers' favored stunt was a simple inside loop called "Tex." A 1976 *Sports Illustrated* article detailed how tackles Webb (6'5", 249 pounds) and Elam (6'4", 253 pounds), launched the initial charge with a diagonal outside burst that opened the seams for Hart and Hardman's pass rush. "We want the element of surprise," coach Monte Clark said. "The blocker's been lining up across from someone and BOOM. Suddenly he's got a different guy in his face."

Hart and Hardman were close friends, though different in personality. The introverted Hart tried his best to stay away from the media while Hardman was talkative and quotable. A natural-born pass rusher, he was a first-round pick by the 49ers in the 1970 draft. "I came from the back of the pack at North Texas State," Hardman told the *San Francisco Chronicle*. "I only started two or three games my junior year, but I played next to Mean Joe Greene and got my appetite whetted for getting to the quarterback."

The 6'3", 255-pound lineman would go on to make life rough for opposing quarterbacks during a 12-year career, including from

1970 to 1979 with the 49ers. He made the Pro Bowl in '71 and '75 and capped his career by winning a Super Bowl ring with the 1980 Raiders. Hardman retired after the 1981 season. Though the statistic is unofficial, the 49ers give him credit for some of the greatest single-season sack totals in team history: 18 (in 1971), 17 ('72) and 15 ('75).

But he saved his Hollywood theatrics for the big screen. "Big Mean" had no patience for the modern on-field celebrations. "I can't stand people getting joyous over mediocre accomplishments," he told the *Chronicle*. "A guy gets up and does jumping gymnastics, and he might not make another tackle for two weeks."

63 Len Eshmont

Almost everyone associated with the 49ers has heard of Len Eshmont. The award named after him is the most prestigious honor handed out in the locker room each season. It goes to the player who "best exemplifies the inspirational and courageous play" of Eshmont. Past honorees include Leo Nomellini, Bob St. Clair, Joe Montana, and Jerry Rice.

But even those who have won the award know little about the man himself. Defensive lineman Bryant Young, who captured the honor an astonishing eight times, is mostly unaware of the Eshmont's contribution to the franchise. "I don't know him. I just know what the award represents—courage, leadership, inspiration, everything you read about it," Young said. "Basically, that's what he stood for."

That's true. But there was so much more.

A nimble halfback/fullback, Eshmont was part of the original 49ers in 1946, playing with the team through 1949. Before paving the way for 49ers leaders, he paved the way to the opponent's end zone. Eshmont scored the first touchdown in franchise history. The score came on September 8, 1946 when Frankie Albert passed to running back Johnny Strzykalski, who lateraled to Eshmont for a 66-yard touchdown against the New York Yankees.

Eshmont gained 1,181 yards and tallied 232 carries in his four-season career with the 49ers. He also led the team in kickoff return yards in each of his first two seasons. And, of course, Eshmont carved his niche as a leader. In a description that would later be just as fitting for award-winners like Len Rohde, Roger Craig, and Justin Smith, Eshmont played through pain, spoke up when the team was down, and pushed players with his relentless work ethic. "You've heard of the power of suggestion?" said Garland Gregory, a guard for the 1946 and 1947 teams. "Len had some powerful suggestions."

Raised in the tiny Pennsylvania mining town of Atlas, Eshmont was a sensation as a high school player. Mount Carmel High still gives out an annual Len Eshmont Award, too. Nicknamed "the Atlas Antelope," he went on to play at Fordham University—a major power of the era—and left a legacy there, too. In 1938 Eshmont became the first sophomore to win the NCAA Division I-A rushing title. As a senior in 1940, he led the team to the Cotton Bowl where the Rams fell to Texas A&M 13–12. Eshmont was named an All-American that season.

He became the 36th overall pick of the New York Giants in 1941 but played just one season before being commissioned in the U.S. Navy. He served as a physical education instructor at pre-flight schools around the country—including a stop at St. Mary's in California, where he would team with Albert to form a power-house on a local military team. Eshmont was the only player in the nation to be selected to the all-service teams three years running, from 1942 to 1944.

After the war he joined the 49ers and played with them until 1949. Going on to stints as an assistant coach at the Naval

Len Eshmont Award Recipients

Year	Position	Name	Year	Position	Name
1957	QB	Y.A. Tittle	1986	QB	Joe Montana
1958	FB	Joe Perry	1987	WR	Jerry Rice
1959	HB	J.D. Smith	1988	NT	Michael Carter
1960	S	Dave Baker		RB	Roger Craig
1961	DT	Leo Nomellini	1989	QB	Joe Montana
1962	DE	Dan Colchico	1990	DE	Kevin Fagan
1963	T	Bob St. Clair		LB	Charles Haley
1964	DT	Charlie Krueger	1991	WR	John Taylor
1965	QB	John Brodie	1992	QB	Steve Young
1966	HB	John David Crow	1993	WR	Jerry Rice
1967	HB	John David Crow	1994	QB	Steve Young
1968	LB	Matt Hazeltine	1995	FB	William Floyd
1969	CB	Jimmy Johnson	1996	DT	Bryant Young
1970	S	Roosevelt Taylor	1997	DT	Dana Stubblefield
1971	LB	Ed Beard	1998	DT	Bryant Young
1972	DE	Tommy Hart	1999	DT	Bryant Young
1973	S	Mel Phillips	2000	DT	Bryant Young
1974	T	Len Rohde	2001	RB	Garrison Hearst
1975	CB	Jimmy Johnson	2002	SS	Tony Parrish
1976	DE	Tommy Hart	2003	LB	Julian Peterson
1977	S	Mel Phillips	2004	DT	Bryant Young
1978	RB	Paul Hofer	2005	DT	Bryant Young
1979	RB	Paul Hofer	2006	DT	Bryant Young
1980	DT	Archie Reese	2007	DT	Bryant Young
1981	TE	Charle Young	2008	WR	Isaac Bruce
1982	WR	Dwight Clark	2009	TE	Vernon Davis
1983	RB/ST	Bill Ring	2010	LB	Takeo Spikes
1984	LB	Keena Turner	2011	DE	Justin Smith
1985	FB	Roger Craig	2012	DE	Justin Smith

Academy and the University of Virginia, Eshmont's life ended abruptly in 1957 when he succumbed to hepatitis at a Virginia hospital. "The father of three young daughters, he had suffered a relapse after undergoing major surgery at the hospital 11 days ago," a UPI report said. "Until the relapse, hospital officials said, the young coach 'appeared to be rallying.'"

He was 39 at the time of his death. The 49ers named the award after him eight days later. "When I heard he died I just couldn't believe it," Strzykalski recalled in *Forty-Niners: Looking Back*, a book by Joseph Hession. "He was a great competitor. That's what made him a good football player. He just loved competition."

64 John Taylor

John Taylor is known for his game-winning touchdown in Super Bowl XXIII, but Taylor was hardly a one-catch wonder. A prolific receiver who spent his 1987 to 1995 career in the shadow of Jerry Rice, the 6'1", 185-pounder was a big-play threat who deserves his moment in the sun.

Then again, Taylor was a guy accustomed to playing on football's back roads. He and his buddies used to hold pickup games at the cemetery because it was the only park in his Pennsauken, New Jersey, neighborhood without broken glass littering the ground. Taylor once said that the only thing kids had to worry about when they caught a pass was running into a tombstone.

Those games featured five future NFL players: Taylor; younger brother Keith Taylor (Washington Redskins defensive back); Billy Griggs (New York Jets tight end); David Griggs (Miami Dolphins linebacker); and Todd McNair (Kansas City Chiefs running back).

The playing surface got better—and so did Taylor. He walked onto the football team at Delaware State and then he started running to the end zone. Of his 100 career college receptions, 33 went for touchdowns. The 49ers saw enough explosiveness to take him in the third round of the 1986 draft, launching the NFL career of one of the league's top No. 2 wideouts.

You know about his best catch. But his best game says more about the player Taylor was. On one memorable night in Anaheim, California, he finished with 11 catches for 286 receiving yards. It happened on December 11, 1989 when the 49ers visited the Los Angeles Rams for a monumental regular-season game: The *Monday Night Football* stage would decide whether the 49ers or their NFC West rivals would win the division and earn a first-round bye in the playoffs.

It started off atrociously for the 49ers, who trailed 17–3 in the second quarter. The Rams tried to put the game away with a fake field goal just before halftime, but holder Pete Holohan's run came up inches short of the goal line.

That left the door open a crack, and Taylor came bursting through. On the 49ers' next possession, a third-down play from their 8-yard-line called for Taylor to run a slant. So quarterback Joe Montana acted quickly, handling the exchange from center and tossing the ball to a slicing Taylor as soon as he could—like a second baseman turning a double play.

As Rams cornerback Clifford Hicks fell, Taylor caught the ball and outran safety Vince Newsome down the sideline. Rice helped by sealing off speedy cornerback Jerry Gray with a nice block, and Taylor made it all the way to the end zone. The 92-yard touchdown cut the deficit to 17–10.

The Rams, though, remained confident. George Seifert told the *San Francisco Chronicle* that Rams owner Georgia Frontiere spent halftime "walking the sidelines with her glass of white wine toasting the Rams' fans because they had a lead." Her optimism was reasonable, considering Los Angeles scored the first 10 points of the second half to push their edge to 27–10.

But after a 7-yard touchdown pass from Montana to Mike Wilson helped narrow the gap, the 49ers were poised to strike again—this time from even farther. Pinned at their 4-yard-line, the 49ers called for another slant. As Taylor blasted hard across the middle, Montana hit him in stride for what would be a 96-yard touchdown catch.

Years later, Montana would use those two big plays to explain the brilliance of the West Coast Offense. He said it didn't require rocket-powered throws—just an understanding of where the ball needed to go and when. "I'm loving it because I've thrown two passes for 10 yards [through the air] but I have 190 passing yards and two touchdowns," Montana said. "It's a matter of just understanding that you have to let the system work. You don't have to use your arm. You just have to use your mind and know where everybody is and big plays will present themselves."

Taylor's second touchdown cut the score to 27–23, and the 49ers capped their amazing comeback when Roger Craig scored on a one-yard touchdown run for the 30–27 final. With home-field advantage secured, San Francisco marched through the playoffs and crushed the Denver Broncos 55–10 in Super Bowl XXIV. Taylor caught a touchdown pass in all three playoff games.

65 Walsh Coaching Tree

Some NFL leaders have a coaching tree. Bill Walsh has a coaching forest.

Having himself studied at the foot of NFL pioneer Paul Brown, Bill Walsh passed along his own innovations and wisdom to a generation of assistant coaches who would go on to transform the NFL landscape. By the time of Walsh's death in 2007, 22 of the 32 NFL head coaches could trace their lineage back to the man who

A mentor to a multitude of successful coaches, Bill Walsh diagrams a play before a 1986 game against the Patriots.

coached the 49ers from 1979 to 1988. "In the recent or modern history of the NFL, no coach has been more influential and innovative than Bill Walsh," Baltimore Ravens coach Brian Billick told USA TODAY. "That includes his coaching on the field and his thoughts and actions on how franchises can work together to win championships."

Seven former assistants from Walsh's staffs went on to serve as head coaches: George Seifert (two-time Super Bowl winner), Mike Holmgren (one-time Super Bowl winner), Ray Rhodes, Bruce Coslet, Sam Wyche, Mike White, and Dennis Green.

In turn these men hired coaches and passed along Walsh's lessons regarding the West Coast Offense. As it spread around the league, Billick was among those who campaigned for a name change because he considered the "West Coast Offense" a misnomer. "We should call what many teams currently run exactly what it is—the 'Walshian Offense,'" Billick said.

Name a coach, and chances are you can trace a line back to Walsh in just a few of steps a la Six Degrees of Kevin Bacon. Test your friends and see if they can do it with, say...Pittsburgh Steelers coach Mike Tomlin.

Tomlin had served on the Tampa Bay Buccaneers staff of Tony Dungy...who had served as a Minnesota Vikings defensive backs coach under Dennis Green...who had served as the 49ers wide receivers and special teams coach under Walsh from 1986 to 1988—and before that as the running backs coach for Walsh's teams at Stanford in 1977 to 1978.

Kansas City Chiefs coach Andy Reid? He worked as a Green Bay Packers assistant under Holmgren, who was Walsh's quarterbacks coach from 1986 to 1988 and a 49ers offensive coordinator from 1989 to 1991.

Mike Shanahan and Jeff Fisher? They both worked under Seifert, Walsh's defensive backs coach from 1980 to 1982 and defensive coordinator from 1983 to 1988.

The coaching tree doesn't even count another major contribution to the profession. Walsh created the Black Coaches Summer Program, in which he invited African American coaches to training camp to watch how he ran his organization and let them take part in coaching. Herm Edwards, Lovie Smith, and Marvin Lewis were among the camp participants who went on to become NFL head coaches. "The essence of Bill Walsh was that he was an extraordinary teacher," NFL commissioner Roger Goodell said in a statement after Walsh's passing. "If you gave him a blackboard and a piece of chalk, he would become a whirlwind of wisdom. He taught all of us not only about football, but also about life and how it takes teamwork for any of us to succeed as individuals."

66 Hearst's Burst

There was already plenty of offense between the 49ers and New York Jets on September 6, 1998 at Candlestick Park. Both quarterbacks threw for more than 360 yards. Three wide receivers had 100-yard games. The score was 30–30 at the end of regulation.

As it turned out, that was merely the warm-up act.

Garrison Hearst made it an overtime for the ages by blazing 96 yards to score the winning touchdown, the longest rush in 49ers history. "That will go down in history as one of the great, great runs of all time," 49ers coach Steve Mariucci said. "What a finish."

The previous long had been an 89-yarder by Hugh McElhenny on October 5, 1952.

Hearst, a college sensation at Georgia where his numbers rivaled Herschel Walker's, experienced a frustrating start to his NFL his career. The Phoenix Cardinals selected him with the No. 3 pick in the 1993 draft, but injuries and dubious supporting casts kept him from showing his talent in anything other than occasional flashes.

With the 49ers, however, Hearst would finally establish sustained success. Signed as a free agent in 1997, he became the team's first 1,000-yard rusher since Ricky Watters in 1992. Hearst scored four touchdowns during that '97 season, topping the total of his entire career to that point. Hearst would go on to spend five seasons with the 49ers, including a then-team record 1,570 yards during the 1998 season. (Frank Gore established the new mark of 1,695 in 2006.) Hearst broke out that '98 year, starting with the game-winner against the Jets on opening weekend.

The play that secured his place in 49ers lore was called 90–0. It came after the Jets failed on their first two cracks in overtime and with the 49ers pinned at their 4-yard line. Mariucci called for the 90–0, an inside trap, thinking it might buy the offense about four yards. "Steve [Young] looked at me like, *You've got to be kidding*," Mariucci said. "We were just trying to come off the goal line. We were just trying to make a little room and get a first down."

The play began with center Chris Dalman blocking down on one defensive tackle and right guard Kevin Gogan blocking down on the other. Hearst's job was to watch the direction of the blocks: When the linemen pushed their opponents left, Hearst bolted to the right. "That's a key," Young said. "If they don't get the down block, it's a loss of two. It's really the old '80s pulling trap."

The next block came from left guard Ray Brown, who pulled to his right and took out middle linebacker Dwayne Gordon. Another key block came from fullback Marc Edwards, who nailed left defensive end Rick Lyle to help spring Hearst free.

After that it was a convoy to the end zone.

Hearst was joined in his 17-second sprint by wide receiver Terrell Owens and left tackle Dave Fiori, who served as the running back's bodyguards. "I couldn't have done it without them," Hearst said. "When I was running downfield, I had a whole lot of red jerseys around me."

The hardest part for Heart wasn't the run. It was enduring the giddy celebration when players started piling on top of him. "I was just trying to breathe," Hearst said.

67 Drink Carmen Policy's Wine

Carmen Policy grew up in Youngstown, Ohio, where shipments would arrive each fall with rejected wine grapes from California. Residents in his Smokey Hollow neighborhood, many of them Italian-Americans, awaited these shipments as if it were a holiday, racing to railroad yards to load up on the fruits of this faraway harvest.

His neighbors created their homemade wines using old family recipes. Those wines were often crafted in November and released in April. Each was a labor of love—even if love was in the eye of the glass holder. "Everybody thought theirs was the best," Policy said with a laugh, "but it was really dreck."

Years later, Policy learned firsthand about the planning and dedication it takes to create something more magically enduring. 49ers masterminds Eddie DeBartolo and Bill Walsh taught him that greatness came from setting an exacting standard and settling for only the best ingredients. In pursuing excellence, Policy said, "You don't cut corners."

With Policy aboard as a top executive starting in 1983, the 49ers went on to win Super Bowls after the 1984, '88, '89, and '94 seasons. Those teams were the toast of the town—and San Franciscans don't toast with dreck.

These days Policy owns a gorgeous vineyard in Napa Valley that produces his Casa Piena label, a 100 percent Cabernet Sauvignon that exhibits profound depth and character—much like his best rosters. Policy and his wife, Gail, approach their current task the same way the 49ers approached their glory years: assembling the best talent. His team includes Thomas Rivers Brown, one of the most

sought-after winemakers in the Napa Valley (and a former *FOOD &*
WINE winemaker of the year) and heralded vineyard manager Jim
Barbour.

The Policy Vineyard, located in Yountville, California, is a
14½-acre property once owned by Charles Krug. Upon purchasing
the land in 2003, Policy's first act was to rip out all the old vines.
He was building this franchise from the ground up. First came an
exhaustive planning phase. Then for three or four years, the grapes
were simply thrown on the ground and tilled back into the earth.
"The first good wine requires four to five years under your belt
and another five or six years before the revenues hopefully exceed
expenses," Policy said. "Patience? It drove me nuts at first."

A one-time attorney, Policy argued a case before the U.S.
Supreme Court by the time he was 33. He met DeBartolo when he
won a lawsuit against the DeBartolo Corporation during a trial in
Youngstown. DeBartolo hired him as 49ers counsel in 1979 to write
up a contract for the team's new coach (some fellow named Walsh).
By 1990 Policy was the CEO and president of the franchise. Because
they celebrated in Napa often during that time, Carmen and Gail fell
in love with the region and began plotting their retirement.

Then again, "retirement" is the wrong word. They are hands-
on owners. "It brings out the competitive juices, but in a different
way," Policy said. "Here you're not really staring down your competition. You want everybody to do well in the Napa Valley because
when they do well it enhances the entire region. You're competing against yourself. You're competing against the elements—the
weather, the ground."

Policy knows what it takes to make a winner. His NFL peers
voted him the Executive of the Year award in 1994. *GQ* once
named him one of the most influential people in sports.

And to his delight, he's not the only sportsman making a go
of it in Napa. His fellow winemakers include Hall of Fame pitcher
Tom Seaver ("He does everything but drive the tractor," Policy

said), Indy Car driver Randy Lewis, and fellow football friends such as Fran Tarkenton, John Madden, Rick Mirer, Jimmy Cefalo, and Dick Vermeil. "You'll be surprised how many people love wine and sports," Policy said. "Maybe it's the good life."

Finding a bottle of Policy's wine requires patience, creativity— and ample cash. There are no tours of the Casa Piena vineyard. (It's on his private estate.) And the team produces a little more than 1,000 cases a year.

Outpost Wines, atop Howell Mountain above Napa Valley, is among the places that offers tastings. Bottles are also available at casapiena.com. Which year to try? Policy said the 2008 vintage was "phenomenal" and 2010 was a "bang-up year." But he also said to keep an eye on a promising young newcomer. "I'm telling you, 2012 is going to go down as one of the great vintages of the Napa Valley," Policy said.

68 Vernon Davis

To steer clear of the drugs and alcohol that was taking down so many of his friends in his rough Washington, D.C., neighborhood, Vernon Davis spent a lot of time lifting weights as a teenager. That's easy to believe now. The 49ers' record-setting tight end has the physique of a bodybuilder. "If you had his body," his first 49ers coach, Mike Nolan, quipped, "you'd throw yours away,"

But it took a few years for the 6'3", 250-pound Davis to truly flex his muscle in the NFL. Atop young Davis' hard body was a hard head. The sixth overall pick out of Maryland in the 2006 draft was strong, fast, and talented, but those skills were undermined by his bad routes, unreliable hands, and erratic temperament.

But then Mike Singletary yelled at him.

Singletary's infamous "I Want Winners" rant on October 26, 2008 became something of a punch line. Often forgotten is that it worked. The target of the former head coach's ire that day was Davis, who had committed a silly personal foul penalty and was banished from the field. Singletary going berserk is easy to find on the Internet, but only Davis and Singletary were there for the more significant conversation that ensued. "Tears were shed," Davis recalled years later at Super Bowl XLVII.

Davis said that he demanded a trade; Singletary said fine. In that instant Davis realized just how easy it was for Singletary to toss him to the curb. Davis had thought he was "the franchise," but he had made himself irrelevant. "That moment it started to click for me," Davis said. "I said, 'I have to put my teammates first because if I don't I'm going to lose all I have. I have to focus and I have to be different.'"

The next year Davis caught 13 touchdown passes, made his first Pro Bowl, racked up 965 receiving yards, and erased the bust label that had followed him over his first three seasons. Teammates elected him as the winner of the Len Eshmont Award, the prestigious honor that goes to the 49ers player who "best exemplifies the inspirational and courageous play" of its namesake.

You want winners? You got one. "I knew Coach Singletary was trying to use a disciplinary action with me and I fed into it," Davis said. "It made me a better man, a better teammate, and a better leader for my team. It helped me become the player I am today."

Beyond the production Davis grew up emotionally. He was named a team captain. He was vocal in support of teammates such as quarterback Alex Smith, who came under fire. Even during prolonged stretches when he vanished from the game plan, such as late in the 2012 regular season, Davis didn't grumble—let alone demand a trade. The guy, who once had dropped too many passes to count, stuck around after practice to work on his hands by catching passes shot from a Jugs gun.

And when it mattered, he delivered. After that quiet 2012 regular season, Davis had five catches for 106 yards and a touchdown in the NFC Championship Game against Atlanta. Then in a loss against the Baltimore Ravens, he tied a Super Bowl record for tight ends with 104 yards (on six catches). That was Davis' fourth career 100-yard game in the postseason, tying Keith Jackson's NFL record for most by a tight end. Among all players only Davis and receiver Larry Fitzgerald registered four 100-yard receiving games over their first five career playoff games.

"Putting my teammates first was the best thing I could have done," Davis said. "Once I did that, things started to happen for me. I started to see the game differently. It wasn't about me anymore."

69 Master of the Funky Chicken Dance

Merton Hanks' famous chicken dance started with Big Bird.

The 49ers' defensive back was watching *Sesame Street* with his oldest daughter, Maya, in 1995 when Bert and Ernie mimicked the way pigeons walk. Merton and Maya started doing it, too, bobbing their necks back and forth in a comic dance.

On November 12 of that season, the 49ers traveled to Dallas for a game they were supposed to lose. With Elvis Grbac making an emergency start at quarterback, most figured the powerhouse Cowboys would crush the 49ers. But Hanks set the tone early by returning a fumble 38 yards for a touchdown. When he got to the end zone, he suddenly felt the urge to dance again. It was poultry in motion.

The 49ers went on to win 38–20 at Texas Stadium. And the Chicken Dance became Hanks' signature move. "At first when he was doing it, I thought, *C'mon*," teammate Marquez Pope told *The San Francisco Examiner*. "The fans really love it, and he connects with them that way. So I figured you have to give the people what they want."

Hanks had plenty of opportunity to strut his stuff. During a 49ers career spanning 1991 to 1998, the former Iowa standout made four Pro Bowl teams. A fifth-round pick in the 1991 draft, Hanks racked up 31 interceptions in a San Francisco uniform, which ranks as fourth best in team history. He was finger-pickin' good.

But his dance—later to be emulated by the likes of Shaquille O'Neal—often overshadowed the more important parts of Hanks' game. He was relentless in his preparation. And from the instant he arrived in the NFL, he would swoop toward the game's legends as if they were a wobbly pass over the middle. He sought out the likes of Deacon Jones (who advised him on how to handle his rookie year), Ray Nitschke (who gave him advice on balancing football and family), and Lester Hayes (who taught him to keep notebooks on opponents). Throughout his career Hanks kept charts on the tendencies of opposing offensive coordinators, making sure to update his files whenever the play caller switched teams.

Hanks was more than just comic relief. "You don't want to be known just for something goofy," Hanks told *The Examiner*. "You know that you have to do something good before you can celebrate. You have to earn it. It's predicated on hard work and being prepared."

Hanks had been an All-Big 10 selection at the University of Iowa but slipped in the draft because of his slow 40-yard dash times at the Combine. He ran it in 4.74 seconds, a lackadaisical performance that *Sports Illustrated* once compared to "showing up at a job interview without pants."

Merton Hanks, a four-time Pro Bowler at safety, performs his memorable funky chicken dance in 1996.

But Hanks' play at Iowa captured the notice of defensive backs coach Ray Rhodes and scouting director Tony Razzano, who pleaded—sometimes at a shout—until George Seifert relented and took Hanks with the 122ⁿᵈ overall pick. Hanks would go on to look plenty fast as one of the most dynamic defensive backs of his time. "Mert covers more ground than anyone else at his position," 49ers quarterback Steve Young told *SI*. "And his quick changes of direction surprise a lot of quarterbacks."

After his playing career, Hanks went on to serve as the NFL's senior manager and assistant director of operations. But perhaps he—not Jerry Rice—should've been the one who ended up on *Dancing With the Stars*.

70 Dexter Manley vs. Bill Walsh

In early March 2012 with the New Orleans Saints' "Bountygate" scandal still fresh in the news cycle, former Washington Redskins defensive lineman Dexter Manley went on a Washington, D.C., sports radio show and said NFL bounty systems were old hat. In fact he accused Bill Walsh of running one with the 49ers. "He's dead and gone now," Manley said. "But he had bounty programs. Yes, he did."

As Manley's charge started making the rounds on the Internet, I called as many former 49ers as I could. They defended Walsh vehemently, denouncing the accusation as ridiculous. "Absolutely not true," Carmen Policy avowed.

Walsh's son, Craig, blasted the comment, too but had a theory as to why Manley said it. On a *Monday Night Football* game played November 17, 1986, tight end Russ Francis delivered a legal crackback block that demolished Manley and opened up a huge lane for running back Wendell Tyler. Then Francis did it again.

While writing the Manley story, I tried to reach Francis, a three-time Pro Bowl selection, for more details. I came up empty. But it turns out, he was worth the wait.

About a month after my story came out, Francis—then 59 and living in Hawaii—started sending me e-mails with the subject line: "Bill Walsh—The Rest of the Story."

Francis, like several readers at the time, pointed out that I'd missed an important element of the backstory—that Manley had boasted to the press that he was going to knock Joe Montana out of the 1986 game. Among the 100 things you should know about the 49ers: Don't ever, ever, ever mess with Bill Walsh. What follows is Russ Francis' e-mail to me, reprinted verbatim, with his permission:

> Dan, I have just been sent the "bounty" story you wrote. Nice piece. I know that it is hard to get all of the facts correct from a time so long ago. Or so it seems... You got most of it right, and I thank you for that.
>
> Here is my side of it:
>
> I remember that hit on Dexter like it was yesterday, because I was intent on hitting him so hard he would remember it for all of his tomorrows. From the sound of things, and the tenor of his comments, it looks like it is still working. Here is the true story.
>
> Ole Dex left out the part about him being quoted in the paper the week of that game when he opened up his mouth, left his brain disengaged, and told the world that he was going to take our QB, Joe Montana, out of the game when we played the Redskins.
>
> We liked Joe. What the heck did he expect? Did he not think our coach and our team was going to respond?

Bill Walsh was much too classy a gentleman, and he had put together, along with John McVay and Eddie DeBartolo, a much-too-talented team to ever begin to need to issue an order to knock a player out of the game. That was par for the course with guys like Ronnie "BoBo" Lott, Keena Turner, Hacksaw, and just about every other player on the team. And they did not need any cheap shots. They all came straight at you and delivered with serious intent.

Dexter flatters himself to think he was thought to resemble anything akin to a real force on the field. Dexter was a very good player for a period of time, and he most certainly did his best to deliver the biggest hits possible on his opponents every chance he got, so his contorted recollection matches what I remember about what he looked like on the ground after those hits. And it is difficult to understand and borders on comical.

I hit him clean and hard. Twice and no flag. I did not get compensated for those hits. I did them for free. No bounty, no foul. End of story. Case closed, next case.

Dexter did not get near Joe Montana that day. Just the way Bill wanted it to be. Now there was a man among men. Bill Walsh, our mentor, our friend...and not just for winning championships, but for his almost elegant way of handling so many diverse personalities and egos, with class, grace, and true leadership.

Even though this was eons ago, any slight, whatsoever implicating one of the icons of the NFL will not be permitted—most certainly not by such an unmanly attack by Manley on a man who elevated the fortunes and the standard of character and opportunity of his players as Bill Walsh did throughout his entire career.

I will not stand by, nor will any of Bill's players, and listen to someone who so patently gets it so wrong, and shed a tainted light on one of our own who shared so much of his brilliance with so many of us.

If this were a tongue-and-cheek shot across the bow from one player to another, so be it. But this is personal, and Mr. DM, and use those initials any way your creative imagination will allow, is so far out of touch with the game that he deserves to be called on it in spades.

Sorry for the novel, but I am in motion from far out on the left side of the formation, picking up speed, I see Joe glance at me to time his cadence just right, and he did, and I don't really hear the hut, or final command for Fred Quillan to snap the ball, and I see DM lift off the ground, out of his stance, and start his acceleration to the QB, and as he rises, moving quickly now, he glances back to hear, not see, the explosive impact brought to him courtesy of the entire 49er organization in the form of messenger #81.

The message is swift, and it is painful. Both intended. Both accomplishing the goal. No more problem with Dexter.

And please feel free to quote me on this or my previous message.

Be well and aloha

—Russ

71 Dallas Heartbreak

Part of the reason the The Catch felt so good in 1981 is because how bad Preston Riley's drop felt in 1972. Against the same Dallas Cowboys, an onside kick popped out of Riley's hands, and the hearts of 49ers fans crashed to the floor.

This heart-wrenching defeat marked a third consecutive playoff loss to Dallas. And this knockout punch hurt so much that it took the 49ers nearly a decade to get up off the canvas. "That probably ended our run," 49ers running back Ken Willard said. "That was heartbreaking. And if you look at the records, Dick Nolan's reign was pretty much over after that."

That 30–28 loss to Dallas in the divisional round game at Candlestick Park on December 23, 1972 came after it looked as if the 49ers were on the verge of payback after consecutive losses in the NFC Championship Game. They led this one 21–6 in the second quarter and were up 28–13 with nine minutes to go. "Even with five minutes to go, I didn't think any of us felt we had a chance to win," Cowboys guard Blaine Nye admitted in *The Sporting News 1973 Football Guide.*

And then the sure thing unraveled. The 49ers collapsed just as they had in their 1957 playoff defeat to the Detroit Lions. This time it was Roger Staubach, who rallied his team back from the brink of extinction, delivering two touchdown passes in the final 1:30. "It's hard to analyze a game like this," 49ers quarterback John Brodie said, "because I'm not quite believing it myself."

The game started in the most promising way imaginable. Vic Washington returned a kickoff 97 yards for a 7–0 lead. After that the Cowboys did what they could to help, committing three turnovers inside their 35 that led to three 49ers touchdowns. It looked increasingly as if coach Dick Nolan had finally cracked the code to his nemesis. The 49ers had already walloped Dallas 31–10 on Thanksgiving Day. This looked like another rout. "They were laughing at us, making fun of us during the game," Cowboys safety Charlie Waters recalled years later for ESPN. "They were really enjoying having the upper hand on us. They didn't think there was any way [we'd come back] because our offense was sputtering. We were doing absolutely nothing."

But the punch lines turned into a punch in the gut, as Staubach added to his legend as Captain Comeback. Having led the Cowboys to the Super Bowl championship a year earlier, Staubach took over for a struggling Craig Morton late in the third quarter.

With the Cowboys still down 28–16 in the fourth quarter, Staubach first hit Billy Parks for a 20-yard touchdown pass, cutting the deficit to five with 1:10 left in the game. That's when the trapdoor fell open. Cowboys kicker Toni Fritsch, an Austrian import with a gift for trickery, lined up to the left. But as he approached the ball, he slung his right foot behind his left and delivered a goofy-looking squib kick. The 49ers were expecting an onside kick, and Riley was well positioned on the front lines because of his reliable hands. But the ball deflected off of him, and Mel Renfro recovered the ball for the Cowboys at midfield. "I don't know what happened," Riley said in the locker room.

Staubach had a theory. "It was like we deserved it," he said. "It was all positive thinking down there. Everyone knew we were going right back out again."

Staubach promptly directed another scoring drive, this time connecting with Ron Sellers from 10 yards out to give the Cowboys their first and only lead 30–28. The 49ers, though, still had 52 seconds remaining. It proved to be just long enough for more frustration.

More Dallas Soap Opera

In a replay of their 1970s trilogy, the 49ers and Dallas Cowboys met three consecutive times in the postseason during the 1990s. Each matchup occurred in the NFC title game, and each produced the eventual Super Bowl champion.

January 17, 1993: Cowboys 30, 49ers 20 at Candlestick Park

Cowboys quarterback Troy Aikman shredded the 49ers by connecting on 24-of-34 passes for two touchdowns without an interception. Deep threat Alvin Harper was the surprise contributor, slipping free for three catches for 117 yards, including a 70-yarder that set up the clinching touchdown. 49ers quarterback Steve Young, trying to emerge from Joe Montana's shadow, threw for 313 yards but also threw two interceptions, prompting fans to wonder if he could win the big one.

January 23, 1994: Cowboys 35, 49ers 21 at Texas Stadium

Young took abuse from the disappointed fan base again, but the 49ers defense had a hard time stopping the Cowboys. Aikman completed 14-of-18 passes for 177 yards and two touchdowns. Dallas pulled away with 21 consecutive points in the second quarter thanks to a 4-yard run by fullback Daryl Johnston, an 11-yard run by Emmitt Smith, and a 19-yard catch by tight end Jay Novacek.

January 14, 1995: 49ers 35, Cowboys 28 at Candlestick Park

Young reached his first Super Bowl thanks in part to some daring early bootlegs that kept the Cowboys defense off-balance. (Young finished with 10 rushes for 47 yards). Defensive back Eric Davis got the 49ers rolling with a 44-yard interception return for a touchdown. Ricky Watters caught a 29-yard pass from Young, and William Floyd had 1-yard touchdown rush. That gave the 49ers a 21–0 lead, and they held on to help Young get that monkey off his back. The quarterback celebrated with an exuberant victory lap.

Cowboys defenders Tony Casillas and Charles Haley, a longtime 49er, take down Steve Young during the NFC Championship Game in 1993. Dallas has been a repeated playoff nemesis of San Francisco.

Brodie connected with Riley for a sideline catch at the Dallas 40 to stop the clock with 11 seconds left. But 49ers tackle Cas Banaszek was called for holding, bringing the ball back to the San Francisco 30. Brodie's next pass was intercepted.

Riley remains the eternal goat, but he was hardly alone. The 49ers managed only 255 yards of offense that day—56 below their regular-season average—and the defense failed time and again to put the game away. Bruce Gossett missed field goals of 40 and 32 yards. "They ought to get off of poor Preston," defensive lineman Cedrick Hardman told the *San Francisco Chronicle*. "He just made the last of a lot of errors that day. I did more to lose that game than he did."

72 Randy Cross

Like icons John Elway and Ray Lewis, longtime 49ers lineman Randy Cross went out on top. He rode off into the sunset with a victory in Super Bowl XXIII. As his final act, Cross blocked for the 11-play, 92-yard scoring drive capped by Joe Montana's touchdown pass to John Taylor to defeat the Cincinnati Bengals 20–16 on January 22, 1989.

Now *that's* how to make an exit. "It was perfect. It's what you dream of being able to do when you're a young kid growing up. That was something out of the movies," Cross told 49ers.com. "It was the perfect time to step away. It was kind of a special feeling to walk off that field and look around that stadium in Miami, soak it in because it was the last time I'd ever do it."

Cross understood better than most how much it meant to go out a winner, having started his career as a loser. Drafted as a center out of UCLA in 1976, he broke in during the dark days of the pre–Bill Walsh era. The 49ers went 8–6 during his rookie season before plummeting toward consecutive finishes of 5–9, 2–14, 2–14, and 6–10.

But along the way, Cross stumbled across his big break both literally and figuratively. He sustained a fractured ankle in game nine of 1978 and missed the rest of the season. By the time he'd healed up for the '79 opener, Walsh was in charge. Cross' fifth head coach in four seasons had the wisdom to move the 6'3", 259-pound mauler to guard in order to make better use of his foot speed. "That move enabled me to blossom as a professional," Cross told UCLA.com.

The franchise blossomed too. The 49ers won three Super Bowl championships (1982, 1985, and 1989) over the span of Cross' 13 seasons. He was the 49ers' Offensive Lineman of the Year in '86,

'87, and '88 and was voted the 49ers' Man of the Year in 1985 for his work in the community.

Born April 25, 1954 in New York, Cross grew up in Southern California and first became a star at UCLA. He was a two-time All-American with the Bruins and played on the 1976 Rose Bowl championship team, meaning he finished his college career in style, too.

The 49ers took him in the second round (42nd overall). Asked to name his career highlights, he picked erasing a 28-point halftime deficit to beat the New Orleans Saints 38–35 on December 7, 1980 and being on the field for The Catch in the NFC title game against Dallas. And, of course, he fondly remembers his trio of Super Bowl triumphs. "All three of my Super Bowls were favorite memories," Cross told 49ers.com. "I have three kids, too. You don't pick a favorite kid, and it's the same when it comes to picking a favorite Super Bowl."

By the 1988 season, however, Cross knew his magical ride was about to come to a full stop. It was on the plane ride to Miami for Super Bowl XXIII that Cross plopped down next to Walsh and told him that this would be the final game—just as it was for the coach. "Yes, I knew that was it for me," Cross told UCLA.com. "I know I could have played three or four more years, but it wouldn't have been at the level I wanted."

Cross promptly made a seamless transition to the broadcast booth, serving as an NFL analyst for NBC Sports before moving on to CBS. He'd gotten a head start on his second career by doing color commentary for USFL games during the final years of his NFL playing days. Even then Cross began sending audition tapes to the networks in hopes of catching on.

Whenever he decides to hang up his microphone, however, it will be tough to top his exit from the NFL. "I chose to end it on the perfect stage," Cross said.

73 The Grab

Thirty years after Dwight Clark's fingertips earned their place in football lore, the modern 49ers gave the franchise the ultimate anniversary present: Vernon Davis made a heart-stopping catch in the end zone to cap another classic NFC playoff game. The only question this time around was what to call it. "The Catch" was taken. So was "The Catch II." This one demanded at least a tad more originality. "You've got to call it 'The Grab,'" Davis said.

By any name the play provided one the most exhilarating finishes in the history of the 49ers. The 49ers actually rallied twice in the final minutes to pull off a 36–32 NFC divisional playoff victory against the New Orleans Saints on January 14, 2012. "It's history, legendary, anything you can describe," Davis said.

Let's start at the end: Facing a 32–29 deficit as time ticked away, quarterback Alex Smith marched the 49ers close enough to take a shot at the end zone. On a third-and-4 play from the 14-yard line, the quarterback spotted his tight end with a sliver of room at the center of the goal line.

Smith rifled the ball to Davis, who clenched it as he endured a wicked and immediate blow from Saints safety Roman Harper. It was an unlikely recipe for a game-winning touchdown: A much-maligned quarterback threading a beauty to a tight end once mocked for his unreliable hands.

The victory propelled the 49ers to the NFC Championship Game. As if immediately understanding the magnitude of his journey, Davis was in tears by the time he reached the sideline. Coach Jim Harbaugh welcomed him with a hug. "History was going through my mind," Davis said. "It was us against history. Us against *No*. Us against *Can't*. And we managed to pull it off."

In a play known as The Grab, tight end Vernon Davis hauls in the game-winning touchdown against safety Roman Harper and the Saints on January 14, 2012. (AP Images)

The 49ers had practiced the play design, called "Vernon Post," a few times during the week but always with Davis lining up on the other side of the formation. It worked every time. The rehearsal also let Smith know that he'd have to throw the ball with authority. "I knew it was going to be a bang-bang play," Smith said. "It wasn't going to be a lob ball."

The Grab was merely the closing scene of an epic game that included four lead changes over the final 4:02. Led by the prolific

Drew Brees, the Saints were coming off consecutive 600-yard games but safety Donte Whitner let New Orleans know right away that yards against the 49ers would be hard-earned.

On the Saints' opening drive, Brees tossed the ball to Pierre Thomas on a third-and-6 play from the 7. That's when Whitner demolished the running back with a stadium-rattling hit that jarred the ball loose. As the 49ers recovered the fumble at the 2, a man who knew something about hard hits rose to his feet. "It brought me out of my chair," Ronnie Lott said. "It also brought back memories…[Whitner] set the tone. As my son said, 'Down goes Frazier!'"

The Saints, however, were too talented to stay on the canvas for long. Brees, who threw for 5,476 yards and 46 touchdowns during the regular season, got rolling late. He hit running back Darren Sproles for a 44-yard touchdown with 4:02 remaining to give the Saints a 24–23 lead. That's about the time the teams started trading touchdowns the way tennis players return serves. Smith countered the Sproles scamper with his own legwork. On a third-and-8, the 49ers rolled the dice and called for "QB-9"—a designed scramble to the left side of the line. The 49ers were betting that the Saints would be blitzing from the right. New Orleans did, and Smith blazed 28 yards for a touchdown, drawing a cheer from the Candlestick Park crowd loud enough to drown out six years of boos.

The euphoria lasted less than a minute as Brees hit tight end Jimmy Graham for a 66-yard touchdown with 1:37 to play. All that did was set the stage for The Grab. The 49ers became the first team in playoff history to take leads twice on touchdowns in the final three minutes, according to the Elias Sports Bureau. "This," Harbaugh said, "was an all-day sucker."

74 The Nolans

When San Francisco hired Mike Nolan as its head coach in January 2005, his youthful face looked familiar to much of the 49ers' old guard. Former linebacker Dave Wilcox, who was in the audience at the press conference, had to resist the urge to make the kid fetch him some Gatorade. That's because Wilcox and company remembered Mike Nolan as the plucky little ball boy for *their* coach, Dick Nolan, who had guided the team from 1968 to 1975 and twice led them to the brink of the Super Bowl.

Mike was the coach's son, the pipsqueak who used to help defensive lineman Charlie Krueger pull off elaborate locker room gags like taping quarterback George Mira's practice uniform high up on a pole. "Now, I turned on the TV the other day, and I couldn't believe it," Mira told me after the Nolan hiring. "That kid is now the head coach of the San Francisco 49ers."

This news was no prank: Dick Nolan and Mike Nolan became the fourth father-son coaching duo in the history of the NFL. Neither coach reached his ultimate destination by taking the team to the Super Bowl. But both left a lasting impact on the franchise, for better or worse.

Born March 26, 1932, in Pittsburgh, Dick Nolan played quarterback at White Plains High School in New York. He went on to become a standout defensive back at the University of Maryland and was part of the school's 1953 championship team. The Giants took Dick Nolan as a fourth-round draft pick in 1954, and he spent seven of his nine NFL seasons in New York. He also played for the Chicago Cardinals and Dallas Cowboys.

After retiring in 1962, he became an assistant with the Cowboys. Three years later, when a young running back named

Dan Reeves was trying to make the team, Nolan campaigned passionately to get him on the roster; Reeves parlayed that chance into an eight-year playing career. Years later, when Reeves was coaching the Denver Broncos, his training-camp roster included a rookie defensive back named Mike Nolan—and Reeves cut him. "I don't think Dick ever forgave me for that," Reeves later said, laughing. "He called me up after I cut Mike and said, 'Okay, I see how it is. I save you, and you cut my son?' He was joking, of course."

Dick Nolan took over as the 49ers head coach starting with the 1968 season, replacing Jack Christiansen, who had gone 7–7 the previous season. Nolan had helped build the 49ers into a perennial contender by the early 1970s when the team won three consecutive NFC West championships. Quarterback John Brodie was the MVP in 1970, the same season Nolan earned NFL Coach of the Year honors after going 10–3–1.

But even those glorious seasons ended in anguish when the 49ers finished one game short of the Super Bowl after the 1970 and 1971 seasons. "He was a class act, the kind of guy who stood by his word," offensive tackle Len Rohde said. "I know we didn't have any Super Bowl rings. We didn't win a championship. But some things are more important, and I think that was the case with Dick. He treated people honestly. He was straightforward and fair."

Krueger echoed those sentiments. "I played for him for six years, and they were the best six years of my football life," he said. "I just have a lot of respect for him. He was a decent man, just and fair. You can't say that about a lot of coaches."

Mike Nolan never enjoyed the success his father had. Taking over the team during a sustained low point in franchise history, his teams went 4–12, 7–9, 5–11, and 2–5 before he was fired midway through the 2008 season and replaced with Mike Singletary. Mike Nolan is most remembered as the 49ers coach, who tied his fortunes to quarterback Alex Smith, the No. 1 pick in the 2005 draft.

All along, the son tried to honor his father. When the NFL's contractual obligation to Reebok apparel thwarted Nolan's plan to wear a suit and tie on the sidelines —just as Dick Nolan had— Mike brokered a compromise: He had Reebok design his suit.

75 Jesse Sapolu

Jesse Sapolu was a team player all the way. "If individual awards were important to me," he said, "I would have signed up for tennis." Instead, the offensive lineman wound up with a grand slam of the NFL sort, winning four Super Bowls during a 49ers career that spanned 1983 to 1997.

Along the way Sapolu proved time and again that his unselfish approach wasn't just talk. For one thing he moved from center to guard without complaint in 1994 because he recognized that doing so might help the 49ers win another Super Bowl. (It did.) For another, Sapolu put his life on the line every time he took the field, revealing only after his playing days that he had a torn aortic heart valve that left him dangerously short of breath at times. Caused by rheumatic fever in his childhood, the condition also led to an enlargement of his heart that required two surgeries, including one during his playing days. That's why his 2012 autobiography is appropriately titled *I Gave My Heart to San Francisco*.

A symbol of grit and determination during an era dominated by more famous names, the feisty Sapolu began his NFL career as an afterthought. In 1983 the 49ers drafted him in the 11th round, usually the territory for training camp bodies and practice squad material. To put it another way, there were 61 offensive linemen taken in that NFL draft; Sapolu was the 53rd.

But the 6'4", 271-pound native of Western Samoa blossomed under the guidance of offensive line coach Bobb McKittrick. Both men embraced the science of the smash. The reason Sapolu could swap positions so seamlessly—he was a Pro Bowl player at center in '93 and at left guard in '94—was because he approached each task with the precision of a diamond cutter. "The best technician and most fundamentally sound lineman I have ever coached," McKittrick said. "Sapolu would have been selected to nine or 10 Pro Bowls if we did not move him around on the line."

The former University of Hawaii star started at left guard for the '88 champs and at center for the '89 champs. He switched back again after the '93 season even after getting his long overdue individual recognition. It was at the Pro Bowl in Hawaii that season that McKittrick and then-coach George Seifert approached Sapolu with a plan: They wanted Sapolu to go back to guard so that they could target New York Giants center Bart Oates in free agency. The switch had the added benefit of allowing the 49ers to fill the gap left behind by guard Guy McIntyre, who was headed to the Green Bay Packers as a free agent.

Sapolu, as usual, stonewalled his ego at the line of scrimmage. "Your family is asking, 'Why'd you do it?' Your friends are asking, 'Why'd you do it?' They're almost saying you're stupid for making [the move] because now you're in the Pro Bowl," Sapolu said. "But those people don't have to weigh the importance of the Pro Bowl compared to the Super Bowl. If our chances were hurt because I was selfish enough to stay, it would have been something lingering in my heart. It's thinking of that that made me willing to make the sacrifice."

Besides, Sapolu had bigger things to worry about, even though he kept them to himself. He was just four years old when he contracted rheumatic fever. The disease ripped a small hole in his heart valve. Because the valve failed to close properly, Sapolu's heart worked harder. The walls of his heart eventually grew larger, causing shortness of breath as he detailed in his book and in an interview with KNBR radio in 2012. "I would feel like I was drowning at times," Sapolu said.

The University of Hawaii monitored his condition throughout his college career, but the lineman wanted to keep his health status under wraps. The 49ers discovered it during a physical and kept close tabs on him as well, regularly dispatching him to experts at Stanford University Medical Center. As Sapolu detailed in his KNBR interview, he learned to take short breaths during times of exertion. Still some of those two-a-day training camp sessions under the burning sun in Rocklin, California, scared him. He sometimes prayed for his heart to calm down between one practice and the next. "When we were conditioning, I was afraid because I couldn't take a deep breath all the way through," he said. "I learned to take shorter breaths just to survive."

Considering the seemingly fragile nature of his health, his NFL durability is astounding. Sapolu appeared in 22 playoff games for the 49ers—one short of Jerry Rice's team record.

After retirement one of the NFL's greatest self-made (and self-less) players began teaching young players how to maximize their skills. Sapolu runs a Men in the Trenches academy for linemen. And on his website sapolumeninthetrenches.com, he uses the best possible phrase to describe the sacrifices he made to be part of the 49ers. "I would do it again," he writes, "in a heartbeat."

76 The Har-Bowl

A fan base accustomed to magical Super Bowl endings and confetti-covered parades barely knew how to deal with the frustration of coming up short. A day after the Baltimore Ravens beat the 49ers 34–31 in Super Bowl XLVII, the angst was so widespread that a local radio station asked listeners, "Would it have been better if the 49ers had not gone to the Super Bowl at all?"

That's how much it hurt when San Francisco's last-gasp drive stalled at the 5-yard line with two minutes remaining in New Orleans. The team had three chances at close range to pull off the kind of frenzied miracle the 49ers Faithful had come to expect. But there would be no Dwight Clark this time. No Joe Montana. No John Taylor. No John Candy.

Only heartbreak.

Quarterback Colin Kaepernick understood immediately that it wasn't supposed to end like this for the 49ers. After the game he was asked how long the loss would sting. "For the rest of my life," the 25-year-old said.

Billed as the Harbaugh Bowl because it pitted sibling head coaches against each other—John (Ravens) and Jim (49ers)—the family feud angle became a mere footnote by the time the crazy game reached its white-knuckled conclusion. The 49ers had been 5–0 in Super Bowls and aiming to tie the Pittsburgh Steelers for most rings by winning their sixth championship. They almost got there, too, except…well, except for a lot of things.

The 49ers were a mess in the early stages of the game, blowing assignments on defense such as when Jacoby Jones slipped past defensive back Chris Culliver for a 56-yard touchdown catch. There were gaffes on special teams, as Jones blazed through everyone to score on a 108-yard kickoff return. That helped the Ravens, led by quarterback and Super Bowl MVP Joe Flacco, build a 28–6 lead after the first play of the second half.

But then the Superdome had an electrical malfunction. The power went off without a flicker of warning, leaving the stadium in darkness for 34 minutes. When the lights finally came back on, the 49ers looked like a high-voltage machine again: Michael Crabtree's

31-yard touchdown catch made the score 28–13, Frank Gore's six-yard run made it 28–20, and David Akers' 34-yard field goal made it 28–23. "That's when it started to look like a football game," linebacker Ahmad Brooks said.

Had the 49ers actually completed the rally from a 22-point deficit, it would have been the largest comeback in Super Bowl history, surpassing 10-point comebacks by the Washington Redskins in Super Bowl XXII and the New Orleans Saints in Super Bowl XLIV.

Instead, players and fans were left wondering about five fateful yards. On first-and-goal from the 7, Kaepernick handed the ball to LaMichael James for a 2-yard gain. On second-and-goal from the 5, the quarterback threw an incomplete pass intended for Crabtree. He did the same thing on third down, too.

So on fourth-and-goal with the Super Bowl hanging in the balance, the quarterback scanned the Ravens and identified them in a Cover-0 defense—no safeties back and all the defenders at the line of scrimmage. Kaepernick called an audible to a fade to Crabtree, his go-to receiver.

But that pass fell incomplete, too, albeit with a lot of bumping and grabbing by Ravens cornerback Jimmy Smith. "A lot of contact," Crabtree said. "Had the ball been a little lower and given me a chance to make a play, I'm sure [a penalty] would have been called. It's frustrating. It was a game-winning touchdown. It makes you sad. It's the Super Bowl."

77 Joe Montana's Comeback

Known for his cool in the face of impossible odds, Joe Montana nearly surrendered on this one. Frustrated and feeling helpless,

Montana was close to calling it a career after a devastating back injury in the fall of 1986. "Honestly there were times I wanted to give up," Montana acknowledged years later.

Instead, to the surprise of no one, he engineered a stirring comeback. Montana capped an excruciating rehabilitation process by returning to the field on November 9, 1986. Montana completed 13-of-19 passes for 270 yards and three touchdowns to lead a 43–17 victory against the St. Louis Cardinals.

But it almost never happened.

While facing the Tampa Bay Buccaneers in the '86 season opener on September 7, Montana rolled out to his left. Just before going out of bounds, he twisted his body to make an off-balance throw. As he let go of the ball, he grabbed his back. Just like that, the career of the reigning Super Bowl MVP was at a crossroads. Doctors discovered that a ruptured disk was putting pressure on the sciatic nerve in his left leg. One told him that a comeback would be tough and that the rehab would be brutal. "[My wife] Jennifer was always trying to keep me calm about it," Montana said. "But football was something that I had been doing all my life, and it was going away."

Montana found this comeback much more difficult than—say, a two-touchdown deficit. The rehabilitation work was painful, and the progress was slow. Fortunately, he had a no-nonsense physical therapist who wouldn't let him feel sorry for himself. "When I was ready to give up, she would just start ridiculing me, trying to embarrass me so that I would work out," Montana said. "Whatever she could say, it didn't matter. She'd say, 'Oh, you're giving up after two Super Bowls? That's soooo courageous. You're soooo tough.' Because it was not an easy process back, learning how to walk again."

But he made it back. Montana trotted on to the Candlestick Park field in Week 10 and promptly connected on a trio of touchdown passes—all to Jerry Rice (45 yards, 40 yards, and 44 yards).

The crowd went berserk: Their hero had returned—even if he didn't exactly feel like Superman. "When I got back out there, I was probably 182 pounds at most," Montana said. "The wind blew, and I was moving."

In his second game back, he threw for 441 yards against the Washington Redskins. He was voted the AP Comeback Player of the Year in 1986. In retrospect, Montana finds it hard to believe he almost walked away. "You can't describe the excitement that comes from that game on Sunday," he said. "Whenever you hear someone say, 'Gosh, why doesn't he just retire?' Well, just go play the game one Sunday and be at that level. It's like a kid with candy. If he's never had candy, he doesn't have any idea what he's missing. The minute you give him candy, he wants more, right?"

78 See the 49ers Play Abroad

Before heading off to see the 49ers play at Wembley Stadium in 2010, longtime fan Jerry Cadagan and his wife, Kris, wondered how many other fans might make the trek. So the residents of tiny Sonora, California, enlisted the help of a few popular 49ers bloggers and extended a worldwide invitation: If you're heading for London, let's get together.

It resulted in a Red and Gold melting pot. Fans arrived from England, Italy, France, Ireland, Scotland, Sweden, Switzerland, and Germany—all of them speaking the same language (fluent Montanese.) About 90 international delegates crowded into Waxy O'Connor's pub to swap stories about the 49ers' past and present. "It was amazing to see so many people from so many different

Road Warriors

How do you make sure a team is ready for the pressure cooker of a hostile crowd? Turn up the heat. That's essentially what Bill Walsh did by moving 49ers training camp away from the gentle breezes of the Bay Area.

In 1981 Walsh moved camp to Sierra College in Rocklin, California, where the oppressive summer heat of the Sacramento Valley helped forge the 49ers' steel. "Bill Walsh was not someone who tolerated mental errors," running back Roger Craig said. "The heat is what kept us focused. When it's 105 degrees, and it's the hottest practice of the year, you don't want to start jumping offside."

The 49ers won their first Super Bowl that season.

And soon they would establish themselves as the greatest traveling show in the history of the NFL. At one point from 1988 to 1990, San Francisco won 18 consecutive road games. It's an NFL record that might never be broken. The only team to come within a Hail Mary was the New England Patriots, who won 12 straight from 2006 to 2008. The 49ers remain the kings of the road.

Craig understood that their talent was the biggest reason for the way his units dominated away from Candlestick Park. But he said the atmosphere at Rocklin certainly helped. The team trained there from 1981 to 1997, which is to say that all of their Super Bowl victories came while spending training camp in the heat. The 49ers relocated their training camp to the University of the Pacific in Stockton, California, from 1998 to 2002 before settling in for good at Santa Clara. "When you train at home, the tendency is to stay in a relaxed mood. It gets to be routine," Craig said. "You want to be somewhere where all you can do is focus on football. It gets you excited for the year."

places," Cadagan said. "You think of yourself as a faithful fan. And then you meet somebody from Sweden who gets up at 5 AM to watch the 49ers on their computer."

Some teams have a strong passing game. The 49ers have a strong passport game. Not only is owner and co-chairman John

York on the NFL's international committee, the team jumps at chances to play on the world's stage.

They have played 11 times internationally, including two regular-season games. Under York's direction the 49ers became the first team to play a regular-season game outside the borders of the United States. That happened on October 2, 2005 when the 49ers took on the Arizona Cardinals in front of an estimated 100,000 fans at Azteca Stadium in Mexico City.

The 49ers took another road trip—this time 5,371 miles—in 2010 when they headed to Wembley Stadium. The 49ers defeated the Denver Broncos 24–16 on Halloween in front of a sellout crowd of 83,941. They liked the experience so much that the team arranged to return to London for a game against the Jacksonville Jaguars on October 27, 2013. CEO Jed York said the 49ers enjoy playing the role of "ambassadors for the NFL." General manager Trent Baalke said, "Competing on an international stage is a great opportunity for our football team."

In the light of the 49ers' globetrotting ways, we checked in with Cadagan, a natural-born event organizer, to provide some advice for those looking to tag along. The retired lawyer and newsletter publisher said the key is to stay a few extra days. "Make sure it's not just about football," he said.

In 2010, for example, he and Kris flew from San Francisco to London's Heathrow Airport on Thursday in advance of the Sunday game. Then they stayed another three days for sightseeing, including jaunts to Paris, Stonehenge, Windsor Castle, and a night of theater with *Mama Mia* in London.

To secure game tickets, he used craigslist before leaving the U.S. to score club seats in block 242, row 12. Tickets are also available through 49ers.com or at (415) GO-49ERS. "Being a 49er fan doesn't mean you should limit your world travels to places you read about in *1,000 Places to See Before You Die*," Cadagan said. "Be creative and plan your own overseas trip and cheer on the Niners at the same time."

Cadagan was already thinking about another trip to London for the 49ers' 2013 game. His itinerary so far? "Do the town and then watch the Jaguars slink out of Wembley Stadium in fast retreat."

78 Alex Smith

On April 23, 2005, just a few minutes before commissioner Paul Tagliabue announced the year's No. 1 draft pick to a national television audience, coach Mike Nolan reached for the phone at the 49ers' Santa Clara offices and placed a call to the NFL draft headquarters in New York. "Are you ready to go to work?" Nolan asked.

"I'm ready to go to work," Alex Smith replied.

Little did the polite kid from the University of Utah know he was signing up for eight years of hard labor. Alex Smith's career in San Francisco turned out to be a soap opera of struggles, injuries, boos, benchings, and occasionally flickers of promise. "If you're a quarterback very long in this league," Smith said, "you'd better have thick skin."

By March 2013 when the 49ers traded him to the Kansas City Chiefs for a pair of draft picks, the San Francisco base remained deeply divided over Smith's legacy. Did the No. 1 pick fail the 49ers? Or did the 49ers fail the No. 1 pick? Smith played for four head coaches and seven offensive coordinators during a 49ers career that lasted from 2005 to 2012.

The first five seasons were the worst. He went 19–31 as a starter with a 72.1 quarterback rating and 51 touchdown passes against 53 interceptions. At his worst Smith looked mechanical and overmatched. His book smarts rarely translated to the playing field where the best quarterbacks thrive on instincts and natural reactions.

His final two years were the best. Smith went 19–5–1 with a 95.1 passer rating and 30 touchdown passes against 10 interceptions under coach Jim Harbaugh. At his peak Smith played with efficient precision, having learned how to move the chains with high-percentage throws while avoiding turnovers. Smith once went a franchise-record 249 consecutive passes without an interception, shattering the old mark held by Steve Young (184).

Ultimately, all it got Smith was one last benching and a ticket out of town. "I feel like I have a lot of football ahead of me," he said on his way out the door. "I don't feel like this is my last opportunity. I feel like there's more out there for me."

In the final tally, Smith played 80 games. Only four 49ers quarterbacks played more: John Brodie (201), Joe Montana (167), Young (150), and Y.A. Tittle (112). Smith lost his 49ers job for the final time during the 2012 season when the concussion he sustained against the St. Louis Rams opened the door for Colin Kaepernick, who led the team to Super Bowl XLVII.

In a way it was a fitting finale for Smith, because from the start 49ers fans were often in search of somebody else. The 2005 NFL Draft also offered Aaron Rodgers, a lifelong 49ers fan who grew up in Chico, California, and played just down the road at the University of California at Berkeley. The 49ers considered Rodgers but chose Smith over him. Rodgers slid all the way to No. 24 where the Green Bay Packers nabbed him as the heir apparent to future Hall of Famer Brett Favre. After a three-year apprenticeship, Rodgers was on his way to becoming the 2010 Super Bowl MVP and a full-fledged star.

Smith, in contrast, was thrown to the wolves in Week 5 of his rookie season when Nolan decided the best time for the kid to make his debut was against quarterback Peyton Manning and the Indianapolis Colts' league-leading defense. Smith responded by

The K.C. QB Connection

When the 49ers traded Alex Smith to Kansas City, the quarterback was following in the well-worn footsteps of other San Francisco passers who went from the West Coast city to the Heartland town.

1993: Joe Montana, safety David Whitmore, and a 1994 third-round pick were traded to Kansas City for the Chiefs' first-round pick in 1993. After trading down twice, the 49ers used the first-round pick to select defensive tackle Dana Stubblefield, the 1997 Defensive Player of the Year.

1994: Steve Bono was traded to Kansas City for the Chiefs' 1995 fourth-round pick.

1997: Elvis Grbac left the 49ers to sign as a free agent with Kansas City.

2013: Alex Smith was traded to Kansas City for a second-round pick in 2013 and a conditional pick (second or third round) in the 2014 draft.

Honorable mention: Quarterback Steve DeBerg, who began his career with the 49ers in 1977, eventually became a member of the Chiefs in 1988 with stops in Denver and Tampa Bay in between.

completing 9-of-23 passes for 74 yards and four interceptions in a 28–3 loss. He would throw one touchdown and 11 interceptions during the 2005 season.

After starting the year 2–1 in 2007, Smith sustained a separated shoulder against the Seattle Seahawks. He missed just two games before becoming entangled with the coaching staff over the way they handled his rehabilitation. Nolan questioned the severity of the injury and wondered whether the quarterback was tough enough to play through pain. Smith, though, would eventually require multiple surgeries.

Even when healthy, Smith never came close to matching the exploits of fellow No. 1 picks like Manning, John Elway, or Troy Aikman. But he still managed to leave his mark on the 49ers simply by enduring whatever was thrown his way with grace and class. "Everybody underestimates what he's gone through," former quarterback and NFL MVP Rich Gannon said. "Take Peyton Manning and give him five different offensive coordinators, a couple of different head coaches, five different quarterback coaches, and see how he does."

Smith was a bad fit with Nolan and the next head coach, Mike Singletary. Smith and Singletary screamed at each other in a nationally televised primetime game against the Philadelphia Eagles on October 10, 2010. But the most painful setback of Smith's career was being benched by Harbaugh, who had been his staunchest ally. By the time Smith recovered from that November 11, 2012 concussion, the coach had handed the job to Kaepernick for good.

Smith watched the final game of his 49ers career—and the biggest game of his life—from the bench. "I'm not going to lie about any of that," Smith said. "It's been tough at times for sure, tough to accept, tough to watch, but we're in the Super Bowl, and this has been an amazing experience. It's a great team. I love being a part of it. I have said it before: It's bittersweet."

80 Ken Willard

As a young baseball star, Ken Willard hit what is believed to be the longest home run in the history of the University of North Carolina. When he connected off a smoke-throwing left-hander from Cornell in 1964, the ball cleared the fence, bounced off the street, conked into a building—and is somehow still rolling into legend. "That's one of the advantages of getting older," Willard said with a laugh when I called him in 2013. "The home run is getting longer."

The best estimate puts the blast at 525 feet, which explains why teams like the Boston Red Sox, Pittsburgh Pirates, and New York Yankees tried to get Willard's name on the dotted line long before the 49ers came along. Fortunately for San Francisco fans, Willard chose to become a battering ram instead of a batter, earning four trips to the Pro Bowl as a fullback during an NFL career that spanned from 1965 to 1974.

Though underappreciated—then and now—Willard remains near the top of the 49ers' all-time lists. At of the start of the 2013 season, he ranked fourth in rushing yards, third in touches (catches plus carries), and sixth in yards from scrimmage. And, of course, he remained a home-run threat: Willard's 61 career touchdowns trail only Jerry Rice, Terrell Owens, Joe Perry, Roger Craig, and Frank Gore in team annals. "I was a pretty good receiver out of the backfield," Willard said. "That helped a lot."

Willard's versatility helped explain how he wound up with the 49ers in the first place. Yankees scout Jack White envisioned him as a first baseman and pressured him to sign with the Richmond Virginians, a Yankees farm team. The Detroit Lions envisioned him as a running back and got him to sign his name on a contract. To prevent Willard from choosing the rival AFL over the NFL, the Lions arranged to give him a $25,000 bonus, a $25,000 salary for his second year, and $27,500 for each of the two seasons if he lasted until the 11th spot in the 1965 draft. "So in 1964, I had actually signed a contract to play for the Detroit Lions," Willard said. "I met a guy in a hotel in Richmond and signed a contract, which you weren't supposed to do. But at that time, the NFL and AFL were fighting each other. And you would sign a league contract. So I signed an NFL contract, hoping I'd be drafted by Detroit."

So when the 49ers, who had the No. 2 pick that year, called to talk money, Willard had a rare commodity for a college player: leverage. This was long before smooth-talking agents, but the kid knew how to play hardball in more ways than one. "I was telling all the teams that wanted me—if it was to my advantage—'I'm not going to play for you. I'm going to play baseball,'" he said. "I was kind of bluffing my way through." Willard was still playing poker on the Friday before the draft. And this is how he remembers his call that day with 49ers president Lou Spadia.

> Spadia: "What is it going to take for you to play for the 49ers?"
> Willard: "What are you willing to give me?"
> Spadia: "Anything but the Golden Gate Bridge."
> Willard: "I want you to give me double the bonus Detroit gave me."
> Spadia: "It's yours."
> Willard: "I'm yours."

The payoff for both was immediate. Willard made the Pro Bowl as a rookie, teaming with running back John David Crow and quarterback John Brodie to power the NFL's top-ranked offense. Willard made the Pro Bowl in 1966, 1968, and 1969, too. Long before Craig popularized catching the ball out of the backfield in the West Coast Offense, Willard showed unusually reliable hands for a 6'1", 219-pound fullback. He caught at least 30 passes in five seasons, including 42 receptions for 351 yards in 1966. The team's overall success would come later. Following the coaching change from Jack Christiansen to Dick Nolan in 1968, they won three consecutive NFC West titles starting in 1970. But like so many others from that era, Willard still cringes at the annual disappointment against the Dallas Cowboys in the playoffs. The worst was the 1972 divisional round game when Dallas roared back to win 30–28 in a game the 49ers had led 21–6. "That probably broke us open more than anything else," Willard said.

Willard was an ironman in San Francisco. By the time he was traded to St. Louis in 1974, he was beginning to feel the wear and tear of all those carries. He sustained the first major injury of his career at Candlestick Park, of all places, when the Cardinals

The Case for Ken Willard's Induction

Sometimes the smartest thing is to simply cede the floor. Let's get out of the way and let somebody more qualified do the talking. The best summation of the 49ers running back's place in NFL history comes from his son, Scott Willard, who sat down at a keyboard in the winter of 2010 in a fit of frustration. Floyd Little of the Denver Broncos had just been elected to the Pro Football Hall of Fame, and the news was bittersweet to the offspring of the 49ers' four-time Pro Bowler.

Little amassed 6,323 rushing yards and 54 total touchdowns and was headed for enshrinement. Willard amassed 6,105 rushing yards and 62 total touchdowns but wasn't even on the radar screen. So Scott Willard switched on his computer and began typing away. This is the note he fired off to the *San Francisco Chronicle*.

Kudos to Floyd Little for finally making it into the NFL Hall of Fame because those of us who grew up in that era vividly remember him as one of the great running backs during the 1960–70s. Thirty-five years is a long time and I'm glad that he is finally able to enjoy the moment and be a young man again reliving all of those memories. As I sat with my father watching the Super Bowl, I knew exactly what was going through his mind as we discussed the life-changing accomplishment of being enshrined in Canton. My dad, Ken Willard, wore #40 and played at Kezar and Candlestick Park for nine years from 1965–1973 & for the St. Louis Cardinals for one year. He had a career very similar career to Mr. Little. My dad, too, is worthy of consideration for enshrinement—as is the great John Brodie, who retired with only Y.A. Tittle and Johnny Unitas ahead of him on the all-time passing list.

Ken Willard retired 35 years ago as the eighth all-time rusher after his knees finally called it quits. In that same year, Floyd Little retired as the NFL's seventh all-time leading rusher.

Willard is currently 66th all-time, four spots behind Little.

You will still find my dad's name in the top 15 of San Francisco's all-time rushing, receiving and scoring lists. He is the last man from his era with his level of accomplishments at his position standing outside the gates to Canton. All of his similar peers have their busts and golden jackets. My dad admired Jim Brown and wanted to be like Jim Taylor in 1965, when he was drafted No. 2 overall—ahead of Gale Sayers, Dick Butkus and Roger Staubach—all members of Canton. My dad also ranks statistically ahead of many enshrined players like Hugh McElhenny, Ollie Matson, Marion Motley, Lenny Moore and the great Gale Sayers. I fondly remember reading that Ray Nitschke once pontificated that Ken Willard was the hardest hitting back in the league.

Comparing Mr. Little's career to my father's is like looking at a mirror. Mr. Little was named to the Pro Bowl five times and my father to four. They were also similar in other categories. In the following examples, Mr. Little's stats are listed first for clarity—carries (1,641 to 1,622), rushing yards (6,323 to 6,105), rushing touchdowns (43 to 45), receiving touchdowns (9 to 17), rushing average (3.9 to 3.8), and yards from scrimmage (8,289 to 8,741).

My dad is tied with Paul Hornung and others at 118th on the NFL's all-time rushing TD; Mr. Little is 173rd.

The 49ers have many players deserving of enshrinement and it is unfortunate that all these old-timers have such an uphill battle in gaining entrance into this esteemed club. San Francisco needs to get behind these legends and help push them forward...Time erases memories and legacies. My father would be thoroughly embarrassed by this note, but I know what it means to him and the HOF is the pinnacle. My hope is that these deserving players have the opportunity to enjoy that moment while they are still with us.

—Scott Willard, February 2010

returned to play there on October 6, 1974. "I left more than my heart in San Francisco," he said. "I left my knee."

That was really the beginning of the end of his career, and he retired soon thereafter. These days he works in the insurance industry, a profession he embarked on as an offseason job while still in the NFL. "I've continued to do that and have enjoyed it," he said. "Nothing is like football, but it's a good way to spend the rest of my life."

81 Keith Fahnhorst

Because he had been a terrific pass-catching tight end for the University of Minnesota, moving to offensive tackle in the NFL was tough for Keith Fahnhorst to swallow—in more ways than one. "I ate until it hurt and then I tried to eat a little more," Fahnhorst told 49ers.com. "I ate anything that was fattening, and it was a battle."

Eventually, that key juncture—let's call it a fork in the road—would pay off. Fahnhorst gained the bulk required to play the new position. Later he'd get some added heft from the two Super Bowl rings he won during his 1974 to 1987 career. Fahnhorst played 193 games at tackle—more than any 49ers lineman besides Len Rohde (208). The starter for a pair of 2–14 stinkers, he blocked for some lousy teams and he paved the way for some of the greatest Niners moments of all time.

And to think it happened by a fluke.

Fahnhorst had dreams of dancing in the end zone himself when the 49ers took him with the 35th overall pick of the 1974 draft. But when a labor dispute prevented veterans from joining camp that year, 49ers head coach Dick Nolan asked the rookie to play a little offensive line until the vets came back. Fahnhorst cringed a bit, wondering if he'd ever see his tight end position again. His wife had a more dramatic reaction. "Oh God," she said, "you're going to get fat."

Fahnhorst recalled his transformation from making catches to paving the way for The Catch during an extended interview with the team's website. "I'd like to say it was me who got the franchise turned around," he joked. "But it had a little more to do with Bill [Walsh] and obviously Joe [Montana] and Dwight [Clark] and the rest of them."

But Fahnhorst did his part. Listed at 6'6", 273 pounds, he became a dominant force as the 49ers right tackle for more than a decade. He was a first-team All-Pro in 1984—arguably the 49ers' finest season—and was also a key figure in the locker room. "Keith Fahnhorst was a great leader. I loved him," running back Roger Craig said. "He was like the team spokesman."

And Fahnhorst did receive his moment in the sun. In 1975 against the Los Angeles Rams, the second-year player got to show off his soft hands by snaring a pass from quarterback Steve Spurrier. His final totals: one catch, one yard, one heck of a career.

82 Steve Wallace

Steve Wallace helped open eyes about the importance of the blind side. The 49ers' left tackle for the better part of a decade was in charge of making sure Joe Montana and Steve Young stayed upright. Plenty of other maulers did the dirty work over the years, but Wallace was the first to be compensated like a star, landing a five-year, $10.7 million extension—unheard of for a tackle in the late-1980s. "Joe had won two Super Bowls," Wallace told *The Birmingham News*, "so the 49ers had to pay for him and his insurance policy—me."

In essence, Wallace was cashing in on Bill Walsh's frustration. The 1987 season had all the makings of a Super Bowl year. The 49ers went 13–2 during that strike-shortened season and entered the playoffs as the NFC's No. 1 seed. More than that, they entered the postseason on a roll, having won their final three regular-season games by a combined score of 124–7. But a not-so-funny-thing happened on the way to the championship: The Minnesota Vikings upset the 49ers 36–24 in the divisional round because Vikings pass rusher Chris Doleman made life miserable for Montana and later Young.

Doleman, who would later play for the 49ers, pushed around left tackle Bubba Paris, registering two sacks of Montana and knocking him down several other times. That ticked off Walsh, who was sick of seeing his Super Bowl plans derailed by edge rushers like Doleman and (in previous years) Lawrence Taylor. So Walsh made a decision that would forever underscore the importance of pass protectors.

Paris was out, and the smaller, more fleet of foot Wallace, who had been splitting time over his first two seasons, was in. He started every game in 1988, including a 34–9 playoff victory against the Vikings as the 49ers went on to win their third Super Bowl title. "I can remember a lot of parts of that ride, going against talented defensive ends like Chris Doleman, Richard Dent, Kevin Greene, Lawrence Taylor, and all of the other All-Pros. I just found a way to shut them out, one by one," Wallace told 49ers.com.

Wallace, who was 6'4" with 285 pounds and a mean streak, mostly handled opposing pass rushers all by himself. "The one thing I started noticing was that Bill Walsh started leaving out the tight end and the running back to help me and kept them on their own assignments. His thing was, 'You block that guy,' and nothing else was said about it," Wallace said. "The funny thing about it in

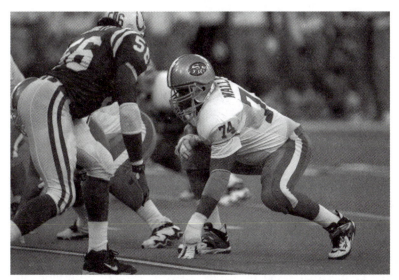

A great pass blocker, offensive tackle Steve Wallace was known for his double helmet-looking, Procap headgear, which provided cushioning to protect against concussions.

looking back was that most teams had to have that extra protector over there, but I didn't know any better."

Drafted in the fourth round (101st overall) in 1986, Wallace first made a name for himself by blocking for Bo Jackson at Auburn. During 12 seasons in the NFL, he was named All-Pro three times (1992 to 1994) and won three Super Bowl championships ('88, '89, and '94.)

He was doing his homework in advance of his final title, Super Bowl XXIX, when he heard a former rival make an on-air prediction. "I heard [former New York Giants quarterback] Phil Simms saying, 'The San Diego Chargers should beat the San Francisco 49ers, and this is the reason they should beat them right here: Leslie O'Neal, the [five-time] Pro Bowler should dominate Steve Wallace,'" Wallace told 49ers.com. "I had about 10 phone calls immediately asking, 'Did you see that?' I'm sitting in my room by myself thinking, *My God.* But I believed in myself and I knew that I'd be ready to battle."

Suffice to say, Wallace took Simms' crystal ball and smashed it to pieces. The 49ers blasted the San Diego Chargers 49–26, and O'Neal was a nonfactor.

Besides stuffing pass rushers and opening holes, Wallace tried to open minds. Because a series of concussions threatened to force him into early retirement, he experimented with a Procap helmet. Essentially, it was a regular helmet but fortified with Styrofoam. It looked like he was wearing a helmet on top of his helmet. "It was a double helmet, and it was heavy," Wallace told *The News*. "But that thing was like having a rubber cushion."

With increased scrutiny on the long-term effects of concussions, Wallace urged the NFL to explore the idea of wearing the helmet that saved his career 20 years earlier. "Why not take a look at this? The whole idea of the Procap is what NASCAR uses to cushion walls at races," he said. "Why not have the extra protection? Guys are dying earlier; guys are losing their memory. Something needs to be done."

83 Keena Turner

Keena Turner likes to remind people that he won only four Super Bowls. *Only* four Super Bowls? "You know what's really interesting? I spend more time thinking about the ones that got away," Turner said, smiling wide. "We should have won six."

Lest you accuse the former Pro Bowl linebacker of being greedy, understand that such mentality explains why the Bill Walsh–era teams won all those other rings in the first place. Satisfaction was not to be tolerated. Walsh banished it from the premises. "There was this never-ending pursuit of perfection," said

Turner, who played for the 49ers from 1980 to 1990. "Because perfection was something you could never attain. You could never be satisfied, and that meant you were always motivated because it never was enough."

Turner didn't understand Walsh's philosophy at first. Heck, he didn't know who Walsh *was* at first. On the day that the 49ers selected the Purdue star in the second round of the 1980 draft, it was linebackers coach Norb Hecker who called to give Turner the news. Turner was so elated he put on a 49ers cap and danced around campus. There was only one problem. "When I hung up the phone, I thought Norb Hecker was the head coach of the 49ers," he said. "That shows you how much I knew about the team and what was going on."

Turner soon learned exactly who was in charge. That was driven home during a seminal moment late in his 1980 rookie season. The 49ers were in the midst of an eight-game losing streak when Walsh summoned Turner and two other young players into his office. None were stars. They were mostly special teams players trying to establish themselves. Walsh's message was simple: "I need more." He did not elaborate on what "more" meant. You either understood or you didn't. "One of the players in that meeting was released a week later," Turner said. "I remember the impact that had on me as a young player. It was a realization about what it took in terms of effort and dedication and production and commitment. That stuck with me for the rest of my career, and I would always reference that meeting when I went about preparing every year."

By the next season, the 49ers began to truly understand what "more" meant. The influx of young talent—Ronnie Lott, Eric Wright, Carlton Williamson, Dwight Hicks—along with the emergence of Joe Montana propelled the 49ers to their first Super Bowl championship. Turner also helped the 49ers win titles in '84, '88, and '89. All along, Turner embraced the notion of chasing perfection. In 1984 he made the Pro Bowl team. He had four interceptions that season, tying a team record for most by a non-defensive back (shared by fellow linebackers Jim Fahnhorst in '86 and Frank Nunley in '74). Turner finished his career after 153 games. Among 49ers linebackers only Matt Hazeltine (176 from 1955 to 1968) played in more contests.

When I asked Turner to pick his favorite Super Bowl memory, it should come as no surprise that he fixated on something he should have done better. "The simple answer is to say, 'Winning the four Super Bowls is a great memory,'" he said. "But what haunts me is that I was almost the goat. In Super Bowl XVI, I missed a play."

On a third-and-short late in the third quarter against the Cincinnati Bengals, Turner didn't hear the play call and was still on the sideline when Pete Johnson rumbled for a first down against the 49ers' 10-man defense. It could have been worse. Johnson only picked up two yards, and the 49ers promptly let Turner off the hook with the greatest goal-line stand in Super Bowl history. "What if they had scored on that play?" Turner said. "My career would have been over!"

Turner calls his association with the 49ers a "30-year love affair." And there's no end in sight. Having played his last snap in 1990, he remains an integral part of the organization as the vice president of football affairs. Turner works closely with the team's alumni, a role he learned under the tutelage of popular former alumni director R.C. Owens. "Hopefully you also walk away better prepared for the rest of your life," Turner said. "Whether that's financially or emotionally or mentally, you want to walk away with a skill set that helps you lead a productive life. Hopefully we care about other people. We take care of our families, and then hopefully you leave some kind of mark."

84 J.D. Smith

Because of his speed and strength, J. D. Smith could play almost anywhere on the football field. For a while that was his problem. Smith wanted to carry the ball. But before he could land that full-time gig, he played defensive back...kick returner...linebacker... and safety. And after all that, he became one of the best running backs in 49ers franchise history.

Dubbed the "Cinderella Workhorse" by longtime team historian Donn Sinn, the patient Smith began his career with the Chicago Bears before playing for the 49ers from 1956 to 1964. The 6'1", 205-pounder made Pro Bowls in 1959 and 1962 and was the second 49ers rusher after Joe Perry to register a 1,000-yard season.

Smith still ranks highly on the franchise's all-time lists, including sixth in rushing yards with 5,535. He is tied with six other players for most rushing touchdowns in a season, scoring 10 in 1959. Smith's path, though, was as long and winding as a broken-field run. Drafted in the 15th round by Chicago in 1955, the college fullback figured he would receive an opportunity as a runner after showcasing his stuff at North Carolina A&T.

But after spending the 1955 season fulfilling his military service, he arrived for his first NFL training camp in 1956 to find a backfield overflowing with talent. The Bears needed another runner like they needed a hole in the line. Chicago already had Willie Galimore, Bobby Watkins, J.C. Caroline, Perry Jeter, and Rick Casares. That year the Bears would lead the NFL in total offense, rushing offense, and rushing touchdowns. Smith's dreams of running were dashed; "Papa" George Halas moved him to defensive back.

As Sinn recounts in his terrific biography of Smith for *49ers Magazine*, the keen eye of 49ers head coach Frankie Albert might have rescued the runner from the brink of obscurity. Four games into the '56 season, the Bears tried to sneak Smith through the waiver wire, so that they could put him on the taxi squad. Instead, Albert spotted the name and placed a call. And as soon as Smith heard the magic words—*The 49ers will look at you as a ball carrier*—Smith was ready to pack his bags and head west. The franchise sealed the deal on November 15, 1956. To make room for him on the roster, Bill "Tiger" Johnson retired as a player and joined the 49ers' coaching staff. (Johnson would later be known as the coach who got the Cincinnati Bengals head coaching job over Bill Walsh, but that's another story.)

Even with the 49ers, though, Smith had to wait. By the time he arrived for his first practice in '56, the team's secondary was in such dire straits that Smith was called upon to play five games on defense. He had zero carries. In 1957 Smith played 12 more games on defense—and had zero carries. But he also received a chance to show what he could do with the ball in his hands, finishing third in the NFL with a 26.3-yard average on kickoff returns.

Smith finally kicked down the door and ran through it in 1958. After being eased in sparingly at running back, he dazzled in Week 11 against the Green Bay Packers, racking up 113 rushing yards on seven carries that included an 80-yard touchdown jaunt. It was the 49ers' longest run of the season.

By 1959 coach Red Hickey designated Smith as the left half-back alongside fullback Joe Perry, switching Hugh McElhenny to flanker. Smith blossomed into an NFL star that season, rushing for 1,036 yards to finish second in the league behind Jim Brown. He topped the 100-yard mark in five games, averaged 5.0 yards per carry, and registered 10 touchdowns.

For five consecutive seasons (1959 to 1963), Smith would be the 49ers' leading ground gainer. He was fast, he was powerful, and, of course, he showed tremendous patience.

85 Show Me the Money

Accounts differ regarding what former 49ers strong safety Tim McDonald actually said to inspire one of the most repeated lines in Hollywood history. But everyone knows the final result. In the 1996 blockbuster *Jerry Maguire*, fictional receiver Rod Tidwell (played by Cuba Gooding Jr.) tells his agent to "Show me the money!"

In 2005 the American Film Institute ranked it as the 25th greatest movie quote of all time. "Show me the money!" checked in just ahead of Mae West's "Why don't you come up sometime and see me?"

Cameron Crowe, the writer/director of *Jerry Maguire*, said the Tidwell line came from following around McDonald, who was a free agent in 1993. "He was actually at an owners' meeting to be paraded through the lobby to get his price up because he was a free agent," Crowe told the *Toronto Sun* in 1996. "He said, 'I've got a wife and I've got kids and I've been beaten up for five years here in Phoenix and now I'm a free agent. Show me the money.'"

McDonald's representative at the time, superagent Leigh Steinberg, whose own life helped provide the framework for the movie's title character, said McDonald's original line was much more subtle. "Cameron was with us at the 1993 NFL meetings in Palm Desert, [California,] and we were showing Tim off to some team executives, hoping that someone would take a liking to him and want to bid for him," the agent told *Sports Hollywood*. "I was walking him around, showing him off to the teams because he was quite tall for a safety." (A very similar scene takes place in the movie.)

"So then Cameron was in Tim's room one night, asking him what he was looking for in the process. CNN's *Money Line* was on the TV in the background, and Tim answered 'the money.' Now, Tim meant a lot more than cash. He meant respect and a home and a whole lot of values beyond a salary, but he gestured to the screen and Cameron laughed and wrote the line, 'Show me the money.'"

McDonald's version is that he uttered the immortal phrase mostly out of exasperation. After six years with the Cardinals, he was shopping for a new team. Prospective employers kept skirting the salary issue by showing off their training sites, offices, and other amenities. "Finally I leaned over to my agent and said," McDonald recounted for *San Francisco Chronicle* columnist Gwen Knapp in 1998, "'At some point, somebody's going to have to show us the money.'"

However he said it, it paid off for both him and the team. The 49ers signed the talented and heady defensive back to a five-year, $12.5 million deal that made him the highest-paid defensive back in league history. McDonald responded by making the Pro Bowl three more times (for a total of six by the time he retired after the 1999 season). He fortified the San Francisco defense to match its already potent offense, helping the 49ers defeat their playoff nemesis, the Dallas Cowboys, en route to winning Super Bowl XXIX.

Far from the brash and emotional Tidwell character of cinema, McDonald was a man of balanced temperament. One of his greatest assets was his intellect, which allowed him to read opposing defenses. He wasn't exactly greedy either. During his first season in San Francisco, he donated $22,000 to the Boys and Girls Clubs of the Bay Area—$2,000 for every 49ers victory. "In other words, he is the antithesis of the Hollywood character," Knapp wrote.

Drafted out of USC in the second round (34th overall) by the St. Louis Cardinals in 1987, McDonald arrived in San Francisco with the reputation as a steady playmaker. He registered 40 interceptions and 16 fumble recoveries in his career.

Given his on-field smarts, it's no surprise that he found a second career in coaching. His stops included a distinguished tenure as the head coach at his alma mater, Edison High in Fresno, California, and one season as the secondary coach at Fresno State. The New York Jets signed him as their defensive backfield coach for the 2013 season.

As for the fictional Tidwell, that snippet of dialogue has continued to shadow Cuba Gooding Jr. like a shut-down defender. On the DVD commentary for *Jerry Maguire*, Gooding says: "That line has haunted me ever since. I can be at a funeral, and in the back you'll hear some [jerk] go, 'Show me the money.'"

86 49ers-Giants Rivalry

Because his hand gleams with three Super Bowl rings, it's easy for Roger Craig to wave away the ghosts. So the answer to the question is "No." He's not haunted by his infamous fumble against the New York Giants in the 1990 NFC Championship Game at Candlestick Park. "It was never anything I worried about," Craig said. "I had too many other great plays to think about."

Such is the nature of the ferocious 49ers-Giants rivalry, a heavyweight slugfest, in which dominance sometimes changed hands in an instant. At the rivalry's peak, the teams' playoff series launched four Super Bowl champions over a 10-season span (from 1981 to 1990).

Through 2013 the teams had met eight times in the postseason to tie the NFL mark for the most playoff showdowns. But the frequency only tells a fraction of the story. The games tended to be high-drama epics fraught with peril and animosity. "We had a great rivalry back then, and those were some hard-fought games," Craig said. "They didn't like us, and we didn't like them."

In a matchup of two legendary players who faced each other repeatedly during the playoffs, Giants linebacker Lawrence Taylor bears down on quarterback Joe Montana. (AP Images)

Here is a chronological recap of one of the NFL's greatest playoff rivalries.

January 3, 1982: 49ers 38, Giants 24 at Candlestick Park, divisional round

The 49ers hadn't made the playoffs since 1972, but that was nothing compared to the Giants' last playoff appearance in 1963. In his first career postseason game, Joe Montana gave a glimpse of the magic to come, completing 20-of-31 passes for 304 yards and two touchdowns, including a 58-yarder to Freddie Solomon.

The Giants, whose coaching staff included assistants Bill Parcells, Bill Belichick, and Romeo Crennel, managed to climb to within 24–17 after three quarters. But the 49ers iced it on Ronnie Lott's 20-yard interception return for a touchdown. "That was the one that started the rivalry, the hatred," former Giants linebacker Carl Banks, a rookie that season, told SI.com. "And I say that in loving terms. Those 49ers, those guys on the West Coast, they were so good that you hated them. And it started because there was a different type of arrogance about them. They were kind of finesse, but they also didn't back down."

December 29, 1984: 49ers 21, Giants 10 at Candlestick Park, divisional round

The Giants, now coached by Parcells, were still no match, at least not this season. The 49ers went 15–1 during the regular season and were en route to their second Super Bowl title. In this one Montana threw touchdown passes to Dwight Clark and Russ Francis for a 14–0 lead.

The Giants pulled to within 14–10 when linebacker Harry Carson intercepted a Montana pass and returned it 14 yards for a touchdown. But Joe Cool answered with a 29-yard scoring strike to Freddie Solomon, making it 21–10 for the final score. There was no more scoring as the second half turned into a defensive struggle on a muddy field.

December 29, 1985: Giants 17, 49ers 3 at the Meadowlands, wild-card round

The 49ers sneaked into the 1985 playoffs by winning five of their last six to finish 10–6, but that express train ran into a brick wall in the wild-card round. Giants running back Joe Morris dashed for 141 yards on 28 carries while, in a rarity, the 49ers' big guns went silent.

Montana was sacked four times, lost a fumble, and threw an interception. Jerry Rice had just four catches for 45 yards. And Craig, coming off his 1,000/1,000 (rushing yards/receiving yards) season had only 23 yards rushing and 18 receiving. A 21-yard field goal by Ray Wersching represented the 49ers' only score.

January 4, 1987: Giants 49, 49ers 3 at the Meadowlands, divisional round

The most lopsided playoff loss of the Bill Walsh/Joe Montana era hurt in more ways than one. Jim Burt, New York's brutish nose tackle who would later play for the 49ers, knocked Montana out of the game in the second quarter with a concussion. Adding insult to injury, linebacker Lawrence Taylor intercepted the pass Montana threw as Burt crashed in and returned it 34 yards for a touchdown to make it 28–3.

Montana had come back from midseason back surgery, but this time he was done after Burt's blow knocked him unconscious. "It was clean," Burt said, "but I don't feel good about it." *The New York Times* ranked the game No. 3 in its 2009 countdown of the Giants' greatest moments at the Meadowlands.

January 20, 1991: Giants 15, 49ers 13 at Candlestick Park, NFC Championship

This is among the most painful defeats in 49ers playoff history as San Francisco appeared en route to keeping its three-peat hopes alive. They held a 13–12 lead late in the fourth quarter. Instead, Craig fumbled as the 49ers were trying to grind out the clock, giving New York one last chance with 2:36 remaining. The Giants' seven-play drive ended with Matt Bahr blasting the winning 42-yard field goal as time expired.

Craig, though, said he's never looked back. "It was just one play," the four-time Pro Bowler said. "That's part of the game. It wasn't meant to be. Joe [Montana] got hurt. The defense couldn't stop them. There's never one play where you win or lose. You win and lose as a team."

In the fourth quarter, Giants defensive end Leonard Marshall blasted Montana from the blind side. The hit, which Montana has called one of the hardest of his career, bruised his sternum and stomach, injured his ribs, and broke his hand. As a result this game represented the last start for Montana in a 49ers uniform. Steve Young would assume the reins for the rest of the game and Montana's career.

January 15, 1994: 49ers 44, Giants 3 at Candlestick Park, divisional round

The 49ers lost three out of their last four in 1993 to finish the regular season 10–6, but they rebounded to pummel the Giants in their playoff opener and led 23–3 by halftime. Ricky Watters scored five touchdowns and ran for 118 yards, and Steve Young picked apart the Giants secondary by connecting on 17-of-22 passes for 226 yards. The 49ers intercepted two of Phil Simms' passes and limited the Giants to 41 rushing yards.

January 5, 2003: 49ers 39, Giants 38 at 3Com Park, wild-card round

In one of the wackiest games in NFL history, the 49ers trailed by as much as 38–14 largely because they had no answer for Giants receiver Amani Toomer, who caught three touchdown passes. New York held its 24-point margin with four minutes to play in the third quarter, and the Giants started celebrating a bit too early. "Oh, they talked so much trash," former 49ers center Jeremy Newberry recalled.

Instead, the 49ers roared back behind Jeff Garcia, who kept finding receivers Terrell Owens and Tai Streets to take a 39–38 lead. But the drama was just beginning. With six seconds left in the game, New York long snapper Trey Junkin botched the snap on a 40-yard field goal try. The holder, Matt Allen, had the wherewithal to heave a desperation pass in the general direction of anybody.

The officials correctly flagged the Giants for having an ineligible man downfield but missed the pass interference committed by 49ers defensive end Chike Okeafor, who had hauled Rich Seubert to the ground. (The NFL later issued a statement acknowledging a botched call. The offsetting penalties should have meant that the down was replayed.)

The nuttiest thing? Junkin had spent his entire career trying to raise awareness about the value of having a reliable long snapper. "And he did it," 49ers veteran long snapper Brian Jennings said, tongue in cheek. "A spectacular job of it. He threw himself on the grenade. That brought a lot more recognition to the position."

January 22, 2012: Giants 20, 49ers 17 (OT) at Candlestick Park, NFC Championship

The 49ers let another Super Bowl trip slide through their fingers as they led 14–10 in the third quarter before things went hauntingly awry. Giants kicker Lawrence Tynes drilled a 31-yard field goal in overtime. But he did so only after return man Kyle

Ricky Watters' High Five

In the days leading up to an NFC playoff game against the New York Giants on January 15, 1994, running back Ricky Watters kept his yap shut. With all the attention on Giants' star rusher Rodney Hampton, the normally talkative Watters promised he'd let his play speak on his behalf.

Then he answered with a roar.

Watters scored five touchdowns to lead the 49ers to a 44–3 demolition at Candlestick Park. "Everybody was saying Rodney Hampton was going to come in here and control this game," said teammate Dexter Carter, one of Watters' closest friends on the team. "Ricky may not say much about it, but I'm sure that had a lot to do with it. Ricky had a great day."

Watters, the 49ers' second-round draft pick out of Notre Dame in 1991, made the Pro Bowl in each of his three seasons in San Francisco. His outburst in the playoff game against the Giants was the unquestioned high point. He scored his first touchdown on a one-yard run off right guard. No. 2 was a carbon copy. No. 3 went off right guard for two yards. He ran left and cut back up the middle for six yards on touchdown No. 4. The capper came from two yards out, right up the gut.

Watters would later gain infamy as a Philadelphia Eagle for a selfish quote—"For who? For what?"—when asked about his unwillingness to risk bodily harm in order to make a catch. But after his big day with the 49ers, he was quick to share credit. Watters said he could sum up his day this way: "Offensive line."

Watters did his part, too. On one run he planted linebacker Lawrence Taylor, his hero, with a straight arm to the head. That was Taylor's thanks for having earlier told Watters he was running great. "I should have told him he was running like (crud)," Taylor said.

Williams fumbled a punt deep in 49ers territory, his second miscue of the game.

Filling in for injured punt returner of Ted Ginn Jr., Williams came up to field a Steve Weatherford punt but backed away at the last minute. After the ball barely touched Williams' right knee, Giants wide receiver Devin Thomas recovered it at the San Francisco 29, setting up New York's go-ahead score. Williams, however, responded by returning the ensuing kickoff 40 yards. That helped set up David Akers' game-tying field goal to force overtime.

But in overtime Williams gave the ball away again when linebacker Jacquian Williams stripped him at the 19 to set up Tynes' field goal. "You have to take full responsibility for that, which I do," Williams said. "It's something I made a mistake on. I'll move through it, I'll promise you that."

The rest of the team could have spared him the agony, but they never got going either. The offense converted only 1-of-13 third-down chances, and the defense couldn't stop Giants slot receiver Victor Cruz (142 receiving yards). "We're going to move forward as a team," Williams said. "Everyone has come to pat me on the back and the shoulder to say it's not me."

Within a year the 49ers were back in the Super Bowl.

87 Colin Kaepernick

Colin Kaepernick was a fourth grader at Dutcher Elementary School in Turlock, California, when a teacher assigned him to write a letter to his future self. Though just 5'2" and 91 pounds at the time, the kid saw bigger things ahead. So little Colin wrote, "I think in seven years I will between 6 ft to 6-4, 140 pounds and I hope to go to a good college in football, then go to the pros and play on the Niners or the Packers, even if they aren't good in seven years."

As it turned out, Kaepernick wound up living his dream almost to the letter. And though he grew up to be big (6'4") and strong (230 pounds) and fast (4.53 seconds at the Scouting Combine), he continues to treat the NFL gridiron as if it were a playground back home. To this day his friends from Turlock call him "Bo" as in Bo Jackson because Kaepernick was that same type of multi-sport freak.

- Basketball? It was his leaping ability on the court one night at John H. Pitman High that helped persuade Nevada coach Chris Ault to extend a football scholarship. He recognized that the kid clearly had the athleticism to run his Pistol offense.
- Baseball? He went 11–2 with a 1.27 ERA, fired two no-hitters in high school, and said he was once clocked at 94 miles per hour. The Chicago Cubs drafted him in 2009 but never came close to signing him. "I couldn't even get him to throw for me," scout Sam Hughes said. "His heart was set on football."
- Four-square? His high school principal, Rod Hollars, said that huge crowds would gather to watch lunchtime games featuring Kaepernick and future Fresno State running back Anthony Harding.
- Football? Well, that was where the games ended and the legend began.

The 49ers took him in the second round (36th overall) of the 2011 draft with the idea that they could groom him behind the scenes for a few years. He was supposed to be raw, but coach Jim Harbaugh, a one-time Pro Bowl quarterback, had played catch with Kaepernick during a pre-draft workout and walked away thinking he had the seeds of something special.

The 49ers were content to let Kaepernick sit for the first two seasons, but in Week 10 of the 2012 season, starter Alex Smith sustained a concussion. That opened the door for Kaepernick to make his first career start against the Chicago Bears on *Monday Night Football.*

Rather than shrink from the big stage, Kaepernick promptly carved up the league's second-ranked scoring defense for 243 yards, two touchdowns, and no interceptions. He attacked without hesitation, making quick decisions and improbable throws. "The guy can throw so hard, so far. It really just makes you step up your speed, your focus. It brings the best out of all of us," wide receiver Michael Crabtree said "He's like a pitcher. The guy's got a cannon."

By the time Smith was healthy, the 49ers had a decision to make. The eight-year veteran was the safe choice, having guided the team to the NFC title game just a year earlier. In his last healthy game of 2012, Smith completed 18-of-19 passes for 232 yards and three touchdowns to earn NFC Offensive Player of the Week honors. Still a decision loomed. But the 49ers suspected an even higher level within reach with Kaepernick. Late that November, 49ers CEO Jed York dropped by the head coach's office. "What are you thinking?" York asked.

"My gut says Kap," Harbaugh replied.

With that the 49ers pinned their Super Bowl hopes on a neophyte with only a handful of career starts. Risky? Sure, and Kaepernick wobbled in losses at St. Louis and Seattle. But the bigger the stage, the better the kid played. Against Tom Brady and the New England Patriots in a December 16 *Sunday Night Football* contest, Kaepernick engineered a 41–34 victory by throwing four touchdown passes. In his first career playoff start, he bolted for 181 rushing yards against the Green Bay Packers. In the NFC Championship Game that followed, Kaepernick fell behind 17–0 to the Atlanta Falcons before calmly directing a 28–24 victory.

Kaepernick's magical run ended in Super Bowl XLVII when the 49ers' offense came up five yards short on their last-gasp drive and lost 34–31 to the Baltimore Ravens.

But Kaepernick threw for 302 yards, one touchdown, and one interception in that game, and his 15-yard touchdown run was the longest by a quarterback in Super Bowl history.

Even in defeat the 49ers walked away from the 2012 season feeling like there would be better days ahead. "He's a new generation type of quarterback," former running back Roger Craig said. "I call him the Avatar quarterback because he plays like he's not real. The way he runs, it doesn't look like he's that fast. But you blink, and all of a sudden he's 10 to 15 yards in front of you. He's a 21st century quarterback."

A 21st century quarterback? Maybe the 49ers should write a letter to their future selves.

88 1986 Draft

Whenever NFL executives study college game film, time a prospect's 40-yard dash, or work the phones looking to swap picks, they're trying to do exactly what the 49ers accomplished in 1986. That was the year Bill Walsh delivered a draft class with an emphasis on *class*. At the peak of his creative powers, the Hall of Fame coach combined his keen eye for talent and his knack for deal making to restock the franchise. Eight of the 14 players Walsh scooped up that day would start in the team's Super Bowl XXIII victory against the Cincinnati Bengals just two years later.

With Walsh exchanging commodities like a bond trader, the 49ers maneuvered for extra picks and came away with (deep breath)

Charles Haley, John Taylor, Tom Rathman, Kevin Fagan, Don Griffin, Steve Wallace, Tim McKyer, and Larry Roberts (exhale). For sheer depth and quality, the 1986 Draft ranks among the best team hauls ever. It happened only because Walsh made six draft day trades with four different teams, repeatedly trading down for more and more picks. "There was a lot of laughing because we were wheeling and dealing like we were in one of those boiler room operations," Walsh told the *San Francisco Chronicle* for a story on the 10-year anniversary of the draft bonanza. "We had a lot of things going at once. We'd have four people waiting on the line at one time and we'd decide who to make the trade with. And all of them thought they were really basically ripping us off."

The 49ers originally owned the 18th pick of the first round. But that didn't last long. Walsh figured it was a deep draft and let it be known that he was all ears for teams willing to deal extra picks. The 49ers coveted Auburn defensive end Gerald Robinson, but he went 14th to Minnesota. They also had an eye on running back Ronnie Harmon, but he went 16th to the Buffalo Bills. After that, the wheels were in motion. By the time the day was done, the 49ers had…

- Swapped first-round picks with the Dallas Cowboys, dropping to 20th and picking up an extra fifth-round choice.
- Traded that No. 20 pick, plus their own 10th-rounder, to Buffalo to add second and third-round picks.
- Flipped that second-round pick from Buffalo to the Detroit Lions for second and third-round picks.
- Flipped that third-round pick from Detroit for a first-round pick in 1987 plus a 10th rounder.

"This brought together all the resources we had to evaluate talent," Walsh told the *Chronicle*. "Our coaches, our scouts, our willingness to open discussions with every team in the league, our willingness to have any number of exchanges occurring concurrently, it was the 49er organization at its best."

89 Red Hickey's Shotgun

Bill Walsh was not the first 49ers head coach with an innovative streak. Red Hickey, who coached the team from 1959 to 1963, helped popularize the shotgun formation with his audacious play calling.

Hickey, though, did not invent the shotgun. The Pro Football Hall of Fame traces the play's origins back at least as far as Pop Warner's Double-Wing-B formation, which had been introduced at Stanford some 30 years earlier. Other teams had used a short punt formation numerous times over the years.

But Hickey pulled the trigger for a new generation. While gearing up for a November 27, 1960 game against Baltimore, Hickey fretted over the Colts' ferocious pass rush led by defensive tackle Eugene "Big Daddy" Lipscomb. As a way to diffuse the pressure, Hickey positioned his quarterbacks seven yards deep for the snap rather than under center. Running backs lined up on either side or positioned at a slight angle just in front of the quarterback. "People thought I was being goofy," Hickey said in *Stadium Stories: San Francisco 49ers* by Dennis Georgatos. "Well, if it works, you aren't so goofy. I was convinced that the offense we had just wasn't good enough. So I started playing around with some ideas in my head. I wanted to have something that I could confuse them, keep the other teams guessing, and by golly, that's what the shotgun seemed to do."

In its debut the shotgun kept the Colts guessing just long enough for the 49ers to pull off a 30–22 upset. John Brodie started the game at quarterback but left after a tough hit from Lipscomb. Bob Waters stepped in and directed the victory. Frank Morze deserves credit as the lucky center who handled the deeper snaps.

Including that game the 49ers won four of their final five that season to salvage a 7–5 season.

With that success Hickey kept right on innovating. In 1961 the 49ers used one of their three first-round draft picks to add rookie Billy Kilmer, a nimble-footed running quarterback from UCLA. That allowed the coach to try a three-quarterback shuffle, in which Brodie, Waters, and Kilmer entered the game on an alternating basis. Hickey sent in plays with each new man. The 49ers started the '61 season 4–1, including a 49–0 victory against the Detroit Lions and a 35–0 rout of the Los Angeles Rams the following week. "We were killing guys," receiver R.C. Owens said in *Stadium Stories*. "We were the talk of the football world."

As that '61 season went along, however, the 49ers and their shotgun formation started shooting blanks. The Chicago Bears hammered the 49ers 31–0, kicking off a stretch of four winless games (including a tie against Detroit). The Bears had provided the blueprint for how to stop the shotgun. Linebacker Bill George moved up to the line of scrimmage, and his presence allowed the Bears to gain penetration by going through the center and to the quarterback. Hickey surrendered and returned to a traditional pro-style offense for the final weeks of '61.

Though best remembered for his time in San Francisco, Hickey later helped one of the team's rivals. In its obituary of Hickey on March 31, 2006, the *San Francisco Chronicle* noted that Cowboys coach Tom Landry hired Hickey to teach Roger Staubach the shotgun offense. The scheme, which Landry modified and called the spread offense, helped launch Staubach's career in the early 1970s. Much to the chagrin of the 49ers, the Cowboys would go on to make five Super Bowls that decade.

90 John McVay

Football is a game of unsung heroes. The running back gets the glory, not the lineman who made the block. The kicker gets credit for the game-winning field goal, not the guys who delivered the perfect snap and hold.

With that in mind, say hello to John McVay.

As an executive, who worked two stints for the 49ers from 1979 to 2004, his fingerprints—though not his face—are all over the team's five Super Bowl victories. McVay's official titles included general manager, vice president, and assistant to the president. His unofficial title was indispensable resource for Bill Walsh, Eddie DeBartolo, and Carmen Policy. "John was the glue to our organization," offensive lineman Randy Cross once said.

Born January 5, 1931, McVay grew up around greatness. During his playing days, he was a center on the football team for Miami (Ohio) where his coaches included Woody Hayes (who would gain fame by winning five national titles at Ohio State) and Ara Parseghian (who won two national titles at Notre Dame).

As a high school coach for several teams in Ohio during the 1950s and '60s, McVay mentored Alan Page, the Central Catholic (Canton) High star who would go on to a Hall of Fame career as a defensive tackle for the Minnesota Vikings and Chicago Bears. McVay later coached at the University of Dayton from 1965 to 1972. That's where he met an energetic young football mind who would hold the key to his future: Eddie DeBartolo Jr. "He'd run around with our football players," McVay told *The Sacramento Bee*, "fun guy even then."

After a successful head coaching stint in the World Football League, McVay encountered a rarity for him: a patch of bad luck.

He spent two-and-a-half forgettable seasons (1976 to 1978) as the New York Giants head coach. The team went 14–23 under McVay, and the last straw came right after a potential breakthrough in '78. "We were right on the verge," McVay told the *San Francisco Chronicle*. "We were 5–3 and then we were 1–7. We got a bunch of guys hurt and then we had that stupid fumble."

That stupid fumble is among the most famous blunders in NFL history. While sitting on the ball to preserve a lead against Philadelphia, Giants quarterback Joe Pisarcik botched a handoff to Larry Csonka, and Eagles safety Herman Edwards scooped up the fumble, racing for the winning touchdown.

Disgruntled Giants fans burned their tickets in the parking lot; McVay was eventually fired. "Worst moment," McVay told *The Bee*. "But things turned out okay."

Things turned out impeccably. In 1979 the 49ers added McVay to the front office where he became a key voice in the draft and in free agency as the 49ers built their dynasty. He was named NFL Executive of the Year in 1989.

With the 49ers seeking a sixth title in Super Bowl XLVII, *Bee* reporter Joe Davidson ventured out to McVay's home in Granite Bay, California. Davidson asked the longtime executive to compare and contrast the old generation of 49ers greatness to the new wave. McVay, who had just turned 82, said Walsh would be delighted with the 49ers' rebirth under coach Jim Harbaugh and quarterback Colin Kaepernick. "People want to tell me that Jim Harbaugh is another Bill Walsh, and that's not so because Jim is himself," McVay said. "I've spoken to him at length—very impressed. I do see similarities and some of the same qualities. Jim's very strong willed and so was Bill. Bill was intense, and Harbaugh is definitely intense. And that kid Kaepernick is amazing. He's a specimen, runs like a gazelle…Bill would've loved him."

Davidson discovered that McVay's home features a room adjacent to the house that McVay calls "the Dungeon." The room includes life-size cutouts of Joe Montana and Steve Young, scores of team photos, season logs, and mementos of each of the club's five Super Bowl seasons—four in the 1980s and the 1994 campaign.

Among the items is an autographed photo from Walsh. The inscription reads: "My lasting friend. You are the master."

91 Buck Shaw

Before becoming the first head coach in 49ers history, Lawrence "Buck" Shaw really did win one for the Gipper. Shaw was a tackle at Notre Dame and spearheaded the offensive line that blocked for the great George Gipp. Together they helped lead Knute Rockne's undefeated Fighting Irish teams in 1919 and 1920.

Rockne later nudged Shaw into coaching, giving him an unsolicited recommendation for a college job. But Shaw realized instantly he was not a fiery halftime orator in Rockne's mold. "When I discovered that I wasn't, I dropped the histrionics," Shaw said. "Heaven help you if you try anything insincere on today's players."

Instead Shaw was a genteel general, the thoughtful man behind a string of powerhouse teams both in the college ranks and the pros. It was his success at Santa Clara University in 1936 and 1937 that put him on the national radar as a coach. Those Broncos teams went a combined 18–1 and won back-to-back Sugar Bowls, both times upsetting LSU. By 1942 when Santa Clara briefly suspended football, Shaw's record was 47–10–4, a mark that made him one of the most respected figures in Bay Area sports at the time. His rising stock did not escape the notice of a Santa Clara alum named Tony Morabito, the 49ers' original owner, who later lured Shaw to serve as the team's first coach. Author Dan Maguire wrote in *San Francisco 49ers* that it was "well known in many circles" that in 1941 Shaw had turned down an offer from his alma mater, Notre Dame, because he preferred to stay in or near San Francisco.

Shaw took the reins as the fledgling team was born into the new All-America Football Conference in 1946. Shaw called the shots for such early stars as Frankie Albert, Hugh McElhenny, and Y.A. Tittle. In all Shaw went 71–39–4 (.645) as the 49ers head coach through 1954. "I had more fun playing football from 1951 to 1954 with San Francisco under Shaw and with Frank than I did before or after," Tittle wrote in a 1964 essay for *Sports Illustrated*. "Shaw could create a relaxed mood at practice during the week because he was a very gentle, friendly man who never raised his voice to his players. He was successful with this method, and it made the 49ers a happy club. I don't want to get into any arguments about how you should coach; some very tough coaches have been successful, too. But it's a lot more fun with the relaxed winners than with the tough winners."

Nicknamed the "Silver Fox" because he was prematurely gray and with movie idol looks, Lawrence Timothy Shaw was born on a farm in Mitchellville, Iowa, on March 28, 1899. He played all of four games in high school before heading off for a season at Creighton University and then Notre Dame. With the Fighting Irish, Shaw starred as a 6'0", 175-pound tackle, playing on both the left and right sides. He also converted 38 of 39 extra points during his varsity career that lasted through 1921, a Notre Dame record that stood until 1976.

Shaw's coaching career began in 1924 when Rockne gave him a strong endorsement for a position at North Carolina State. A stop in Nevada followed and then came an assistant's job at Santa Clara.

Unlike his mentor Rockne, however, Shaw tended to discourage his players from going into coaching. "You're a teacher without tenure," Shaw said. "The history teacher doesn't have to send his class out before 64,000 people on Saturday to compete against classes from other schools, classes, which may have better material than he has. But you send your class out, and your status keeps changing, according to what happens to it out there."

In the pros, starting with the 49ers in 1946, Shaw got a reminder of just how ruthless his profession could be. Morabito declined to renew his contract in 1955, relieving him of his duties after the 49ers managed a 7–4–1 finish despite injuries to key players such as McElhenny. "He has been given 100 percent authority, not 99 percent but 100. Four out of the past five years, the 49ers have either folded completely or lost the big one," Morabito said on the day he announced the news. "It's time we tried something else."

Shaw later went on to coach the Philadelphia Eagles to an NFL championship in 1960. He was the only coach ever to defeat Vince Lombardi's Green Bay Packers in a title game.

92 Recite the "I Want Winners" Speech

Mike Singletary's legendary rant from October 26, 2008 is the stuff of YouTube legend. In one angry, fiery, passionate—and hilarious—30-second clip, the 49ers coach earned a spot on the Mount Rushmore of crazy coaches right there next to Jim "Playoffs?!" Mora, Herm "You Play…to Win the Game" Edwards, and Dennis "They Are Who We Thought They Were" Green.

Anybody can belt out Singletary's famous line—"I want winners!"—but the key is to master the lyrical rhythms of a coach gone mad. (For the oratory style, it might help to remember that Singletary is also an ordained minister.)

First let's set the stage. Singletary, who had just coached his first NFL game, was ticked off at tight end Vernon Davis for drawing an unnecessary roughness penalty during a 34–13 loss to the Seattle Seahawks. After the call, Davis tried to avoid his coach when he ran to the sideline. That only made things worse. Singletary got in the tight end's face and gave him an earful.

He wasn't done. Singletary later walked over to Davis on the bench. And with 10:41 to play in the game, the coach banished his player to the locker room.

Now cue the soundtrack. This is the full text of what happened in the postgame news conference:

Reporter: What happened between you and Vernon Davis?
Singletary: Vernon…It was something that I told everybody at the very beginning of the week. I would not tolerate players that think it's about them when it's about the team. And we cannot make…we cannot make decisions that cost the team. And then come off the sideline and it's nonchalant? No. You know what? This is how I believe, okay? I'm from the old school.

I believe this: I would rather play with 10 people and just get penalized all the way until we've got to do something else—rather than play with 11 when I know that right now that person is not sold out to be a part of this team. It is more about them than it is about the team.

Cannot play with them. Cannot win with them. Cannot coach with them. Can't do it! I want winners! I want people that want to win.

The Seahawks game is also remembered for another embarrassing incident. During halftime—as the 49ers trailed 20–3—Singletary dropped his pants and pointed to his backside while berating the team. He later explained his motivation in a prepared statement: "I used my pants to illustrate that we were getting our tails whipped on Sunday and how humiliating that should feel for all of us. I needed to do something to dramatize my point; there were other ways I could have done it, but I think this got the message across."

During his turbulent, three-season tenure, Singletary went 18–22 and was fired before the last week of the 2010 season. The 49ers would hire Jim Harbaugh in 2011, and he would lead them deep into the playoffs, including a 2012 Super Bowl run, during his first two years at the helm.

93 Tom Brady and The Catch

Before he grew up and started his own football dynasty, little Tommy Brady got a firsthand look at greatness. The future New England Patriots star was a frequent visitor to Candlestick Park. "When I was four years old, my dad brought me to as many 49ers games as were possible," said Brady, who was raised in San Mateo, California. "We'd tailgate in the parking lot and then head in. Our seats were pretty high up on top of the stadium. You needed binoculars just to see what was going on, but there was nothing more thrilling than watching legends like Joe Montana and Steve Young. I think everybody wanted to be like those two guys."

Brady's football education included the master class. He was there on January 10, 1982, the day Montana tossed a high-arching miracle in the end zone to Dwight Clark. Most people remember that game for "The Catch." Brady remembers it for something else. "I had to have a foam finger," he recalled with a laugh, recalling his fixation on the souvenir. "I had that in my mind. And once a kid has that in their mind, that's all they want. For the entire half of the game, I kept complaining to my parents that everybody had a foam finger but me. My parents finally broke down and got me one just to shut me up."

Brady told that story at a 2012 fund-raiser while in the presence of his idol. Montana responded by recounting the struggles the 49ers had during his rookie season when the team went 2–14. "We were getting fingers," Montana told Brady. "But they weren't those big ones."

But the 49ers, like many other teams, let Brady slip right through their fingers. During the 2000 NFL Draft, San Francisco passed on the local product, selecting Giovanni Carmazzi from Hofstra University in the third round with the 65th overall pick. Carmazzi would never attempt a regular-season pass in his two years with the 49ers. Brady, selected three rounds later with the 199th pick, is bound for the Hall of Fame.

94 Burnt Toast

With his white hair and dizzying intellect, Bill Walsh often elicited comparisons to a professor. Football was his chemistry lab. He understood how different elements would react to each other—and what might make the whole dang place blow up.

Joe Montana marveled at the way Walsh could defuse a combustible situation. On September 8, 2011, Montana shared a story during an intimate fireside chat with his fellow residents at the Millennium Towers in San Francisco. As neighbors gathered round, Montana opened up with surprising candor about how Walsh's genius extended beyond Xs and Os. "The thing that Bill brought with him was this belief in each other," Montana said. "Ronnie Lott used to say it best: 'You don't have to like the guy next to you, but you have to be able to trust him out on the field.' We're all going to make mistakes, but it's how the guys around you react. It's that group that brings it back together."

In other words, everyone had to buy into the team concept. And if someone didn't? "If there were any *me* guys on our team, they did not last very long," Montana said. "There's one story I talk about all the time. There was a defensive back. I'd rather not say a name, but you'll probably know once I get going."

Joe Fonzi, a television reporter who moderated Montana's chat, interrupted to ask if the player happened to wear jersey No. 22. "Yes, he did," Montana said. "And he just kept going and kept going. It was all about him unfortunately."

Defensive back Tim McKyer happened to wear No. 22 while with the 49ers from 1986 to 1989. He had a terrific career, winning three Super Bowls (two with the 49ers) and twice ranking among the NFL's season leaders in interceptions.

But then there was that chemistry issue.

Montana, without ever confirming the player by name, picked up the story. He said what No. 22 really wanted was for Jerry Rice to respond to any questions about the best defensive back he faced by answering with the name of the guy Rice lined up against in practice every day. "He called himself 'the Blanket,'" Montana said. "Well, one day he got beat for three touchdowns. And the next day, he comes into the locker room. We can be brutal in the locker room. There's a blanket hanging in his locker, and it's got three holes on it. Then he got really mad, which is the worst thing you can do, because the next day there were three pieces of burnt toast on the blanket."

Players continued to tease the Blanket—until he went undercover. "It got to the point where when we were in Atlanta for a game," Montana said, "he was so distraught he wouldn't even come out of the hotel. We had to go into the hotel because he wasn't going to come out and go to the game. And then he was gone after that."

McKyer's final season with the 49ers was under George Seifert, who had succeeded Walsh as head coach. Seifert, while defensive coordinator, had more patience with the high-maintenance cornerback than anyone on staff and often tried to broker peace. But once Seifert became head coach, even he reached his limit with disruptions.

The 49ers started shopping McKyer after the 1989 season and wound up sending him to the Miami Dolphins for a 1990 11th-round choice and a 1991 second-round choice. McKyer played for seven teams during an NFL career that lasted through 1997. His career highlights include a 96-yard interception return for a touchdown against the 49ers in 1995.

For the 49ers of that era, though, it was all about chemistry. "If there was any guy that upset the balance of that team, Bill Walsh, Carmen Policy, and Eddie Debartolo took care of it fast," Montana said. "That was a big part of that nucleus."

95 Michael Crabtree

Michael Crabtree always played quarterback while growing up in Texas. Still he had his favorite receivers. As a kid he was a big fan of Terrell Owens and Michael Irvin. And he was so enamored with

Randy Moss that he and his friends in Dallas turned his last name into a verbal taunt. If one of them made a leaping grab over a cornerback, he'd turn to the hapless defender and say, "You just got Mossed."

Crabtree kept the phrase in his lingo even once he reached the NFL. It made for some amusing moments on the Santa Clara practice field in 2012 when Moss arrived as a free agent. "It's funny when you catch a ball over somebody and tell the DB, 'You got Mossed,' and Moss is standing right there next to you," Crabtree said.

But by the end of their first season together, opposing defenses were closer to crying than to laughing: Crabtree, the first-round draft pick in 2009, finally blossomed as the go-to guy the 49ers had always envisioned—in part because his childhood idol played the role of mentor.

With Moss pointing the way, Crabtree led the team with 85 catches for 1,105 yards, becoming the 49ers' first 1,000-yard receiver since Owens in 2003. Dusting off the explosive run-after-catch ability he had last shown at Texas Tech, the 6'2", 215-pounder also caught nine touchdown passes that season, five of them on third down. Along the way, coach Jim Harbaugh said that Crabtree had the best hands of any receiver he'd ever seen.

Crabtree really took off once the team made a midseason quarterback switch from Alex Smith to Colin Kaepernick. The receiver's breakthrough night came in a *Sunday Night Football* game against the New England Patriots on December 16 when Crabtree had seven catches for 107 yards and two touchdowns.

He Mossed a lot of defenders that night. "Michael really has all the skills to be a complete wide receiver," Moss said. "He just needed somebody really older, someone who has really been through what he has been through, to be able to get him down that path."

Crabtree's development as an NFL threat was several years in the making. He got off to a rocky start as early as 2009's draft day when concerns over his attitude prompted a top five talent to drop all the way to No. 10. In fairness Crabtree really is a mercurial personality.

Hundreds of Records

A franchise with an impressive postseason history established a new—if quirky—milestone in a 45–31 victory against the Green Bay Packers on January 12, 2013. In that divisional playoff game, the 49ers became the first playoff team in NFL history to have two 100-yard rushers, Colin Kaepernick (181) and Frank Gore (119), plus a 100-yard receiver, Michael Crabtree (119).

He can be intensely private in the locker room and a recluse with the media. He is a tough person to read.

His rookie season began with a 71-day holdout, which some speculated might last all season. Crabtree's performance on the field was curtailed by injuries and by his poor chemistry with Smith. But the perception of him as a high-maintenance personality—"a diva," as he was famously described by a rival coach—turned out to be hogwash. "I told people they were stupid for saying that. It was absurd," Texas Tech coach Mike Leach told me. "This is a guy whose job is football, whose hobby is football, and whose passion is football. Michael really believes, like John Wooden used to say, that you should 'make each day your masterpiece.' His masterpiece is on the football field."

With the 49ers Crabtree was a dedicated worker, arriving before practice each day and coached himself through drills. He was trying to improve his burst, so he could get an extra step on defenders. He soon emerged as a safety valve for young Kaepernick. "When he's in the huddle, he'll say, 'Look for me, I can make a play,'" said tight end Delanie Walker, who contributed during the 49ers' Super Bowl run in 2012. "We need somebody to speak up, and he's been doing it."

Crabtree, though, suffered a setback in May of 2013 when he tore his Achilles tendon. He'll need that work ethic now more than ever.

96 Attend a Pasta Bowl

When Bill Walsh dressed up as a bellhop before the 49ers' first Super Bowl, he did so as a prank. He was just trying to keep the team loose. But once a year, 49ers stars really do provide the best customer service in town.

At the team's annual Pasta Bowl—hosted in cooperation with the Silicon Valley Leadership Group—players, coaches, executives, and alumni work as waiters, dishing up family-style Italian food in the name of a good cause.

Your waiter for the night might be Dwight Clark (ask him about "The Catch" of the day), Aldon Smith (arrange for a sack lunch), or Colin Kaepernick (ask him to pass the salt). The 49ers make sure everyone's plate is full before sitting down and joining the table for dinner. "You get to have a great dinner, conversations, take pictures, get autographs—all of that," said Joanne Pasternack, the team's director of community relations and the 49ers Foundation. "It's such a unique opportunity. And in the process, we donate around $200,000 each year to Bay Area charities through the event."

Tickets for the Santa Clara Convention Center ballroom event aren't cheap ($249 in past years) and can be hard to come by. Corporate sponsorships are also available. But this is an easy choice for your things-to-do list. Just ask the 10-year-old who showed up one year in a Frank Gore jersey and wound up sitting with his idol. When the kid started rattling off his knowledge of Gore's career stats, the running back was amazed. "I think you know more about me than I know about myself," he said.

The 49ers always have held annual season kickoff fundraisers, but the Pasta Bowl, born in 2007, has taken things to a new level. It takes place almost immediately after players check in for training camp, which means that the roster—and wait staff—is around 90.

Each table at the Pasta Bowl seats 20 with two spots reserved for the 49ers' VIP hosts. A table in 2012, for example, featured a pair of legends—Vernon Davis and Tom Rathman. But Pasternack said it can be just as fun to get "the guy who might get cut next week" because the event marks his debut in a 49ers uniform. The rookies are as thrilled to be there as the fans.

And when you go, bring your appetite. Pasternack said Ricky Jean-Francois remains the greatest waiter of all time because he dished out "Ricky-sized portions"—big enough even for a 295-pound defensive lineman.

Pasternack said all of the money goes to the charitable 49ers Foundation, which in turn writes checks to Bay Area nonprofits that fit the 49ers' mission of keeping kids "safe and on track and in school." For information call the 49ers main line at (408) 562-4949 and ask to speak to someone from the 49ers Foundation. Or go to 49ersFoundation.com.

97 The Alphabet Backfield

When it comes to the 49ers basics, it's not the ABCs you need to know. It's Y.A., C.R., J.D., and R.C. That eye-chart of a combination formed the so-called "Alphabet Backfield" for the 49ers in 1959. Y.A. Tittle was the quarterback, R.C. Owens was the flanker back, J.D. Smith was a running back, and C.R. Roberts was the fullback. Such a collection of first names posed a challenge for Red Hickey's staff.

One of the several 49ers players in 1959 with initials as their first name, R.C. Owens was known for his ability to catch alley-oop passes. (AP Images)

At least initially. "The coaches would always get us mixed up," C.R. Roberts recalled with a laugh. "Someone would say, 'R.C.' And they'd mean C.R. and vice versa. So we had a real problem with that."

In 2012 I called Roberts, who was then 76, to help explain the origins of the 49ers' version of *Sesame Street*. As it turned out, the Alphabet Backfield had a special place in history for reasons that went beyond their two-letter first names. Roberts thinks the group may have invented the high five. "Three from the Alphabet were black," Roberts said, referring to himself, Owens, and Smith. "The first time we saw all the black guys—the backs and the ends and R.C. and all the guys—on the field at the same time, God, it was really a good feeling. We just slapped hands and carried on. So we think that's where that high fiving came from. This was in the '50s, and we'd never seen it before. We'd get on the field and slap hands. We'd slap it up, down low; then it went up high."

Cornelius Roberts was "C.R." for most of his life. Even his parents called him that. He didn't even know his full first name until he looked it up on his birth certificate while in high school. Roberts originally dreamed of becoming a fighter pilot. But during his freshman year at USC where he was part of the ROTC program, an optometrist discovered that Roberts had astigmatism. He would still be allowed to fly—but taking controls of a fighter jet was out of the question. "That crushed me," he said.

Roberts settled for a college career as a terrific USC tailback, one who made history in 1956. When the Trojans played a road game against the University of Texas at Austin, it marked the first time a black player competed against a white player in that state. Roberts racked up 251 rushing yards—and was cheered as he left the field.

Roberts' lifelong devotion to civil rights complicated his journey to the 49ers. (He made his pro debut in Canada because— in part—he viewed the NFL as racist.) The New York Giants drafted him in the 14th round in 1958, but he didn't fit with that roster and he often grumbled about the cold weather. "So when my displeasure with all of that stuff was displayed, they traded me to Pittsburgh," Roberts said. "And I thought Pittsburgh was a hell-hole. So I was there for about 10 plays and left."

At long last he found his home in San Francisco. That '59 team finished 7–5 thanks to a big boost from the backfield: Smith rushed for 1,036 yards and 10 touchdowns. (Both marks were second in the NFL behind Jim Brown.) The Alphabet Backfield was still on the roster for one more season—also a 7–5 finish—but was broken up by 1961 when Tittle was traded to the New York Giants.

So who came up with the Alphabet Backfield nickname? Roberts said he "didn't even realize the significance of that until maybe four or five years out of pro ball when people talked about it." He said the moniker didn't stick until a newspaper trivia contest featured the Alphabet Backfield and promised more than $1,000 in prize money. "That was a big deal then," Roberts said. "So, maybe that's what really got it going."

For the record the non-alphabet version of that 49ers backfield was: Yelberton Abraham Tittle, Cornelius R. Roberts, Raleigh Climon Owens, and J.D. Smith (whose name really did consist of initials only).

98 Ted Kwalick

When Vernon Davis caught 13 touchdown passes in 2009, he broke the 49ers' single-season record for touchdowns by a tight end. The mark had stood for more than 35 years. Somehow, though, Ted Kwalick wasn't too heartbroken about being surpassed. "I didn't even know I had the record," he said with a laugh.

Kwalick established the mark in 1972, the best of his three consecutive Pro Bowl seasons. The 6'4", 226-pounder hadn't even been monitoring Davis' touchdown progress in 2009 because he was sure that Brent Jones had passed him years earlier. As it turned out, Jones had only tied Kwalick's mark with nine touchdowns in 1994.

So Kwalick was happy to usher in a new king. For one thing he admired the unusual athleticism Davis brought to the tight end position. For another, Kwalick had a profound appreciation for Davis' early career struggles. He'd taken that road himself.

Kwalick, too, was a ballyhooed first-round draft pick who failed to make an immediate impact. The 49ers took the All-American from Penn State with the No. 7 pick in 1969, but he had two catches as a rookie and only 10 the following season. "I thought I would step in and play right away," he said, "but the NFL is a rude awakening."

Kwalick said quarterback John Brodie once told him that tight end is the second-hardest position to learn—after quarterback. A tight end must learn not only the nuances of passing routes, but also the blocking assignments for the running game. Kwalick, Brodie, receiver Gene Washington, and other offensive players would meet at the quarterback's house every Wednesday night to go over game film. "It takes a while to figure it out," Kwalick said. "Maybe some guys can step in right away, but for the other 98 percent of us there is an adjustment period."

It took three seasons of study, but Kwalick's light came on in 1971. And all the lights illuminated the following season. With Washington providing a reliable deep threat on the outside, Kwalick sprang loose for career highs in touchdowns (nine), receiving yards (751), and average yards per catch (18.8). Only Kwalick's teammate, Washington, (12) and Rich Caster of the New York Jets (10) had more touchdown catches that season.

Kwalick's career with the 49ers lasted from 1969 to 1974. He made three consecutive Pro Bowls starting in '71. He finished 10th in the NFL in receiving yards in '72 and '73—not too shabby for a tight end of that era.

After retirement, Kwalick went on to be the founder and president of ProTech Voltage Systems, a clean electrical energy business, in Santa Clara, California. As for his place in 49ers history? Kwalick has nothing to lament about a record he was unaware of in the first place. "I have a feeling Vernon is going to score a lot more touchdowns," he said.

99 Neon Deion

Like many flings this one ended up with a bad breakup. Deion Sanders spent just one season in San Francisco—a torrid, tumultuous affair that ended bitterly as "Prime Time" spurned the 49ers for the rival Dallas Cowboys.

But they'll always have 1994.

That's the year Sanders blew into San Francisco in search of one thing—a ring. At the start of the love affair, everyone seemed happy. Sanders had one of the best seasons of his Hall of Fame career while in a 49ers uniform, intercepting six passes (for an NFL-best 303 yards) and winning NFL Defensive Player of the Year.

It worked out okay for the team, too. The 49ers won Super Bowl XXIX that season when they beat the San Diego Chargers 49–26. Naturally, Sanders had an interception on the big stage. During that sparkling season, Sanders was at his high-stepping, attention-seeking best, never more so than on October 16, 1994 in Atlanta. That's when Sanders returned to face his original team, the Falcons, and re-introduced himself by returning a Jeff George interception 93 yards for a touchdown.

Sanders wasn't the type to go quietly. Over the last few yards of that interception return, he slowed down, broke into a stiff-legged high step, walked the final yard, and then started dancing.

How's that for Southern hospitality? "I've been humble all week," he said after the 42–3 victory. "But now I've got one thing to say: This is my house! I built this! I don't care if I'm with the Falcons or not. This is my house, and it will always be my house."

Who was going to argue with him? Apparently Falcons wide receiver Andre Rison. He and Sanders fought earlier in the game, trading punches like a couple of bantamweights. 49ers linebacker Ken Norton Jr., whose father had been the famous boxer who defeated Muhammad Ali and broke his jaw, scored it 10–9 in favor of Sanders.

After the 1994 season, the 49ers were on the receiving end of a few Sanders shots. The cornerback signed a seven-year, $35-million deal with the Dallas Cowboys and won a title during his first year with his new team. After Dallas beat Pittsburgh in Super Bowl XXX, he began bad-mouthing his ex. "I don't remember the 49ers," Sanders said. "I don't even want to think about the 49ers. Don't upset this moment."

100 Hardy Brown

Before he died in 1991, former 49ers linebacker Hardy Brown liked to tell the story about the time retired Rams star Bob Waterfield was struck by a Volkswagen while crossing the street. Waterfield was okay after the accident, but as he picked himself off the pavement, shaking off the aches and bruises, the quarterback said, "I thought Hardy Brown was in town."

Hardy "the Hatchet" Brown kept 49ers opponents looking both ways from 1951 to 1955. Fueled by rage from childhood trauma and equipped with a shoulder-to-the-head technique that could knock opponents senseless, Brown played with an uncommon malice. "Everybody feared him," longtime 49ers star Gordy Soltau told *The San Francisco Examiner*. "You whispered 'Hardy Brown' to them, and they began to shiver at the sound. Nobody could hit the way he could. If TV had been in when he played, he'd be immortal."

The origins of Brown's violent streak are easy to trace. He was four years old when his father was fatally gunned down by two men at a neighbor's house in Kirkland, Texas. Hardy was in the room. Four months later he was also there when a family friend murdered one of his father's killers. His mother sent him to live at the Masonic Home, an orphanage in Fort Worth, Texas, when he was five. Brown spent the rest of his childhood there, playing football on its Mighty Mite team. He didn't see his mom again for 12 years—and only then because he needed her permission to enlist in the Marines.

One of the other kids at the orphanage was Dewitt "Tex" Coulter, who would go on to become a fine NFL lineman himself. "Football gave us self-worth," Coulter told *The Examiner*. "When the newspapers came out and wrote stories, they'd refer to us as ragtag kids, and that made us angry. That was pity from above, and we hated it. Football was a way to alleviate that."

Listed at 6'0", 193 pounds, Brown was small for his position, even by 1950s standards. Just try telling that to the people he left in his wake. Because the world hurt Brown, he found a way to hurt back. Brown kept a ledger during his playing days of opponents he'd knocked out of games. His final career tally was 75 to 80 victims. Legend has it that he knocked out more than 20 players in the 1951 season alone. "No, I don't feel sorry for anybody I hit," Brown told NFL Films.

He socked his way to the Pro Bowl team in 1952. An NFL Films special in 2009 ranked him as the fifth most feared tackler of all time. Brown's specialty was delivering a knockout punch with his right shoulder. Brown would essentially coil it up—"like a snake," according to teammate Bob St. Clair—and then strike when the time was right. "In mid-air he'd extend the shoulder and aim it at your Adam's apple," St. Clair told *The Examiner*. "You either got hit in the chest or the face. He destroyed people with it."

Brown broke jaws and cheeks and left opponents with concussions. If he played in the modern era, he'd be broke from all the fines.

So potent was Brown's blow that opponents suspected he must conceal a steel plate in his shoulder pads. Officials would periodically check, only to discover that there was no metal under the uniform—just a linebacker hardened by life. "Pound for pound, inch for inch, he was the toughest football player I ever met," former 49er teammate and road roommate Y.A. Tittle said. "He was so tough... he was damned near illegal."

Acknowledgments

If you want to discover the goodness in people, write a book. My family, friends, co-workers, readers, and rival reporters rallied around this project with what Jim Harbaugh might call an "enthusiasm unknown to mankind."

Luckily, this is the part of the book where I no longer have to rank people. That's great because there's no way I could break a first-place tie between:

The 49ers staff, past and present, starting with longtime historian Donn Sinn, whose knowledge and patience knows no bounds. I've never seen the inside of Donn's head, but I suspect it looks a lot like Kezar Stadium. Jerry Walker, the 49ers media relations man from 1981 to 1993, was gracious beyond belief; the museum at the new Santa Clara Stadium is in great hands with him. The great Kirk Reynolds, the former 49ers PR man now with the Pac-12, remains the gateway to stars like Joe Montana and Steve Young. And, of course, a tip of the cap to the 49ers current media relations staff led by Bob Lange, Mike Chasanoff, and Dan Beckler, who carry on the strong tradition. Taylor Price of 49ers.com wrote several outstanding stories on the players that are honored on the team's "10-Year Wall." I used that series as a resource for this book.

My editors, especially Jeff Fedotin at Triumph Books, whose insightful suggestions shaped this project from start to finish. I'm also grateful to the brilliant Betsy Towner, who reads first drafts the way Montana reads defenses—seeing things no one else can. Betsy has been saving my neck since college and will, I hope, for many years to come.

My newspaper teammates, past and present, whose work echoes throughout every page. The most fun I had on this project was re-reading the greatness of Bud Geracie, Tim Kawakami, Mark Purdy,

Cam Inman, Dennis Georgatos, Ann Killion, Clark Judge, Steve Corkran, Dave Newhouse, Jerry McDonald, Michael Martinez, Nancy Gay, Sam Farmer, Sheldon Spencer, Kristin Huckshorn, and Jeff Schultz, among many other heroes. A special thanks also to Mark Smith, Darryl Matsuda, Leigh Poitinger, Diana Stickler, and Dave Belli.

My rival reporters on the 49ers beat, who set an astonishingly high bar with their reporting and prose. Matt Barrows of *The Sacramento Bee*, Matt Maiocco of Comcast Sports Net, Kevin Lynch of SFgate.com, Janie McCauley of the Associated Press, Eric Branch of the *San Francisco Chronicle*, and Craig Massei of Scout.com are the nicest group of steely-eyed scribes you'd ever want to meet. I'm envious of their talent every day.

My wife, Susan Slusser of the *San Francisco Chronicle*, the best sportswriter in my household—or any household, for that matter. Thanks, Sluss, for your encouragement and for understanding why I couldn't include Bert Jones in the 49ers' top 100.

My friends, Howard Beck (*The New York Times*) and Rachel Wettergreen Wilner (*San Jose Mercury News*), are my greatest journalistic influences.

My parents, Dean and Sherrie, who showed me that being nice and working hard is a pretty good playbook for life. And, finally, this book is for my brother, David, the Joe Cool of our Thanksgiving Day games in Cotati, California. Don't let his skinny legs fool you.

Bibliography

Newspapers
San Jose Mercury News
San Francisco Chronicle
The San Francisco Examiner
The Sacramento Bee
The New York Times

Wire Services
Associated Press
United Press International
Bloomberg News

Periodicals
Sports Illustrated
Time magazine

Websites
49ers.com
ESPN.com
profootballhof.com
Pro-football-reference.com
Profootballresearchers.org

Books
Brodie, John and Houston, James D. *Open Field*. Bantam Publishing. (1975).
Dent, Jim. *Twelve Mighty Orphans: The Inspiring True Story of the Mighty Mites Who Ruled Texas Football*. St. Martin's Press. (2007).
Georgatos, Dennis. *Game of My Life San Francisco 49ers: Memorable Stories of 49ers Football*. Sports Publishing LLC. (October 1, 2007).
Georgatos, Dennis. *Stadium Stories: San Francisco 49ers*. Globe Pequot (August 1, 2005).
Maguire, Dan. *San Francisco 49ers*. Coward-McCann (1960).
Maiocco, Matt and Fucillo, David. *San Francisco 49ers: Where Have You Gone*. Sports Publishing. (2005, 2011).
Newhouse, Dave. *The Million Dollar Backfield: The 49ers in the 1950s*. Frog Books. (November 22, 2000).
Tittle, Y.A. and Setting, Kristine. *Nothing Comes Easy: My Life in Football*. Triumph Books. (September 1, 2009).

Events
"A Fireside Chat with Joe Montana." Hosted by KTVU sportscaster Joe Fonzi. At Millennium Tower in San Francisco on September 8, 2011.
"Salute to Titans" breakfast featuring Joe Montana, Steve Young, Aaron Rodgers, Tom Brady, and Jim Plunkett on June 15, 2012. Hosted by Harris Barton's foundation, Champion Charities.